# Writing Essays
## FOR
# DUMMIES®

## by Mary Page and Dr Carrie Winstanley

# WILEY

A John Wiley and Sons, Ltd, Publication

**Writing Essays For Dummies®**

Published by
**John Wiley & Sons, Ltd**
The Atrium
Southern Gate
Chichester
West Sussex
PO19 8SQ
England
E-mail (for orders and customer service enquires): cs-books@wiley.co.uk

Visit our Home Page on www.wiley.com

For general information on our other products and services, please contact our Customer Care Department within the U.S. at 877-762-2974, outside the U.S. at 317-572-3993, or fax 317-572-4002.

For technical support, please visit www.wiley.com/techsupport.

Wiley also publishes its books in a variety of electronic formats. Some content that appears in print may not be available in electronic books.

British Library Cataloguing in Publication Data: A catalogue record for this book is available from the British Library

ISBN: 978-0-470-74290-7

SKY0F3F1F5B-25BA-4F32-A7FE-42C327BFA273_082621

WILEY

# About the Authors

**Mary Page** has a lifetime of experience teaching international students of all ages (her youngest pupil ever was 8 and the oldest 92!) and from very many cultures, countries and backgrounds. Her career started as a lectrice at the Université de Strasbourg in France, then continued at Eurocentres, Bournemouth. Since 2002 she has been teaching English for Academic Purposes at the University of Southampton whilst also managing the IELTS Test Centre there. During the academic year she teaches Advanced Level English Language to international students, as well as on courses for undergraduate students in teaching English as a Foreign Language. Through the summer months she directs a Pre-sessional course for international students wishing to undertake a degree course at the university. She has a busy life and would like a holiday sometime! Her interests include (unsurprisingly!) teaching academic writing, teacher training, and English as a Lingua Franca. Though she's been teaching for many years she still gets a kick out of helping students to learn and seeing them succeed in their ambitions.Mary's first degree is in French (BA Hons, University of Manchester) and she also holds an MSc from Bournemouth University in Managing Business Information Technology, as well as the RSA Diploma in Teaching English as a Foreign Language and the RSA Certificate in Counselling Skills in the Development of Learning.

**Dr Carrie Winstanley** currently works with undergraduate and postgraduate students teaching different aspects of education, including psychology, philosophy and history. She also teaches and researches with highly able children and is especially interested in those who also have learning difficulties, sensory impairments and/or disabilities. She regularly runs workshops with children and adults in museums, galleries and schools, and is fascinated by learning and teaching in formal and non-formal contexts.

Carrie has taught in Higher Education for a decade, following ten years of teaching in schools (maintained, independent and international sectors). She is also an educational consultant and writer. Carrie holds higher degrees in social justice and education (PhD, London), psychology of education (MPhil, Cambridge), as well as the philosophy and history of education (MA, Surrey), plus an undergraduate degree in education (BHEd, Kingston, CNAA). She was awarded a National Teaching Fellowship from the Higher Education Academy in 2008.

# Dedication

**From Mary:** To my goddaughters, Kitty, Jemima and Cordelia, in the hope that this book will be of use to you in the future.

**From Carrie:** This book is dedicated to all the students whose essays I have ever read and all the tutors and colleagues who have ever read mine.

# Authors' Acknowledgements

**From Mary:** Infinite thanks go to the innumerable students and colleagues over the years from whom by osmosis I have learnt, and continue to learn, so very much about teaching, learning and, in particular, academic writing. I would also like to include all the team at Wiley in this, especially Wejdan Ismail and Simon Bell, who supported me when the going got tough! I'm grateful, too, to Julie Watson at Southampton who first put me in touch with them.

Most of all, thanks go to Lauren, the best of friends, who has kept me laughing with her whacky phone calls.

Not forgetting, of course, for their constant love and companionship, thanks (in the form of an extra can of tuna) to the most wonderful cats in the world, Florence and Theo.

**From Carrie:** I am particularly grateful to a group of friends from Kingston Polytechnic – Kate, Hannah, Veena, Jo and Hilary – we were the best study group I ever had and I learnt a great deal from working with you all back in the distant 1980s. Thanks are also due to the many students and colleagues with whom I have discussed essay writing and study skills over the years.

This project was made possible by Wejdan Ismail and Simon Bell at Wiley; sincere gratitude to them and to my copyeditor Charlie Wilson. I appreciate all the support and the perceptive comments that have kept me on track, juggling this book with 'Dissertations' and with real life too. Thanks also to my co-author Mary Page.

I would not have agreed to undertake this project without the encouraging words of Jack and Danny. I'd also like to thank Ma, Pa, Suzi and Missy for their steadfast support, and Andy for helping me to keep going on difficult days.

# Publisher's Acknowledgements

We're proud of this book; please send us your comments through our Dummies online registration form located at www.dummies.com/register/.

Some of the people who helped bring this book to market include the following:

**Acquisitions, Editorial, and Media Development**

**Acquisitions Editor:** Wejdan Ismail

**Development Editor:** Simon Bell

**Content Editor:** Jo Theedom

**Publishing Assistant:** Jennifer Prytherch

**Copy Editor:** Sally Lansdell

**Technical Editor:** Abbie Langridge

**Publisher:** Jason Dunne

**Assistant Production Manager:**
Daniel Mersey

**Cover Photos:** © altrendo images/ Getty Images (front); © Erik Dreyer/ Getty Images (back)

**Cartoons:** Ed McLachlan

**Composition Services**

**Project Coordinator:** Lynsey Stanford

**Layout and Graphics:** Reuben W. Davis, Melissa K. Jester

**Proofreader:** Susan Moritz

**Indexer:** Cheryl Duksta

# Contents at a Glance

# Table of Contents

# Introduction

• • • • • • • • • • • • • • • • • • • • • • • • • • • • • • • • • • • • • • • • • •

*T*he first thing we'd like to do is offer you our warmest congratulations on having made it to university. The biggest hurdle is over. How many people do you know who don't make it through uni? There are, admittedly, a few who fall by the wayside, but this can be for health or financial reasons, amongst others. The student who fails to complete the course for academic reasons is a rarity. The vast majority of students will get through, and you will surely be one of them! The thing is, though, that we don't want you simply to scrape through with a third, but graduate with the best possible degree – an upper second or even a first. You've made a positive step towards that goal by picking up this book.

At first it might seem a bit scary to have to write a serious 'grown-up' essay and then hand it in to a real Professor, someone who's spent a lifetime researching his area. Fear not. We'll guide you through the stages of writing an essay and warn you of pitfalls along the way. Remember that professors and lecturers were once, years ago, students just like you – we all started somewhere and had to take those first hesitating steps. Years ago, though, there wasn't a *For Dummies* book like this to help people, so you've already got a head start.

Brows furrow and heads droop when the subject of writing an essay is mentioned. Though essays are serious stuff, they don't have to be painful experiences. They *do* have to be challenging and demanding. After all, you wouldn't like to think that you would come through your degree course on the back of essays that were easy and didn't stretch you, would you? But with the help of this book you'll be able to meet the challenges of essay writing and respond to the demands made of you. We help you in a holistic way with all the aspects of writing, not just the words on the page but the where, when, and how of the writing experience, so that you can not only be successful in your writing at university, but even – dare I say it? – actually enjoy it.

This is the book for you, then, when you need help with the words, and also when the words won't come. When you don't know where to start, and when you start you can't finish. When you've got too many words, or too few. We look at typical difficulties you might face, and help you through them. And we hope we even make you smile from time to time, because you're at uni and you should be having the time of your life!

# About This book

You may well have used a *For Dummies* book before and be familiar with our easy-to-use format and our chatty style. If, however, you are a newcomer to *For Dummies* books you might be surprised that such a weighty subject as writing essays can be made so accessible. How do we do it? We break down the subject into meaningful, manageable chunks, and then sub-chunks. What you need to do is think what it is you need to know about writing an essay, and then find the appropriate chunk or sub-chunk from our index. What you don't have to do is read from cover to cover. Home in on the bits that apply to you and take our advice. We try to write as if we were talking to you face-to-face, hence our relaxed and informal style. Our book is here for you to dip into when you need us. Think of it as your support and your friend.

# Conventions Used in This Book

Each chapter of this book covers the basics you'll need and also provides further details and examples that you can skim over if you're pushed for time. We also flag up points in the book where you can cross-reference to different chapters, so that you can read the book thematically if you need to.

For ease of navigation, we use the following conventions:

- *Italic* is used for emphasis, to highlight new words, and terms which the text defines.
- **Bold** text is used to indicate keywords in bulleted lists.
- Monofont is used for Internet addresses.
- Sidebars, the shaded grey boxes you see from time to time, point out information which might come in handy, but doesn't qualify as essential reading.

# How This Book Is Organised

We've divided our book into six parts. Each of the first five parts corresponds to a step in the process of writing an essay, followed by a sixth section, the Part of Tens. In order to help you familiarise yourself with the content of our book and find what you're looking for, we summarise each section here.

## Part 1: Navigating a World of Information

These first three chapters help you to get a feel for what it is you are expected to produce. We look at the difference between writing an essay at secondary school and writing one at university. Essays often break down into one of several basic types, so we show you what you should be aiming towards and – above all – help you to get going. This can be the hardest step of all. It's downhill all the way now!

## Part 11: Researching, Recording and Reformulating

You've got to have something to write about, so these next four chapters help you with the content of your essay. We give you plenty of tips on how best to find your way round your background reading, whether it's from books or online. In addition, we help you to make notes, both from your sources and for your essay. One of the big issues at university, given the ease of the 'copy and paste' function, is lifting, stealing, or plagiarism, whatever you want to call it. Chapter 7 says 'Don't!' in no uncertain terms, but as well as that provides you with the skills so that you aren't tempted to copy someone else's writing in the first place.

## Part 111: Mastering Language and Style

One of the worries we can have about writing an academic essay is whether our language is up to scratch. These three chapters provide a quick brush-up in the building blocks of your essay, the sentence and the paragraph, making sure that you can structure them correctly and then punctuate them accurately, so that your meaning is clear. We also give you advice on how your 'voice' comes across so that you sound appropriately formal and academic.

# Part IV: Tightening Your Structure and Organisation

Now you've got to put it all together. These four chapters divide your essay into a beginning, a middle and an end. Each has its own special features and here we explain what these are and show you what your tutor is expecting to find. In addition you will probably want to use quotations in your essay. Chapter 14 shows you how to do this, and then finish off the whole product with a nice list of references at the end. You're nearly there!

# Part V: Finishing with a Flourish: The Final Touches

Two of these chapters give you tips with the last stage of writing - the one which tends to be rushed. You can gain extra marks by attention to detail in the polishing and perfecting process and we show you how! We then take a positive attitude with the fall-out of the essay, understanding where you went wrong, learning from your mistakes and seeing how you can do better next time if the feedback wasn't quite as good as you'd hoped for. Every mistake is an opportunity to learn!

# Part VI: The Part of Tens

The Part of Tens provides you with two chapters listing helpful pointers to keep your essay-writing on track. Ten Troubleshooting Tips advises you on common problems and what to do if you find yourself in difficulties – for instance, when you've written too much or too little, when you've left it too late, or you have technical difficulties. Ten Tips for Writing Essays in Exams does what it says on the tin.

# Icons Used in This Book

Icons are a handy *For Dummies* way of catching your attention as you run through a page. Icons come in several flavours, each with its own symbol and terms of reference.

This icon does exactly what it says, highlighting helpful hints to ease your essay writing.

Wherever you see this icon there's a point that you should make into a mental or physical note – something for you to bear in mind.

This icon flags up the Don'ts. Things you should avoid doing like the plague. Ignore this icon at your peril.

# Where to Go from Here

You can go pretty much where you like from here. *For Dummies* books are not intended to be cover-to-cover reads, but resources you can dip into as and when you need to. Each chapter is designed to stand alone, delivering the goods on a particular topic. If you really want the lowdown on the whole process, and some ideas on where to go next, you could do a lot worse than read Chapter 1, but never feel that you then have to plod through 2–19 in strict order.

If you want to know more about researching online, check out Chapter 5, for instance. If you're confident that you know what you want to write on, but need to find out how to put the nuts and bolts of your essay together, Chapters 11 to 13 are for you. Chapter 16 shows you how to polish the final item. And so on.

Wherever you go in this book, use it to make writing your essays the most enjoyable experience it can be. Essay-writing should always be a challenge: this book helps it not to be a chore.

# Part I
# Navigating a World of Information

'Isn't it amazing?—They all want the same book.'

## In this part . . .

Getting a handle on what an essay title requires of you is often the toughest step of all, so we cover it thoroughly in this part. We also give you practical tips on how to get stuck in to your essay, and take an in-depth look at the different sorts of essay you might be asked to write. Essays often break down into one of several basic types, so we show you what you should be aiming towards and – above all – help you to get going and keep plugging away.

# Chapter 1

# Mapping Your Way: Starting to Write Essays

*In This Chapter*
▶ Moving from school- to university-level writing
▶ Getting a feel for writing academically
▶ Breaking the writing process down into stages
▶ Achieving success in your essay writing

*Y*ou've probably picked up this book because you're unsure exactly what's expected of you when you write an essay at university. Did your teachers at secondary school explain to you what an academic essay is? Do you know how it differs from other things you've written? You may be someone who writes happily in many situations – for instance you send letters and emails with no hesitation, you have no difficulty keeping a diary or you can write a story from your own imagination. But an academic essay? That's scary!

This first chapter should go a long way to settling any fears you may have about your writing. We make clear how an academic essay differs from the writing you did at school and from other types of writing you may be familiar with. We break the daunting task of writing your essay into manageable chunks and take you through each stage. And we give you some tips on how to gain confidence and write successfully.

## Transitioning to University-level Writing

You write in many different ways when you're at university. You take notes during lectures and seminars, make notes from books and web pages, take part in online discussions and course blogs, and draft essays and reports – as well as writing your shopping list and texting!

Of all your writing activities, the course assignment's the most important. For your assignment, you're set a writing task to do, normally over a period of a few weeks, and the marks count towards your final grade for that unit. Note-taking and blogging are important in that, done well and thoughtfully, they lay the foundations for success in essay writing both in coursework and in exams. But you're assessed on the final product, so that's what you have to give most attention to. You may throw away your notes, and blogs may disappear into the ether, but an essay you're proud of may end up at the bottom of a drawer for you to discover years later and reread, we hope with pleasure.

So, given that essays at university count for so much, why do so many students feel ill-prepared for this type of writing? Basically, writing at each main stage of the education process – primary school, secondary school and university – has a different function. Realising this is the first step to helping you tune in to what's required of you at university. By looking at the big picture, you see how what you write and how you write it changes from phase to phase.

## Writing at school

Primary school teaches you the rudiments of writing. You develop basic literacy in letters of the alphabet and sentences so that you can read and start to write stories and short compositions.

Secondary school assumes that you can use writing to express your ideas and your imagination on paper. You write about the subjects you're exploring in your lessons, and you show the teacher what you've discovered. You have opportunities at secondary school to develop creative writing skills and to begin to analyse topics from your courses in an extended way under the teacher's guidance.

## Writing at undergraduate level

As at secondary school, at university you also have to write essays to show what you know. But now you can't regurgitate what your tutors have fed you. The depth you go into with a subject is reflected in the enormous, seemingly limitless, amount of reading you have to do.

Managing your reading list demands a skill that you may not have developed before university study: critical analysis. With a heightened sense of criticality, you apply frameworks and ideas that experts in the field have developed in order to deepen and extend your knowledge. Many universities give students in their first year support in critical thinking, because this, together with the reading list, is what makes the writing process lengthier and more complex than you've probably known before.

The result of the writing process and your background reading is an essay. As such, your essay relies on a solid bibliography. Your writing at university is based on the research that's gone before. You stand on the shoulders of giants, as Sir Isaac Newton said. You have to acknowledge all quotations from authors and references to their work according to strict guidelines. See Chapter 14 for details on how to reference correctly.

## *Writing at postgraduate level*

To get your head around why you write the way you do at university, thinking about what undergraduate study can lead to may help: postgraduate study such as a master's or a PhD. At master's level you research your subject to an even greater level of detail. Your tutors push you to analyse to the furthest points until you begin to identify gaps in the body of knowledge. This is the basis of the dissertation you write.

If you then go on to a PhD, you make a contribution to the body of knowledge by undertaking a piece of original research, filling in the gaps you identified at master's degree level, if you like, and thus making yourself an expert in this field. People look to you for original thought and comment on your specialist subject. You become an authority. As such, you're expected to have a thorough knowledge of practically everything written on your subject. You read just about every book or paper ever published on it.

From undergraduate level onwards, you can lay the foundation for a career in research. The undergraduate phase you've embarked on is the first step along the road. Most people go no further than a bachelor's degree. A certain number go on to a master's. Very few become doctors in their subject. But if you just think for a moment where the undergraduate degree leads, you can see why universities are keen for you to develop your essay-writing skills.

## Smoothing the transition from school to uni

The transition to university is a difficult one socially and emotionally, in all probability geographically, and for most people, academically as well. You've probably thought long and hard about leaving friends and family behind, and are counting down to freshers' week. But you probably haven't given a great deal of thought to how to manage the academic transition from secondary school to university.

From being top of your class in English, French or history, you're now just ordinary in a cohort of students who seem much more confident and knowledgeable and just downright smarter than you are. And then, when your course starts, you realise you have to write essays and try to convince everyone that you know what you're talking about. How long can it be before they find you out and realise you're a fraud? Isn't stacking shelves in the supermarket a better option?

Relax – everyone's in the same boat and everyone doubts their own ability sometimes. Tell yourself that you've made it, you got the grades, you were accepted, and now you're here to learn. One of the most important things to grasp is the rules of the game you play at university, and a big part of the game is writing essays.

# Getting the Genre Right

If you're unfamiliar with the word *genre*, it's just a way of describing the type of text you're writing. Genres of writing encompass everything from a greeting on a birthday card to an academic essay; in other words, anything you write, by hand or on a keyboard, in any kind of social situation and to anybody under the sun.

The best way to understand the academic essay genre is to compare this type of writing against others you're probably familiar with: creative writing, articles and reports.

The academic genre carries a particular writing style that sets it apart from other genres. Turn to Chapter 10 to find out more about how you can adopt this style in your writing.

## Writing an essay, not creative prose

When you're writing an academic essay, you don't let your imagination run wild and compose stories (unless your course is actually called Creative Writing!). Control's the name of the game. You write to a strict structure and don't deviate. A kind of formula exists for the way you do the introduction, and similarly for the conclusion. What goes in between (the body of the essay) can follow several different overall patterns, and is composed of paragraphs that, once again, fit a particular shape. (Flick to Chapters 12, 13 and 14 for more on how to write each part of your essay.)

You should refer constantly to the work of experts rather than going off on a fantasy of your own. Creativity lies not in flights of imagination but in deep understanding of previous research, and interpreting this in your own way. Though you may not think so, you *do* have room to express your own opinions, but only in the context of what you've read.

You may think of this genre as being like a straitjacket, and in a way it is. But it's actually a pretty easy genre to write within. Once you've got your head around the genre and know what you can and can't do, a lot of decisions are already made for you and you just fit in with everything. You play by the rules.

Just as it doesn't belong in the content of your essay, creativity isn't welcome in how you present it either. An essay printed in a flowery font on petal-pink paper and held together with a daisy chain doesn't impress your tutor. In Chapter 16 we take you through the correct way to present your essay.

## Writing an essay, not a newspaper article

Another type of writing you may have had a try at is journalism. But unless your tutor specifically asks you to write in the style of a tabloid or a quality newspaper for some reason, you need to avoid using features of this genre. A newspaper article isn't an academic essay, and you need to separate the two clearly in your mind.

The first area in which these two genres differ is their structure. Unlike an academic essay, a newspaper article packs as much key information into the headline and the first paragraph as possible, because the writer wants to attract the reader's attention. A reader with very little time skims through the headlines and first paragraphs in order to get the gist of the day's news. To grab the reader's attention and get him or her to continue reading the article, the first paragraph has to contain the essentials and pack a punch. Less important information can be in paragraphs further down, because not everybody reads this far, and often the article ends without any kind of summing up or conclusion.

Not so the academic essay. You don't have to work to grab your tutor's attention, because he or she is going to read your essay anyway. And all of it, too. The introduction to the essay sets the scene and analyses the question you're going to answer. You don't give away the key information in the first paragraph, but divulge that information in a controlled fashion. You make sure that every bit of your essay, every paragraph, contains relevant and meaningful comment, thus building up your argument in a logical and structured way. When you reach the conclusion, you provide some sort of answer to the issue raised in the introduction, and you should to a greater or lesser extent generate a feeling of resolution. You don't think about entertaining the reader (although if your work's interesting, that's a bonus!), but rather focus on answering the question fully with as much relevant detail as space permits.

Style's another factor. With a newspaper article, given the brief amount of time a journalist has to write it, sentences are often short and uncomplicated in structure, paragraphs are short, and language is pretty straightforward because the readership's so wide. In academic style, on the other hand, you have time to deliberate over sentence structure, often resulting in longer and more complex sentences. Paragraphs consist of several sentences that clearly link together. And the writer may also use specialised terminology, because the readership's restricted to a smaller number of people with specialist interests and knowledge.

You can also find in journalism that the language describing an event or a person sometimes appeals to the emotions, because the reporter may be trying to provoke an emotional response in the reader. The writing may have a subjective slant or be attempting to influence the reader in some way. After all, newspapers do have owners, and these owners do have political leanings. Academic writing, in contrast, attempts always to be objective and has what some may consider a cold and distant tone, because to a large extent it avoids subjectivity. This is reflected in the restricted use of the first person pronouns, 'I' or 'we', and a greater use of passive forms such as 'it can be seen that . . .'. (Although academia's been changing of late in this respect, and in some quarters has loosened up a little.)

In keeping with this traditional objectivity, an academic essay takes as its basis the work of researchers and experts who've added to the body of knowledge over the years. You refer continually to authors through referencing and acknowledging sources. You're respectful of your sources, and you aren't arrogant in your argument. Your tutor looks at the extent to which you use your sources, how many you use and the accuracy with which you use your references. He or she assesses you on how skilfully you weave your quotations and references into your argument. In a newspaper report, in contrast, you may notice that direct quotations are often introduced with a simple 'Mr Black said' followed by his exact words, or indirect quotations with a straightforward 'Mrs White told reporters that . . .'.

This is no criticism of journalism, by the way, but a simple statement of fact that the circumstances are different and the features of the genre different as a result. Though we hope that a newspaper article doesn't contain untruthful or libellous information, readers understand that they're reading something written very quickly and that it may contain some bias as a result. Journalists, we hope, don't knowingly write anything false, but circumstances require them to give their own versions of events pretty rapidly. In your situation, however, you have the time to weigh your words so that you produce an academic essay for which you've checked all the facts, and in which you've fully developed the ideas, acknowledged sources and drawn conclusions.

To help you visualise the main differences between essays and journalism, Table 1-1 summarises points of comparison.

| Table 1-1 | Comparing Essays and Articles |
|---|---|
| **Academic essay** | **Newspaper article** |
| Has a beginning, middle and end of equal importance | Is structured like an inverted triangle: supplies information in decreasing order of importance |
| Is written in a formal style | Can be written in a more informal-style |
| Tries to be objective | Can be emotive and subjective |
| Includes references to expert research | Uses quotations that the reader can't verify |

## Writing an essay, not a report

The other genre you may have to use at undergraduate level, especially if you're writing up an investigation, is a report. So where do report writing and essay writing differ?

Essays and reports have some similarities:

 ✔ Both are written in the same style: objective and very focused. Both contain an argument that's clear to follow: sentences and paragraphs flow logically into the next.

✔ Both refer to the previous work of other researchers and present comment and findings in the light of that body of knowledge. Therefore, you give the same attention to the list of references at the end of a report as at the end of an essay.

Where a report differs from an essay is in the inclusion of some extra features. Visually, a report's immediately different from an essay. A report is the product of a piece of research and the different sections of your report correspond to the various stages of that research. It should be easy to spot the sections. Though your tutor may give you instructions that differ in minor details, the usual layout of a report is as follows:

✔ **Title page:** This is pretty self-explanatory!

✔ **Abstract:** You provide an overview of the purpose of the report, summarise how you went about your research and why, and what main conclusions you've come to. You give your reader at-a-glance information that conveys the main gist of your report.

✔ **Table of contents:** You provide an overview, with page numbers, of the different sections.

✔ **Introduction:** You introduce the question you're addressing (as for an academic essay).

✔ **Literature review:** You summarise what you've read from the experts on the topic you're about to research.

✔ **Methodology:** You describe how you went about collecting your data.

✔ **Findings:** You present the results of your data collection.

✔ **Discussion:** You interpret your findings in the light of previous research as described in the literature review.

✔ **Conclusion:** You attempt to answer the question raised in the introduction (as for an academic essay).

✔ **List of references:** You include all your references (as for an academic essay).

✔ **Appendices (if any):** If you've collected more data than you can comfortably contain in the body of your report, you make this into appendices.

The report divides numerically into these sections, and each section begins on a fresh page. Depending on the nature of the report, you can subdivide the different sections into smaller sections, each with its own subheading. The overall effect's thus quite different from an academic essay, where you don't normally use headings or subheadings.

# Crafting Your Essay: Stages in the Writing Process

Now you've got a good feel for academic essays, you need to know how the essay-writing process works. You don't just sit down at the keyboard and produce the finished product in one sitting – or let's say that's unusual or inadvisable. You spread the writing of an essay over a period. You break the process up into manageable chunks, and this helps you to excel at each stage and plan your time so that you don't miss the deadline.

In this section, we divide the process into seven distinct stages. As you become more and more comfortable and experienced with the writing process, you develop and gain confidence in your own individual way of working. You may then modify the process to suit your own preferences. Here we provide a framework for you to begin with.

## Stage 1: Analysing the title

A common criticism of student essays is that the person didn't answer the question. No matter how many times tutors warn students, someone always falls into the trap of not answering the question that they've been set. While you *do* have an excuse (but only a little one!) for not answering the question in the heat and frenzy of an exam, you don't when you're writing an essay, when you have plenty of time to think about and discuss what the essay title requires.

To give a proper answer, you have to understand fully what the question's asking for. To work that out, you unpick:

- ✔ **Keywords:** These explain the topic, for example Shakespeare, sonnets, *As You Like It*, women, and so on.
- ✔ **Function words:** These tell you how you have to treat the subject matter, for example 'compare', 'analyse' or 'discuss'.

Chapter 3 takes you through understanding the title by looking at these important words.

## What writing at university is *not*

Writing an essay at university isn't 'Write all you know about X'. This is what you did when you were much younger and school was more about being told and memorising facts. The more facts you assembled, the more successful you were. You showed that you had knowledge.

Although what you write at university is based on facts or evidence, what you do with this knowledge is what counts now. Your tutor asks you not simply to describe, but to compare, analyse, discuss and suggest. So you read the books, assemble the facts and then do something with them. And what you do with them is what's assessed, not the gathering of the evidence in the first place. You're marked on how well, deeply and accurately you compare, analyse, discuss and suggest.

You arrange an essay at university as an argument, with a question that you state in the introduction, and then develop, and then answer (in part if not wholly) in the conclusion. You don't include anything that's irrelevant to the argument.

This is far removed from 'Write all you know about X'.

## Stage 2: Making a timetable

Planning your time's essential if you're going to get through every-thing you have to do. You structure your time using a timetable. To draw up your timetable, you need to list all the things you have to do in order to be able to write your essay. Have you got all your course notes? Did you miss a session and do you need to borrow a friend's notes? Which books do you need? (Chapter 4 offers advice on getting hold of the necessary texts.)

Next, fill in your diary or calendar with all the commitments you have between now and the deadline. As well as lectures and classes, put in any other work – paid work or study – that you have to do. This should leave you with a rough idea of how many gaps you have in your busy days in which you can slot in work for the essay.

No one can work flat out and not have some pleasure! So include your social life, sports and time for chilling out and relaxing, watching the television or simply getting your energy back.

You need to consider your essay within the bigger picture of all your university work. Make sure you get your priorities right, too, as not all essays, presentations and other tasks you have to do are worth the same. Of course, you want to do your very best in every-thing, but realistically you put the greatest effort into the assign-ments that count the most. That makes sense, doesn't it?

You should now have a realistic idea of how much time's available. Now you can start apportioning blocks of time to your essay. In Chapter 4 we outline a rough guide for dividing your time: 80 per cent on preparation (Stages 1–4) and 20 per cent on writing up and finishing (Stages 5–7). Bearing this in mind, go back to your timetable and calculate when Stage 4 should finish and Stage 5 begin. You have to know when to stop reading and when you have to start writing. This mini-deadline helps you reach the final deadline when you hand the essay in. Then, working backwards from your mini-deadline, you can see how much time you have for all the things you need to read, and you can work out a rough schedule of what to do when. You can amend the timetable as you go along, but do try to meet that mini-deadline so that you can start the actual writing on time.

When you're drawing up your timetable, don't stint the time you allow for Stages 6 and 7. You shouldn't rush these, and you should always allow for the fact that you do your reviewing and checking better after a night's sleep. Stages 6 and 7 shouldn't take place on the day you hand your work in!

Print out your essay timetable and stick it on the wall so that you are continually reminded of where you are in the process and how quickly time's going by.

## Stage 3: Gathering data

What do you need to know and where are you going to get this information from? At home, you should have notes you've taken in lectures, handouts from tutors, maybe a course book and a reading list. In the university, you've got a library with lots of books in it, and also academic journals, many of which may be accessible online. You may not have realised this, but you also have a specialist librarian who knows your subject really well and can make recommendations to you about which books to read.

First, at home, go through all your notes, papers and books, highlighting key information for your essay and making a note of the books you need to find. Then go to the library and find some reading matter, asking for help if need be. Find a nice comfy corner, either at home or in the library, and get down to work.

Make notes as you go through the material, always bearing in mind the essay title. You can so easily get waylaid if you find something interesting to read on an aspect that's only tangential to the essay title. The best thing to do is to make a note of where you found that interesting article, so you can come back to it later when you have more time. Most importantly, keep a detailed record of all the books that you've consulted and any websites you've visited. You have to include a full list of references or a bibliography (see Chapter 14), and suddenly finding that you don't have the information to hand the night before your submission date is extremely annoying.

Chapter 4 helps you with your reading techniques, especially if you're under pressure and time's whooshing by, and Chapter 6 gives you practical tips on note taking.

## Stage 4: Brainstorming and planning

With the mini-deadline looming (see Stage 2), you get to a point when you can't read and research any longer – time to put the books and notes to one side and work with what's inside your head. First you brainstorm (dump the contents of your mind onto paper or the screen), and then you try to make something out of the result by planning.

- ✔ **Brainstorming:** Get those ideas out of your head in whatever way feels best. With practice and experience, you find the way of brainstorming that feels most comfortable and practical in your circumstances. Do you prefer working on paper or the PC (see the 'PC vs Pencil' sidebar later in the chapter on this)? Do you like to make linear notes or use spider diagrams? Do notes on index cards work well for you? How about using colours to organise your ideas?

- ✔ **Planning your essay structure:** Group your ideas together in a logical structure. Think of the plan as like your skeleton. The skeleton holds your body together and gives it shape. Without it you'd be a mess of blubber on the floor. You need your skeleton to stand up straight, and you need your plan to make your essay hang together.

You should already have your timetable pinned up on the wall in the place where you write and study most. Next to it should be your essay plan. Print the plan out and pin it up there. Glancing at both periodically reminds you how quickly time's passing as well as of the shape of the final product.

Finally, when you think you've got all the main points in the right order, go back once again to your essay title and ask yourself whether the plan you have in front of you does actually answer the question you've been set. Look at the broad thrust of your argument and ask yourself whether your line of reasoning is logical, relevant and complete in terms of the question. If it is, move on to Stage 5. If it isn't, you may have to do a little fine-tuning. Don't move on to Stage 5 until you're happy with your plan.

Chapter 6 helps you with brainstorming and organising your material, and Chapter 3 outlines the common structures you use for essays.

# Stage 5: Writing the first draft

If you think of your plan as a skeleton, the next step's to put the flesh on the bones. You have to pull together the little notes, the random jottings, the odd words scribbled here and there to produce the sentences and then the paragraphs that make up the bulk of your essay.

As you write, you make the transition from a private piece of work to a more public one that a number of people may read: your main tutor, other tutors who are moderating marks, or an external examiner. You create your draft by:

- ✓ **Writing for your reader, not for yourself:** You know what you want to say but you can't assume that your reader's following you, so you have to deliver every point you make fully with appropriate development and give examples. Imagine that you're talking to someone who doesn't quite understand or have your background knowledge in the subject. This may help you to develop your point fully so that your meaning's clear.

- ✓ **Guiding your reader:** Don't assume that your argument's obvious. You have to guide your reader through the points you make by using linking words and expressions that point clearly to the line of reasoning you're taking.

- ✓ **Assuming a more academic voice:** Your public consists of academics, and they expect you to write in an appropriate style. This means making your vocabulary formal rather than informal and avoiding anything that sounds too chatty. See Chapter 10 for more on style.

When you come to writing the first draft of your essay, feel free to start with the part you feel most confident about. With a good framework that you're happy with and which you stick to, you now have the luxury of being able to write sections of the essay in the order that seems easiest to you, knowing that, with your plan, you can bring all the bits together at the end to make a cohesive whole. Getting a few paragraphs under your belt as quickly as possible is a good idea, and this gives you confidence to build on for the later, more challenging parts.

When you're doing the first draft of your essay, working with headings is often easiest. Each section and subsection should have a heading. You used them in the essay plan – keep them in when you're writing up the first draft. This helps you to focus on your points, one after the other, and to keep on track. Before you hand your essay in, delete the headings.

Several chapters help you write your first draft. Chapters 8, 9 and 10 help you write well and in an academic style, and Chapters 11, 12 and 13 break the essay down and lead you through forming the introduction, middle and conclusion.

# Stage 6: Revising your draft

Depending on how important it is to you and how much time you have at your disposal, you may make several drafts of your essay (or more likely sections of your essay) until you're satisfied. When you read some chunks back to yourself they may sound really awful – too chatty, clumsy or unclear – so take those parts out and work on your essay until you feel it conveys what you want to say in a manner you're happy with.

If you've been working on your computer for a long time, print out a copy of your essay, go and sit somewhere different and work through it on paper. Sometimes you see things differently when the script's actually in your hands and not on a screen. Use arrows, colours, underlining and whatever signals you need to make to yourself that something's not right. Go through the entire essay making annotations where you have to make changes, and only return to your computer to make those changes when you've got to the end.

Back at the computer, make a copy of your file and label it draft 2. If you have second thoughts about anything you change in the second draft and want to go back to what you said in the first, you can just delete what you don't like in draft 2 and copy and paste over from draft 1. File every draft separately so that you don't lose anything you've written in producing this essay.

When you do make changes, start at the beginning, working your way methodically down the printed page, ticking the alterations as you go along, so that if you're interrupted you know where you are. Then put the essay away. All being well, you're on schedule and can leave the final stage for the next day.

# Stage 7: Checking and polishing

You think you've done the very best you can in the time you've had available to you. Funnily enough, you can always improve on something, and that something may just swing the balance and get you a better mark. If you've been sticking to the timetable you made in Stage 2, you have a day or an evening when you can give your essay that final spit and polish. The main areas to check are content and presentation:

- ✔ **Content:** Edit your essay to ensure that you're being rigorous with your argument and that every point you make, every paragraph you write, adds to the line of reasoning you're pursuing. You have to discard anything that doesn't fit. You don't have the time to do any major rewrites now, so you're stuck with the general train of thought, but you can tweak the odd sentence here and there to soften or strengthen your points.

- ✔ **Presentation:** Pay attention to the detail and proofread your essay, looking for typos and errors. Because first impressions are important, spend some time perfecting the look of the essay as well.

Chapters 15 and 16 take you through the checking and polishing stage.

## The final hurdle: Handing in

Pressure may have been intense, nerves may have been frayed and your fingers may be bitten to the quick. But when you actually get to hand your essay in, you can forget a lot of the stress that went before. When you submit your essay and it's gone, you feel great (for the time being). My goodness! What on earth are you going to do this evening now you've finished? You probably don't need reminding, but can we gently point out that essay number two is looming? So wind down, have fun – you've worked hard and you deserve it! – but be ready to get into essay-writing mode again very soon.

And prepare yourself for feedback on your essay: take a look at Chapter 17.

## Becoming a Successful Essay Writer

You don't just wake up one morning, write your first academic essay and make a brilliant job of it. You get there, as with many things in life, by practice – trial and error.

Writing's something you can't avoid at university. So if you're one of those people who professes to hate writing, think long and hard about how you're going to deal with the writing on your course. You need to practise, clear time for your writing and eradicate those niggling doubts and fears.

## Just write, write, write

Before you even start writing an academic essay, you've got to develop the writing habit, whatever form that takes for you. You've got to write at every opportunity so that writing becomes a natural and frequent occurrence.

## PC versus pencil

Many students we work with use the 'old-fashioned' method of pen and paper for the majority of the essay-writing process. If you're one of these, you may want to consider how useful the PC can be.

✔ **Brainstorm directly onto your computer:** Use mind-mapping software that's designed for the job or the drawing tools in Microsoft Word. Your computer offers a good range of colours, far more than you probably have in your pencil case. Colours are especially useful when you're grouping ideas together, using one colour for one idea. And the bonus is that you can remove highlighting at the click of a button.

✔ **Type your notes up on the PC:** You have no limit on space, you can move chunks around so that you end up with an essay plan without having to start a new document and if you make a mistake or change your mind, that's easy to rectify. Remember, though, that you must save changes as you go along. Your computer's very useful for reordering chunks of text, but mistakes do happen when you're tired and distracted. Returning to work in progress the following day only to find that you've lost something important is so frustrating!

✔ **Use tools to speed up editing and proofreading:** Spellchecking tools are handy (see Chapter 15 for more on this), and a tool such as Find and Replace is wonderful when you realise that you've been using a word wrongly and another one's more apt.

Clearly, working directly onto the computer can save a bit of time, but pen and paper are also comforting. And a program can't do absolutely everything. Think of your PC as a workhorse that enables you to do amazing things in a shorter length of time, but for the fine-tuning you need the thoroughbred – the human brain!

Always keep a pen and a notebook with you, so that you can write at every possible moment. Never go out of the door without them. Keep a diary for the first time in your life, or a journal in which you express your thoughts however you like. Get blogging. Start your first novel! Write first thing in the morning and last thing at night – on the bus, between classes, while you're watching your laundry go around.

Whatever you do, tell yourself 'I'm a writer.' You've got to adopt the mindset of the writer and write at every opportunity, all the time. We're not saying that this is going to be easy, but with perseverance you can change the way you perceive yourself and find a relationship with your pencil you never suspected was possible!

## Giving yourself enough time

If at school you left writing essays to the very last minute and then scraped through with a reasonable pass, don't think that you can get away with the same at uni. The lengthy reading lists and the complexity and depth of the topics you may have to write about make getting away with a last-minute essay rather difficult.

And to be truthful, university isn't about getting by with some scribble you hastily put together the night before. If you're at university, you're there to study at length and in depth over stretches of time that allow you to live with a topic, mull it over, internalise it and make it your own. That way, when you come to give your response in the form of an academic essay, you're doing so after sufficient time to give the subject the consideration it deserves.

If you find writing hard, give yourself as much time as possible. In time, things may well improve and you may pick up speed. But maybe you're always going to find writing difficult, and you just have to live with that, allowing yourself more time than your friends need for writing each essay. Don't be hard on yourself if you do always seem to need more time than your friends. We're all different, and in other areas of your studies you're going to have the edge over other people.

## Changing your mindset

Dwelling on the scarier aspects of writing at university and over-looking the big picture is easy to do. Success is within your grasp if you take a determined and positive attitude. Table 1-2 helps you meet your fears head on.

| Table 1-2 | Tackling Your Essay-writing Demons |
|---|---|
| *If you think . . .* | *Tell yourself . . .* |
| When I hand in my essay, I'll be exposed as an imbecile who should never have come to university. | You won your place at university fairly and squarely and have a right to be there. Many other students are probably feeling exactly the same as you! |
| Writing's such a solitary business – how do I cope? | You have lots of people to talk to! You can discuss assignments with your tutor and your classmates, and although only you write up the final product, you have lots of opportunities for supporting one another along the way. |
| How on earth can I produce assignments of, say, 3,000 words? | You can break any big task down into chunks, and writing's no different; everyone manages to do it in the end. |
| I don't know all the academic words for things, and what I write sounds childish. | You're here to learn, and through reading and attending lectures you pick up the jargon. You soon start writing like an expert! |
| I can't write anything original. | As an undergrad, you don't necessarily have to. You read and acknowledge the work of other writers and researchers who've been there before you and comment on what they've written in your own way and in your own words. Originality can come later (when you're doing your PhD or heading for a Nobel Prize). |

And you may like to write in your own personal worry here and then answer it as if you were speaking to a friend. (Don't leave the right-hand column blank!)

Good! Now you're on your way to changing your mindset.

 Congratulate yourself on already having made a big step forward in discovering how to write at university by picking up this book and showing your determination to succeed.

# Chapter 2

# Getting Going and Keeping Going

• • • • • • • • • • • • • • • • • • • • • • • • • • • • • • • • • •

## In This Chapter
▶ Finding the best conditions to get you working
▶ Getting over the first hurdle and putting pen to paper
▶ Getting by with a little help from your friends

• • • • • • • • • • • • • • • • • • • • • • • • • • • • • • • • • •

*W*hatever the task, the first step's often one of the hardest. For very many people, picking up a book or putting pen to paper can be tough. The trick in many cases is to give yourself the best possible chance to do your best by getting the conditions right for you to be comfortable and successful in your writing.

In this chapter we show you how to overcome your fears about essay writing and feel good about your work, and we give you tips on making the process less daunting than you may imagine. We also provide strategies for the inevitable moments when ideas do dry up and you need to turn the tap on again, and we help you identify what helps you to write happily, efficiently and successfully.

## Getting Ready to Write

A little preparation goes a long way in helping you to find motivation and inspiration. You need to discover how you work best, create a comfortable work environment and pave the way for successful study before you dive in. Read on to find out how.

### Finding out what helps you to work

'Know thyself' is a saying that's served many a purpose since the ancient Greek philosophers first coined it. It must contain some truth for it to have been around so long, and it's a good starting point. For most people to engage in the creative process, whether they're painting a picture, composing music or writing an essay, the conditions have to be right – or at least pretty good. So begin by finding out a few things about yourself: what helps you think, read and write?

Keep a mental note of what you discover for future reference, so that you can enter writing mode more easily and plan your study time effectively.

### Knowing when you work best

Go with your body clock. Are you a lark or an owl? How much sleep do you need to feel good?

This is where you have to be true to yourself and not follow the herd. You may be living in a university hall of residence or sharing a flat with fellow students and feel obliged to go with the general flow of life there – understandably, because most people want to fit in. But with important stuff, you have to do what's right for you.

Many people find the quietness of the hours after dawn conducive to thinking and generating ideas. This means that when you need to write an essay, you have to forgo the late-night movie or the extra pint at the pub with your friends and go to bed early enough to catch what for you are the productive hours of the morning. And we're not talking about getting up at 5 a.m. to work (unless you particularly want to). Just half an hour of peace and quiet before your flatmates get up can be enough over a week or so to capture the creative juices. The section 'Keeping Yourself on Track', elsewhere in this chapter, explains just how useful those half hours can be.

A considerable number of people can work late into the night, even into the wee small hours, and produce good essays. But if you do this, remember that you need to be alert for that 9 a.m. lecture. Margaret Thatcher was said to be able to exist on about four hours' sleep a night, but she's surely in a minority. How many hours do you need?

The message is that, morning, noon or night, whenever you find easiest to write is the time to plan for. Give yourself the best possible chance by observing your own body clock and then – as far as circumstances permit – going with it.

University's the best time of many people's lives. However, sometimes the socialising can take over and blind you to the real reason you're there: to get your degree. So you've got to be tough with yourself at critical times, keep the social life on hold, and listen to the wise voice inside your head that's telling you to knuckle down to your essay. Afterwards you can enjoy the partying so much more.

### Choosing where to work

There you are in the university library, watching all the other students furiously making notes, bashing away on the computer or blowing the dust off ancient tomes. And all you have is an empty sheet of paper and an even emptier head. In these circumstances, the wisest thing to do is to get out.

If ever you're stuck, change something.

The library isn't the only place to work, and you can try other places that may be more stimulating. Here are some ideas:

- A coffee shop: people-watching can be a trigger.
- The local park: the fresh air helps.
- A place with water, such as by a canal, pond or fountain: water flowing suggests thoughts flowing.
- The garden: lie on your back and see the pictures in the clouds.
- The kitchen: cosy!
- Your bed

Try different surroundings and see what works. All you need is a notebook and pencil; then go off and see which environment suits you best.

### Decluttering your area

Are you someone who needs a clear desk in order to focus, or do you thrive amid piles of paper and books? Whatever feels right for you, go with it.

If you're a minimalist, have a clear out. This is symbolic of cleansing your mind of irrelevant thoughts. Get out the vacuum cleaner if you need to. Remove objects that may annoy or distract, like half-eaten plates of food, bank statements, books about the Tudors (when you're trying to write an essay about the Stuarts) or the Valentine card you wish you'd sent.

### Setting the mood

Few people are fortunate enough to be able to turn on their creativity wherever they are, so you need to consider your location and make that as inspiring as you possibly can. Surrounding yourself with the stuff of inspiration can be a great way to boost your mood and make getting down to work slightly less painful!

Consider how your working environment appeals to your senses. Little touches can go a long way to make you feel relaxed, happy and focused:

- **Breathing in aromatherapy:** Try different essential oils to give your environment the fragrance you feel most comfortable and productive with. They aren't expensive and a little goes a long way.

  Good scents to start with are lavender, which can calm you down if you need to focus on your task, and basil, which can stimulate thought if you need a kick start. You don't need expensive burners, just a drop of oil on a tissue.

- **Enhancing the music of your mind:** Some people need quiet in order to think, but others can work better with music in the background. Find the kind of music that either resonates with the thoughts buzzing around in your head or takes you where you want to be. Classical music such as Bach or Mozart may work for you and stimulate your grey cells, or gentle background sounds may maintain focus and peace. Whatever your taste, make sure that you have good headphones so that your choice doesn't disturb your flatmates!

- **Using visual stimulation:** Think of a time and place where you've found creativity relatively easy, and then, within the limits of the possible, try to recreate that place in your study environment. Looking out of your window onto a grey winter's day in Manchester may not stimulate your brain, and you may long for, say, the beaches of Ibiza. OK, so time and your overdraft don't allow you to drop everything and fly off there, but you can pin a picture of a tropical paradise on your wall and be there in your mind in an instant. Close your eyes, feel the seductive heat, smell the exotic flowers, let the grains of sand trickle between your toes and allow that warm creative glow to come over you . . .

## Organising yourself

Don't waste precious study time hunting under your bed for a book, deliberating over biscuits in the local shop, or talking to your friend Ed about the footie results. Spend a little time sorting yourself out before you begin work, and you're more likely to focus without wasting time on bothersome distractions.

### Keeping the essentials to hand

Fetching everything that you need during your writing time, how-ever short that is, helps to keep you focused and on track with your time management. All your writing equipment, food, drink, sustenance, books and lecture notes need to be within reach. In getting up to go and find something, you may well be distracted, and bang goes your writing for that morning. You may also wish to switch off your mobile for the same reason.

Chapter 6 gives you pointers on what tools you need for the job, from a hole punch to paper clips.

### Food for thought

This may be a cliché, but it's one you can't ignore. When you're hungry or thirsty, writing's hard. Heavy meals may send you to sleep, but little snacks, sweets and chocolates can keep you going. Plan to have water with you (many people recommend it) and keep sipping; then take a break now and again to make a cuppa.

Don't overdo the stimulants! Too much tea and coffee can leave you wired. And alcoholic drinks aren't usually recommended when doing serious stuff, but who knows what form your muse may take?

Go shopping before you start writing, so that you're well stocked up on all the little treats that help you along. You don't have to buy calorific biscuits and sweets – you can eat nuts, which although high in calories are nourishing, and fruit too. Your waistline doesn't have to suffer when you're in a writing phase.

### Clearing the decks

Do things that are at the back of your mind – the phone call you need to make, the letter you should have posted yesterday, the washing-up – so that you have nothing to niggle and distract you. The television comes into this category, too. You don't need to interrupt the creative flow in order to watch the latest episode of your favourite show. You can set the timer and record it, or you can probably watch it online.

Turn off your mobile and try to forget about checking your text messages and email. Ask your friends not to get in touch if you want to get your head down and study. Chances are some of them are on the same course as you anyway and need to get on with the same essay. So you're helping yourselves by not distracting one another.

# Overcoming Writer's Block

Your essay-writing process begins with reading, moves on to making notes and then progresses to writing up. You may have no problem finding the motivation to read, and you may make wonderful, clearly organised notes (see Chapter 6). However, at some point you have to start adding words in the form of sentences, and this is where you may face your first real hurdle. Writer's block, or the fear generated by a blank page or screen, is something many students and writers have to overcome at some stage in the process.

Above all, don't beat yourself up. Even famous authors and prolific journalists have times when the ideas don't come. Yet somehow they manage to make a living out of writing! So never feel that you're the only person ever to get stuck. Writer's block's a normal response and it's temporary. You just need to try a few different strategies to find what works for you. Here are a few suggestions.

## Challenging your fears

You may have to tackle some deep-seated fears about writing.

Maybe your essays at school didn't go down well with your teacher, or perhaps your school didn't even teach you how to write an essay, and now you're at uni you find yourself dreading the moment you have to commit your ideas to paper and hand them in to your tutor. You feel scared of what your tutor may say, that he or she may rubbish your humble efforts – after all, tutors are the experts; they've been doing this for years! So you put off starting your essay until the last minute, thus increasing the pressure on yourself.

Relax – you're normal! This behaviour's typical of students the world over. Stop the self-doubts and remind yourself instead that you got to university and you're as good as anyone else.

## Writing something – anything – and rewording it

If you can write something down, you've begun. As the ancient Chinese said, 'The journey of a thousand miles begins with the first step.' However imperfect or stumbling your words, once you look back at them, you see that a strange phenomenon has occurred: the process of writing takes over and generates ideas you didn't realise you had.

Thinking and writing are two independent processes. You don't think something and write down the same thought. The very act of writing produces further ideas and clarifies fuzzy ones. Getting going and writing a few garbled sentences is crucial, even if you discard them at a later stage, because you have to engage with the writing process and let it take over. Trust it, 'It's a kind of magic' (the ancient . . . rock band Queen!).

Begin by writing your name, the date, and the title of the assignment. There. The page isn't blank any more. You've started and you can go on. Write any random thoughts that come into your head, even if what you write is your shopping list. But write *something*. You can delete it later when the real ideas start to roll.

Another way of getting going is to write the title of the essay again, but put it in your own words. Say the title is:

'Compare and contrast $X$ and $Y$. Evaluate their significance with reference to $Z$.'

You write down:

'So I have to make a list of all the things I know about $X$ and all the things I know about $Y$ and see if any are the same. Then I have to look at the things that are different and talk about them. Then I have to think about how important they are when I consider the $Z$ situation.'

So far so good. But you can do a bit more. Go back to the word '$X$' and add an example. Just one. Go back to the word '$Y$' and add an example. Just one. Then go back to the word '$Z$' and write something about it. Just one thing.

Did you find that you wanted to write more than one example each time? Chances are you did, so go on, do it, and before you know it you have a page of ideas to juggle with. You're off!

Get into the habit of always having a pen and notebook on you, so that you can jot down the ideas that pop into your mind at odd moments.

## Talking before you write

Ask yourself what your essay's about, answer the question and then write down what you've just said to yourself. You really don't need anyone to talk to, because what you're doing is verbalising the dialogue that's going on in your head.

Even better, get hold of a small digital voice recorder and record yourself as you babble away. The advantage is you don't have to rely on your memory to know what to write. A recorder's also really useful to have with you if you don't have pen and paper to hand, so that you don't lose those little germs of ideas. Recording yourself talking to yourself may feel strange at first, but you won't regret it when you play your recordings back and discover the nuggets within. You may be amazed and find you can't wait to commit them to paper!

## Visualising the final product

Remember how good you feel when you've achieved something. Reminding yourself of that glow of achievement – the pride you feel and the warmth that goes with it – may give you the courage to face an empty screen. Imagine how satisfied you're going to feel when you've finished. Such visualising may help you to say 'Oh, what the heck' and go for it.

Tell yourself that your essay doesn't have to be perfect immediately (see the sidebar 'Respecting perfection but not letting it hold you back'). When you're revising and editing you can polish your essay and make it really good. The important thing's that you get the work done to the best of your ability and meet the deadline.

## Forgetting about the essay for a while

Time permitting, you should turn your thoughts to other issues and deliberately not think about your essay. When you come back to it after a break, you may be surprised by the number of new ideas that suddenly seem to present themselves.

Don't confuse giving yourself a break from your essay with putting it off indefinitely. The first's to allow the thoughts to form themselves, and the second's a recipe for failing your unit.

# Respecting perfection but not letting it hold you back

Many people hold an idea of perfection in their minds. By all means do your best, but understand that often you have to make do with what you can reasonably achieve in the time at your disposal.

So many students come to tutors like us for advice because they're blocked by overambitious goals. Their aiming high's very heartening, but the reality is that this can set them up for failure. They don't meet the deadline, and assignments spill over from one term into the next, perhaps costing marks and even resulting in ill health.

In the long term, you probably forget your final average grade. What counts is whether you get a degree.

Our advice is to stick to your plan: cut your losses when things don't quite work out with a section you're writing, and instead move on to the next so that you get the essay written and handed in on time, thus avoiding any penalty. Penalties aren't fun.

## *Sleeping on it*

The mind's a wonderful tool. Without you realising, your brain continues to process, categorise and store your thoughts while you're sleeping. Trust your brain to do its work while you get a good night's sleep. It can sort out problems for you and provide a fresh perspective on your troublesome essay when you wake.

 And when you're really under pressure and time's short, don't undervalue a catnap for a quick fix. Watch a cat hunker down, deliberately place a paw over its eyes and shut out the world for ten minutes. Then it stretches, surveys its world and carries on, as alert as ever.

## *Reading something different*

Reading something not directly related to the subject of your essay may help. What about a newspaper or magazine? An article on a different topic can get you thinking, and then all of a sudden the ideas flow and you can't wait to write them down. Your brain's hardwired to make connections, but you've got to give it something to react and connect to.

## Getting your blood flowing

If your brain feels stagnant or you're tired, the best thing to do is to move around. Just walking from one room to another is a start, but we recommend some stretching exercises, yoga postures, or simply standing up, bending over and touching your toes. These get the blood flowing through your body and, most importantly, through your brain.

Don't think that writing's a purely intellectual activity. It has a physical side as well, which can be a trigger for mental activity. The ancient Romans summed this up as 'A healthy mind in a healthy body', and although you don't have to be as fit as an Olympic athlete, your head can benefit from your body feeling good.

You may feel awkward if you're working in a public space such as the university library, but you can walk around the stacks or, if you're restricted to your desk, at least roll your head from side to side, stretch your neck and loosen your shoulders. Just listen to all those crunching noises! These are crystals of tension that you need to shift for your blood to flow, bringing fresh oxygen to your brain and, with it, new perspectives.

## Doing something that makes you feel good

What makes you feel upbeat? The section 'Getting your blood flowing' suggests physical activity, and this may do the trick, but don't restrict yourself to stretching and walking – most importantly, laugh and feel good. Try singing, belly dancing, baking a cake, playing Scrabble, watching a chick-flick or an action movie – anything that helps you get a buzz and puts you in the right frame of mind to continue.

The cheapest and often most effective remedy when you're stuck is a good laugh. You need to loosen up – and who better to chill out with than a couple of mates? Someone cracks a joke, and the tension's gone. When you're back at the keyboard, just remember that joke or think of anything that makes you chuckle, and you can relieve the anxiety of the moment.

Keep a few silly photos of friends or a jokey calendar near your study area to bring a smile to your face when you need it.

Finally, give your body a pamper. Simply taking a shower, washing your hair or splashing water over your face refreshes your body and your brain too. Even just brushing your teeth can make you feel better! After all, your mouth's the vehicle for your voice. Symbolically making your mouth feel clean and revived helps your voice to emerge fresh and sweet on paper.

# Keeping Yourself on Track

Many books, courses and experts on time management exist. Many of us know the theory but find difficulty putting it into practice! At university, tutors have a habit of choosing similar deadlines, for example halfway through the term or at the end of the semester, which means that your essays can stack up if you don't plan ahead. Here's the essence of what you need to do in order to meet those deadlines without causing yourself unnecessary stress.

If you want to improve how you organise your time, check out *Time Management For Dummies* by Clare Evans (Wiley).

## Planning large scale

At the start of term, you get hand-in dates for your various pieces of work, be they essays, reports, presentations or whatever. You need a diary or a wall planner so that you can see how they all mesh together and can identify possible future crisis moments.

Figure 2-1 shows an example from the back page of a student's diary. The university is working on a two-semester system with 10 weeks before the Christmas vacation and two more weeks (Weeks 11 and 12) after the vacation, followed by a 2 week exam period.

The student is studying French, Spanish and Linguistics. The Spanish tutor has asked the students to hand in four short essays, at the end of Weeks 3, 6, 9 and 12. There'll also be a Spanish oral and a written exam in January.

For French there will be three essays to submit (in Weeks 4, 8 and 12), plus a French oral and a written exam in January.

## Year Planner

| | Aug | Sept | Oct | Nov | Dec | Jan |
|---|---|---|---|---|---|---|
| Monday | | | | | | |
| Tuesday | | 1 | | | 1 | |
| Wednesday | | 2 | | | 2 | |
| Thursday | | 3 | 1 | | 3 | |
| Friday | | 4 | 2 | | 4 | 1 |
| Saturday | 1 | 5 | 3 | | 5 | 2 |
| Sunday | 2 | 6 | 4 | 1 | 6 | 3 |
| Monday | 3 | 7 | 5 | 2 | 7 | ④ Start of term |
| Tuesday | 4 | 8 | 6 week 2 | 3 week 6 | 8 week 10 | 5 |
| Wednesday | 5 | 9 | 7 | 4 | 9 | 6 week 11 |
| Thursday | 6 | 10 | 8 | 5 | 10 | 7 |
| Friday | 7 | 11 | 9 | ⑥ Hand in: SPAN 2 | ⑪ End of term | 8 |
| Saturday | 8 | 12 | 10 | 7 | 12 | 9 |
| Sunday | 9 | 13 | 11 | 8 | 13 | 10 |
| Monday | 10 | 14 | 12 | 9 | 14 | 11 |
| Tuesday | 11 | 15 | 13 week 3 | 10 week 7 | 15 | 12 week 12 |
| Wednesday | 12 | 16 | 14 | 11 | 16 | 13 |
| Thursday | 13 | 17 | 15 | 12 | 17 | 14 Hand in: SPAN 4 |
| Friday | 14 | 18 | 16 Hand in: SPAN 1 | 13 | 18 | 15 FREN 3 LING 2 |
| Saturday | 15 | 19 | 17 | 14 | 19 | 16 |
| Sunday | 16 | 20 | 18 | 15 | 20 | 17 |
| Monday | 17 | 21 | 19 | 16 | 21 | 18 |
| Tuesday | 18 | 22 | 20 week 4 | 17 week 8 | 22 | 19 Exams |
| Wednesday | 19 | 23 | 21 | 18 | 23 | 20 |
| Thursday | 20 | 24 | 22 | 19 | 24 | 21 |
| Friday | 21 | 25 | 23 Hand in: FREN 1 | 20 Hand in: FREN 2 | 25 Christmas | 22 |
| Saturday | 22 | 26 | 24 | 21 | 26 | 23 |
| Sunday | 23 | 27 | 25 | 22 | 27 | 24 |
| Monday | 24 | 28 Start of term | 26 | 23 | 28 | 25 |
| Tuesday | 25 | 29 | 27 week 5 | 24 week 9 | 29 | 26 Exams |
| Wednesday | 26 | 30 week 1 | 28 | 25 | 30 | 27 |
| Thursday | 27 | | 29 | 26 Hand in: SPAN 3 | 31 New Years Eve | 28 |
| Friday | 28 | | 30 | 27 LING 1 | | 29 |
| Saturday | 29 | | 31 | 28 | | 30 |
| Sunday | 30 | | | 29 | | 31 |
| Monday | 31 | | | 30 | | |
| Tuesday | | | | | | |

(Sept: "Freshers week" written vertically; Dec: "vacation" written vertically)

**Figure 2-1:** A page from a typical work-planning diary.

In Linguistics, however, there is no exam, just two long assignments, each accounting for 50 per cent of the total mark for the unit. If we look at the way this pans out for the student, the workload builds up gradually with a short essay in Spanish to hand in at the end of Week 3, and another in French at the end of Week 4, followed by a second Spanish essay in Week 6, and a second French one in Week 8. So far so good. But take a look at Week 9. The third Spanish essay and the first Linguistics one are due in on the same day. Given that the Linguistics essay carries 50 per cent of the final mark for that unit, if you were that student you would be foolish to leave the researching and writing of that essay until the last minute, particularly when you'd have another essay due on the same day.

Similarly, there's a potential crisis point at the end of Week 12, when essays in all three subjects are to be submitted on the last day of the semester. The Linguistics one is again worth 50 per cent of the final mark. This serves to remind us that although at first it seems that university vacations are lengthy, in fact you need to use a significant amount of holiday time to study and keep up, especially when you not only have essays to write but exams to revise for. In our example the student has three weeks in which to make merry – but also to work on three essays and revise for the exams.

## Planning small scale

Within the big picture, you need a detailed plan for each individual essay as it comes along. The key to successful planning is to work backwards from the hand-in date, allowing time for the various phases of research, drafting, polishing and so on.

The student whose diary we looked at in Figure 2-1 needs to make a more detailed plan for the crunch points, as shown in Figure 2-2. The first one for her is Week 9, which in practice means looking backwards from the 2 hand-ins in this week to see how she can best manage the workload – *and* have time for relaxation.

Week 7 has no hand-ins, so is a good week to get ahead for the reading for the Linguistics essay. This is a long assignment, of 3,000 words, and the tutor expects each student to do a considerable amount of background reading. The two other assignments are different as they are written in the target language and are much shorter than the Linguistics essay. The essay in French is 700 words long and the Spanish one 500 words.

| | | |
|---|---|---|
| **9 Mon** | | |
| **10 Tue** | Background reading for LING essay | |
| **11 Wed** | | |
| **12 Thu** | | meet Joe & Ollie to discuss LING |
| **13 Fri** | | Plan FREN |
| **14 Sat** | | Write 1st draft FREN |
| **15 Sun** | Plan LING essay | |
| **16 Mon** | | Revise FREN |
| **17 Tue** | DAY IN LIBRARY Write 1st draft LING essay | |
| **18 Wed** | | |
| **19 Thu** | | Check FREN |
| **20 Fri** | | Hand in FREN 2 |
| **21 Sat** | NB: JOE'S BIRTHDAY PARTY! | |
| **22 Sun** | | Plan SPAN essay |
| **23 Mon** | | Write SPAN essay |
| **24 Tue** | DAY IN LIBRARY Write final version | |
| **25 Wed** | | Revise SPAN |
| **26 Thu** | Check LING essay | Check SPAN essay |
| **27 Fri** | HAND IN LING 1 | HAND IN SPAN 3 |

**Figure 2-2:** Small scale planning on a typical diary page

Another thing this student will need to bear in mind when planning is that by the time Week 9 arrives, she will be doing her third assignment in Spanish. In other words the tutor will have given feedback on the first and the second assignments, so the students will have a much clearer picture of what the tutor wants. You begin to get more confident about what is being asked of you and you have a better idea of how long it takes you to produce an assignment. So the student here can be pretty confident that if planning starts the previous weekend (Sunday afternoon, in fact, giving her time to recover from the party the night before!) the first draft of the essay can be written the next day and there will be time to revise and check it through before submitting on Friday. Similarly, there is a clear week available to plan, write, revise and check the second French assignment due in at the end of Week 8.

Given the workload that the Linguistics assignment involves, and the fact that it counts for 50 per cent of the final mark for this unit, it would be a good idea to allocate two Tuesdays, which for this student are free, to solid preparation and writing for this essay, and maybe the university library would be a good place to work. Three weeks should be adequate for our student to read, plan, write, revise and check through. She'll have time to talk to fellow students about the essay, and even arrange to meet her tutor if she has questions. *And* time exists to change things around, deal with setbacks, and really enjoy life at university. It really is all doable!

 Build in slippage time, because things always take longer than you think. Something unforeseen always happens. Life has a habit of intervening and spoiling your beautifully laid plans. Building in some slack means that you can manage the blips better.

# Thinking half hours not whole hours

You often imagine an entire day, or days, of writing, but the reality's very different.

For a start, your brain needs a break to recharge. You often think that you need a good sleep or a decent meal, when in fact a ten-minute doze or a snack can keep you going very nicely, especially when writing gets tough.

You may also be surprised how much you can do in the odd half hour. In this way, you can keep up to speed with your plan and even get ahead! Go on, try it. You may astonish yourself just how deeply you can think, how many ideas you can generate, how much you can actually commit to paper in a grabbed half-hour burst. This can be the way to crack the writing task. And in a difficult moment, you truly appreciate the previous productive half hours.

## Dividing work into manageable chunks

Most tasks – and writing an essay's one of them – can be chopped up into smaller bits that you find easier to do. Don't set yourself a task that's impossible, because you're guaranteeing failure. Writing a section of an essay – a paragraph even – is achievable when sensibly matched to the amount of time at your disposal. The work you complete in half-hour chunks soon adds up. You tell yourself that you can do this little bit, you do it, and you give yourself a pat on the back. Then you feel able to move on to the next little bit.

## Rewarding yourself

You deserve a treat: chocolate, 15 minutes listening to your current favourite band, a lazy soak in the bath, a delicious gossipy chat with a friend, more chocolate, whatever. But congratulate yourself when you've finished a chunk (of work, not chocolate). This way you're associating writing an essay not with hard slog but with the pleasures in life and you're giving yourself something to look forward to.

Scale up the treats and spoil yourself when the whole essay's finished. Promise yourself a good night out or something else you like doing. You're worth it!

# Getting Help: Using Other Students as a Sounding Board

Gone are the days when each student was expected to work in isolation. University spaces are now designed with break-out areas for teamwork, and university libraries are no longer silent cathedrals but have rooms that are designated discussion zones.

Most lecturers nowadays assume that students get together and discuss assignments; indeed, many actively encourage it. The purpose of this is to focus and exchange views so that each individual can truly understand the scope of the essay and what's required, and each can have his or her own take on the issue, confident that it's within the remit of the topic.

This doesn't mean, of course, that you all end up writing the same thing! The purpose of discussing something with your classmates is to flesh out the parameters and work out what everyone's views are. If you do work with a friend in the initial stages, make sure that you write up individually so that the two essays don't end up too 'samey'.

Here are some ways you and your friend can help each other:

✔ Check through lecture notes together and see whether your understanding of the key issues is similar. If not, why?

✔ Exchange websites and book titles. You can save each other a lot of time researching journal articles and the like.

Summarise the content briefly for one another – what may not be of great significance to you in your interpretation of the topic may be of immense value to your friend and his or her take on the subject, so every opportunity you have to exchange views and practical information helps you to firm up and deepen your own perspective.

✔ Exchange scripts with a classmate at the proofreading stage (see Chapter 15) and use each other's fresh pairs of eyes to pick out the little slips that unnecessarily mar your work. This is easier to ask if you've worked together at the start of the process and perhaps made a deal to support one another through it all. Having an arrangement like this also helps you to keep to your timetable, because you don't want to let your classmate down.

# Remembering your tutor's role

If you're having difficulty at any point in the process, whether with interpreting the title, getting going, keeping going or generating ideas, don't forget that most tutors are happy to help you clarify your thoughts. Having to ask your tutor for help is no admission of failure. The majority of tutors want to help their students succeed; after all, reading and grading a pile of unsatisfactory essays is pretty soul destroying. The job's usually a lot easier when the essays are good ones, so asking for pointers and suggestions is in both your and your tutor's interests. So go on, send an email and make an appointment to get some help.

# Recognising What Helps You to Write

When at last you hand in your essay, spend a few moments thinking about the experience and what you can take from it.

✔ How much time did you give yourself to research and write the essay? Was it enough? How much time should you give yourself for the next one?

✔ Where and when did you find it easiest to write? Try to recreate these circumstances for the next essay.

✔ Think about the food you ate, the physical activity you undertook. Did this help or hinder? What might you change next time?

✔ Which of your friends do you like bouncing ideas off? Make a point of working with them again in the future if this relationship can work for you both.

✔ What was your motivation? Was it the short-term promise of a good night out or the thought of being a step nearer your degree? Whatever it was, it worked.

From this point on, you know how to look after yourself and can create the most supportive and stimulating atmosphere. So getting started on your next project and keeping motivated is easier, and, who knows, you may even relish the prospect of writing your next essay!

# Chapter 3

# Working Out the Essay Type

............................................................

## In This Chapter
▶ Analysing the essay title
▶ Structuring your essay
▶ Using common patterns to help you plan your writing

............................................................

*E*very tribe, every culture in the world, has stories. Every one of us has a tale to tell about something that's happened, however big or small. So we all seem to have an innate concept of a narrative with a beginning, middle and end.

An academic essay's rarely a narrative as such, but it does have a beginning (the introduction), a middle (the body or development of the essay) and an end (the conclusion). The story clearly isn't a conventional one, but you, the writer, may benefit from thinking of writing your essay as if you were telling your tutor, the reader, a story. The introduction sets up certain expectations in your reader's mind, and in the conclusion you should make sure that you've met these expectations, so that the reader goes away satisfied. In between the introduction and the conclusion, the story can take several different forms – recognisable patterns that we share with you in this chapter.

So when you embark on your university career and the prospect of writing maybe 50-odd essays over the next three years (not counting exams!) suddenly hits you, don't be dismayed. In this chapter we provide frameworks you can fall back on that help you divide up the essays and make them doable. We show you how to read questions carefully and understand fully what they require of you. And we help you realise that you need to guide your readers gently but firmly along the path of your argument. All your readers really want is for you to entertain them with a well-structured and interesting story.

# Finding Out What to Write About

What to write about seems obvious doesn't it? You read the essay title and then you answer the question, right? If only the task were that simple. At university you often find you have to peel away the layers of meaning to arrive at what your tutor's getting at in the words of the question. Tutors can spend some time composing an essay title in order to get just the right choice and balance of words that challenge you and make you think, without completely mystifying you. They want to get the question right for your level of academic experience, whether you're in the first, second or third year, because clearly tutors make different demands on you depending where you are in your university career.

If at first glance the title seems straightforward, you may be missing something. To make sure you aren't, we advise you to read the title through a couple of times so that you remember it, and then think about it from time to time before you actually start the writing process. This way you give yourself a chance to see deeply into the essay question and avoid rushing into a superficial reading or a misinterpretation of what you need to write. You have to read around and understand the concepts that the essay title refers to in the context of the subject you're studying. If you have any doubts about the way you're interpreting a title, then have chat about it with your classmates or talk to your tutor.

Look up in your course handbook or online what your department's looking for in a first-, second- and third-class degree. To do well, you need to show not just a breadth of knowledge but also, probably more importantly, a depth of knowledge. You need to show that you can dig deeply into your subject and handle subtle distinctions between concepts with confidence and insight.

You need to unpick essay titles so that in your writing you can account for all the threads of meaning they contain. Each thread either gives you the basis for a section of your essay or indicates the approach you need to take. The words in an essay title fall largely into two categories:

- ✔ **Keywords,** which define content
- ✔ **Function words,** which tell you what to do with the content

## Unpicking keywords

You may be surprised to realise that in the academic world, words you thought you understood are used in specialised ways depending on the discipline – whether you're studying philosophy or history, for example – and differently by academics within the same discipline. The difference between the way two experts use a word may be a hair's breadth, but identifying that difference shows depth of insight on your part.

You have to decide on the exact meaning of a word in the context of the subject you're studying. With a word like 'metaphor', for instance, many people first encounter it when studying poetry at school, when you read a poem in class and identify images, similes, metaphors and similar figures of speech. However, at university you go on to discover that different disciplines use the same word with slightly different applications, though the basic meaning remains the same. 'Metaphor' in film studies isn't quite the same as 'metaphor' in applied linguistics, though the two uses share the same root meaning. And even within one area of study you can find subdivisions. Take applied linguistics, for instance, where different types of metaphor exist, such as onto-logical and orientational metaphors. So you need to be very clear indeed what the words in the essay question mean and interpret them accurately in terms of your field of study.

If any possible ambiguity exists in the way you're interpreting a term, state this at the beginning of the essay to make clear how you're using the term in your writing. Skip to Chapter 11 for more on defining keywords and terms in your introduction.

## Looking for function words

After you establish what the keywords and their precise mean-ings are (see the earlier section 'Unpicking keywords'), you can move on to look at the words that tell you what to do: the *function words*. These are largely verbs. Reading them carefully should help your essay to begin to form a shape in your mind, even though the shape may have few details of content in it yet.

Many function words exist, but some are very similar in meaning, and they overlap to a certain extent. Remember, though, that you always have to interpret the essay question as a whole in the con-text of the unit you're taking, while at the same time following the instructions that these function words give you. The old saying about not being able to see the wood for the trees applies here: you have to be able to see the trees (the detailed instructions) without losing sight of the wood (the big picture).

Have a look at past exam questions for your unit. Essay titles often tend to take a similar format over the years. Exceptions always occur, of course, but the nature of the subject usually means that some function words crop up more often than others. Past papers are a good guide to the variety of function words that frequently feature in your subject.

The following list contains some function words, with a few comments and advice on what to look out for when you find them in an essay title. Avoid the traps!

- ✔ **Account for:** This is the same as 'explain' in that you have to give reasons for something happening or why another thing's the way it is.

- ✔ **Analyse:** This is one of those 'big' words that means pulling something apart, and then describing, discussing and giving reasons for what you find, and presenting it all in a methodical and logical way. Imagine yourself looking at your poem, political movement or process under a microscope.

  The essay title may ask you to analyse, but also point you in the direction the analysis should take. When the title presents two items or issues together for analysis, you often need to say what they have in common, but also point out their differences. You don't often have to say only what's similar or only what's different. In an essay at uni, you usually need to say both, and you have to tease out the fine shades of distinction.

- ✔ **Assess:** This is very much the same as 'evaluate', but may indicate a slightly broader view. Both function words are asking you to use your own judgement to state the relative worth of something, so be sure of your facts and make sure that your arguments are solid!

- ✔ **Classify (and justify):** You need to think deeply about the items that you have to discuss and cluster them together thematically. You're then showing that you understand the similarities and differences between the items. Most likely you have to explain your reasons for grouping items together.

- ✔ **Comment on:** This requires you to respond to an issue. You have to pick out the most important points and write around those. Neglecting crucial points in favour of minor ones loses you marks unnecessarily.

- ✔ **Compare and contrast:** When you're writing about similarities and differences, do remember to treat each of the issues under scrutiny equally and give a balanced answer.

- ✔ **Consider:** The danger with 'consider' is that a disorganised writer may dump ideas randomly into the essay. You need to think very carefully about the question and then present your argument logically.

- ✔ **Criticise:** Here you have to discuss and find the flaws in something. But beware! In everyday speech we tend to use 'criticise' with the meaning of 'to say what's bad about something'. Its more specialised meaning, which is what you find in essay instructions, is 'to identify the weaknesses in something', but this doesn't eliminate entirely the possibility of mentioning some of the strengths. You're unwise to be utterly damning and include only negative comments in an essay with 'criticise' in the title. Find good things to say too!

✔ **Define:** Be careful when you define a term. It may be slightly ambiguous and you should be precise about what you take it to mean. Refer to how an expert in the field has used the term, and say that you're using it in the same way.

✔ **Describe:** When a question asks you to describe what something's like, look out for any words that limit your description, such as 'briefly', and make sure that you do just that. You lose marks if the title says 'briefly' and then you describe at length! 'Describe' doesn't mean 'comment on' and you shouldn't do so. You're not being asked for your opinion here.

✔ **Differentiate between *or* distinguish between:** Here your tutor's asking you to focus more on the differences than the similarities. You can briefly mention what the two items have in common in the first section of your essay as part of the background, but what follows should concentrate on the differences.

✔ **Discuss:** This tells you to consider an issue from two (or more) standpoints and present each one in a balanced way with support and examples. You treat different viewpoints equally and weigh evidence for and against fairly. After you've considered these points of view, you come to a conclusion in which you state your personal opinion in the light of all the evidence you've collected. Any conclusion you arrive at should then come across as considered and logical.

✔ **Elucidate:** This is an alternative to 'explain' and means that you have to make what you're writing clear to the reader.

✔ **Enumerate:** Though this means 'give numbers to', don't use actual numbers like 1, 2 and 3. You should use linking words such as 'first', 'secondly' and so on.

✔ **Evaluate (critically):** You may have to evaluate the worth of different suggestions put forward to solve a problem, or evaluate a poem's place in the writer's body of work. But whatever you're evaluating, you're saying how important something is (compared to other suggestions or poems, for instance), and you have to back up what you're saying with hard evidence. The word 'critically' is frequently attached to 'evaluate' to remind you of the fine detail and careful balancing of positive and negative comments required.

✔ **Examine:** This asks you to look at an issue in detail and present your thoughts and comments in a controlled and orderly fashion.

✔ **Explain:** When a question asks you to give reasons for something, make sure that you go into enough detail. Don't assume knowledge on the part of the reader, but rather take the idea back to its roots and detail its development carefully.

✔ **Explore:** Like 'discuss', this asks you to consider a topic from different angles. A clear 'for and against' distinction may not exist. You may or may not be able to establish your opinion when you come to the conclusion.

✔ **Give an account of:** When a question asks you to give an account of something, this is like telling a story. You need to 'describe' but also 'trace', because the account requires a logical order such as chronological (like a narrative).

✔ **Justify:** You may have to state clearly any choice you make or any decision about something's value.

✔ **List:** Do just this! But try to avoid a random list. Group points together and present them in some kind of sequence, maybe by importance, beginning with the most important. Categorising points shows that you've put in some thought and are in control. Take care to develop each point into a fully rounded paragraph: neither list nor enumerate means that you write a couple of sentences around each point. Treat each one as a paragraph (or more) with appropriate linking words within and signposting between.

Steer well clear of bullet-point lists, which are okay in a book like this but aren't acceptable in academic writing (except possibly in an appendix, where you may attach a document such as a questionnaire that contains bullet points).

✔ **Outline:** This means that the topic's too lengthy to describe in great detail, so you should pick out the main points and talk about these. Your selection of the main points is important. It shows that you have a grasp of the big picture. Instructions such as 'outline' (and also 'trace') may be followed by further restrictions such as 'in/with relation to X' which help you to select the points to include in the essay. Writing everything you know about the topic without regard for this restriction loses you marks.

✔ **To what extent?** Not so much a function word as a function expression, this tells you to discuss the issue and evaluate your findings. You come out with an answer that's likely to lean more heavily towards one aspect of the issue than another. Things are very rarely black and white, 100 per cent or 0 per cent. Nor are they often 50:50. Your answer should come down more on one side than the other – in other words a shade of grey.

✔ **Trace:** You can be asked to describe the development of an idea or someone's life, for example. Trace implies a historical approach to the topic. As with 'outline', you may have to pick out the most important points and present them in a logical order. Your selection is crucial.

This isn't a finite list of function words, but it does include the main ones. Do check any new ones that come up and you're not sure about.

What you also find, particularly in exams, is that essay titles are sometimes written not with function words but as questions, for instance 'How valid is X?' or 'What are the implications of Y?'. Sometimes tutors choose direct questions because they think that students respond more quickly to titles with this kind of wording when under stressful exam conditions. They're just another more direct way of setting the question that seems to suit the test situation. If you think a little about the two questions above, you can see that the first one's saying 'evaluate', and the second one 'discuss'. The tutor's simply said it in a more direct way. So don't panic if you're expecting function words and you get a title that's actually expressed as a question instead. Your teacher's trying to help, not hinder! All these function words, expressions and questions are in the title for a purpose: to guide you in your writing so that you deliver what your tutor wants to see. In arriving at your destination – the essay – you take a certain journey, and the instructions in the essay title are like directions, telling you which path to take and how to travel.

# Identifying Different Frameworks

When you get your essay title and you start to think about it, you're hoping to do something good and unique. It certainly will be unique, because nobody else will have written the essay you're going to produce. But this can only ever be true as far as the content (what you put into it) and the expression of that content (the language you use to convey your ideas) are concerned. Those are unique to you. In the structure of the essay, however, you shouldn't be aiming to be unique.

Think of the millions and zillions of essays that people at university have ever written. Each of these doesn't have an individual, unique structure. Putting to one side the essays that ramble without focus and don't lead anywhere, those that have a structure follow paths that others have trodden time and time again. You should by all means strive to be original in your content, but please stick to the tried-and-tested patterns of organisation that we outline in this section when structuring your essay.

Following an essay framework has the added benefit for your tutor that he or she doesn't have to waste effort wondering where you're heading in your answer. If you read or hear the words 'Once upon a time . . .', you know immediately that you're in for a fairy tale. You shouldn't have to worry halfway through whether it's really a fairy tale. Similarly, in the introduction to your essay, you announce the kind of structure your essay has and then stick to it. Once you've announced the pattern your essay's to take, your reader can relax into the content without having to wonder where all of this is going.

## *Knowing what you do for all frameworks*

In the following section we give you general essay frameworks, which you have to subdivide further depending on the total length of the essay you have to produce and the detail you have to go into. The frameworks have three things in common:

- ✔ **They all have an introduction and a conclusion.** How long should these be? We suggest 10 per cent of the total word count for each, giving you 80 per cent for what goes in between. The frameworks that follow show how you can manage the 80 per cent.

- ✔ **They all progress in a linear direction.** This is what makes writing an academic essay in the English style different from ones in other cultures, which present ideas in a more round-about way. An English essay orders its points in a logical fashion in order to present to the reader a line of argumentation that flows uninterruptedly from A to B, and on to C, and so on. It doesn't allow for detours along the way!

- ✔ **They all normally only use one point per paragraph.** The writer develops each point, with examples and quotations where necessary, and then moves on to the next point, starting a new paragraph.

Whatever framework you use, think of your essay as telling a story. The episodes in the story have to follow on logically and smoothly to keep the reader's attention and make understanding your tale as simple as possible. For more information, see 'Making your story flow' later in this chapter or turn to Chapter 9.

# Help! I can't fathom this title!

You're sitting down with the essay title in front of you, and you just can't see what you have to do for this assignment. What now?

The first thing to find out is the hand-in date, so that you know how much time you have to play with and how urgent the situation is. What may well be happening is that your tutor's given out the essay title well in advance of the submission date. Many are very well organised and even distribute essay titles at the beginning of the course, months before you have to submit the work. The essay may look impenetrable to you because the course hasn't yet covered the essay topic in enough depth. Have you got a course schedule? Look at the lecture/session titles over the next few weeks. Does the essay title refer to content you haven't discussed yet, maybe something that's coming up soon? This may well be the case, and so – good news! – we suggest that you put the essay away for a few weeks.

Once the calendar demonstrates that you should be thinking about starting your essay, it's a wise move to discuss the title with your classmates, even if you're pretty sure that you're thinking along the right lines. Checking's always good, and you never know what ideas you may spark off by talking it through with those on the same course as you.

If you're still unsure, go back to your tutor and ask for some clarification, perhaps at the end of a lecture so that everyone on the course benefits. Others are bound to be struggling to understand the requirements of the title if you are. And besides, even if you're pretty sure in your own mind what the title's about, having that confirmed is nice.

## *Examining types of essay*

Frameworks generally fall into one of several basic types. They are:

- ✔ The simple essay
- ✔ The two-sided essay
- ✔ The 'statement and discuss' essay
- ✔ The 'compare and contrast' essay: the block model
- ✔ The 'compare and contrast' essay: the itemised model
- ✔ The 'to what extent?' essay
- ✔ The multi-function-word essay

The function words in the title indicate the form your work should take (flip back to the earlier section 'Looking for function words' for more on these). Whereas in exam conditions you may get a single instruction such as 'discuss X', 'assess Y' or 'outline Z', for coursework – when you have plenty of time to mull over the question, do research and come up with a considered answer – assignment questions tend to have several parts to them, each indicated by a different function word. Often they have only two, for example 'compare and contrast', but they can have as many as five, as in 'describe (a situation), identify (a problem), suggest (solutions), evaluate (solutions) and justify (a choice)'. However many functions words are included, you have to account for them all. And this gives you the form your essay should take.

The following sections take you through each type of essay in turn. We can't be categorical in advising a framework for your essay, because you have to react to the title your tutor sets, but we provide the basic models for you to adapt and tweak according to the circumstances. You can see similarities between the different frameworks. They can have a lot in common, with just a few differences – but the differences are quite significant.

In this book we're dealing with undergraduate essays where the word count is 1,000–3,000 words. Essays longer than this tend to be projects, and when they're a lot longer, say more than 10,000 words, you're in the realm of a dissertation. These longer pieces of writing are subdivided into chapters. The work has a structure of its own, and each chapter may take on a different pattern.

### The simple essay

Take a look at Figure 3-1, which shows the basic pattern of a simple essay.

| Introduction |
|---|
| Paragraph 1 |
| Paragraph 2 |
| Paragraph 3 |
| Conclusion |

**Figure 3-1:** The simple essay.

This is what you need for a fairly short essay of up to 1,000 words. You've probably got a single instruction in your essay title, such as 'describe' or 'comment on'. With 1,000 words, you can take away the introduction and the conclusion, leaving you with about 800 words for the body of your essay. The exact number of paragraphs, of course, depends on the total word count you're allowed and what you're writing about. But this suggests four paragraphs of about 200 words. (Don't take these numbers as a straitjacket you have to force your writing into. They're just rough guidelines to give you an idea when you're new to this kind of writing.)

 Paragraphs don't come out all the same length, but you should look carefully at any that seem very short in comparison with the others and ask yourself whether the point you're making there is fully developed. A short paragraph may send out the message that you haven't worked on it sufficiently. Similarly, any overlong paragraph may in fact contain two points, and you may want to split it. Brevity can be a sign that you should think more deeply over the paragraph's content, or maybe you're getting muddled rather than progressing through the paragraph in the linear way that's the convention in English academic writing. Overly short or overly long paragraphs are therefore not just odd visually but may indicate flaws in the development of your argument.

### The two-sided essay

Figure 3-2 gives you an idea of how a two-sided essay looks.

| Introduction |
| Reason for 1 |
| Reason for 2 |
| Reason for 3 |
| Reason against 1 |
| Reason against 2 |
| Reason against 3 |
| your opinion as conclusion |

**Figure 3-2:** The two-sided essay.

You're probably familiar with this kind of model already. It's the classic 'for and against' or 'state the advantages and disadvantages'. At university the question probably includes a function word such as 'discuss' or 'assess'. If you were asked to talk about this aloud, your ideas would probably spill out of your mouth higgledy-piggledy, and you'd suddenly stop and go back to pick up a point you made earlier. This model essay type imposes order on all of those ideas and presents them in a way that your reader recognises.

In presenting the pros and cons, you should work towards balance. Try to divide the body of your essay into two parts, roughly even in length. Decide on the points that you're going to make 'for' (the advantages or positive points) and work out their order of importance. Cover these points, starting with the most important and progressing downwards until you reach the last point. (Remember: one point per paragraph.) This should account for approximately 40 per cent of your essay.

Now do the same with the 'against' (the disadvantages or negative points): rank them and then write them up, again aiming at about 40 per cent of the total. You should have the same number of points – and so paragraphs – in both sections, and they should be roughly the same length. This should ensure an even-handed treatment of each side of the issue, and the points should balance out – the same number 'for' as 'against'.

If you find that your essay's considerably over length, consider eliminating the last, least important, point in both sections. Make sure that any changes you make to one section are mirrored in the other so that you maintain the balanced effect.

Finally, you draw a conclusion; this is where you should express a view. Don't reveal your opinion until this last part of the essay when you pull all the information together and, in the light of everything you've discussed, come down on one side or the other. You can hedge your opinion, of course, and not be too categorically in favour of one or the other.

### The 'statement and discuss' essay

You find this kind of essay question a great deal in exam papers, because it allows for flexibility in response. You may have a quotation from or about an author or event, or you may get a saying, for example '"Manners maketh man." Discuss with reference to (name of work, author, concept and so on.).' The 'with reference to' is important because it limits the scope of your argument and forces you to focus on a single aspect of your topic.

This essay type basically follows the model of a two-sided essay (see the earlier section on this), but you have to begin by unpicking all the layers of meaning that the statement or quotation contains, and you need to comment on all of these. For instance, if the title includes a quotation, you need to place that in context. This may result in you having your general introduction to the essay immediately followed by a more detailed background paragraph that sets the scene for the comments that follow. These paragraphs probably take the shape suggested in Figure 3-2, and you reach some kind of conclusion at the end, where you can express your opinion.

The body of the essay may not fall neatly into two evenly packaged and weighted sections as you see in Figure 3-2. The way you interpret the opening statement may have an influence on the features you choose to write about and your take on the issue.

### The 'compare and contrast' essay: The block model

This is a type of descriptive essay that asks you to highlight similarities and differences between two works, approaches, concepts and so on. A poor essay simply describes the two items, leaving the reader to pull out similarities and differences for himself or herself. You mustn't leave the reader to do your work for you! What this task requires you to do is to analyse the two items, resulting in a list of salient points that define the ways in which they are similar or different.

You have a choice in the way you present your points, however, and how you opt to organise your work. Figure 3-3 offers you one option, which you may call the block model.

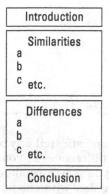

**Figure 3-3:** The 'compare and contrast' block model.

You can see that this diagram is similar in many ways to the one in Figure 3-2 (the two-sided essay), since the body of the essay divides into two chunks of approximately the same length. The first section deals with the similarities, and the second with the differences. Your approach is the same as with the two-sided essay, in that you rank the similarities in order of importance, and then do the same with the differences. You should be looking for the same number of similarities as differences, in order to end up with a fairly balanced treatment of the subject; but don't worry too much if you have more of one than the other, so that one chunk is a little meatier than the other.

With this type of essay you don't have to express your opinion unless you're specifically told to do so. It's a descriptive piece of work, so unless the essay title goes on to tell you otherwise, your personal take on the matter isn't required.

### The 'compare and contrast' essay: The itemised model

Your alternative model for a 'compare and contrast' type of essay is a slightly more difficult one to undertake, so only go for this if you feel on top of your subject and confident of your analysis.

Figure 3-4 shows this second 'compare and contrast' model, which you may call the itemised model.

| Introduction | |
|---|---|
| Point a | similarity |
| | difference |
| Point b | similarity |
| | difference |
| Point c | similarity |
| | difference |
| Conclusion | |

**Figure 3-4:** The 'compare and contrast' itemised model.

You can see that this model's a more sophisticated way of processing and presenting the similarities and differences as you move back and forth between the two items you're writing about – not in a haphazard way, but logically as you deal with one point after another, illustrating each point by reference to each item.

As Figure 3-4 illustrates, the essay organisation isn't driven by similarities or differences, but by points. (Instead of 'point' you may prefer the word 'feature' or 'aspect'.) You take the points one by one, mentioning first the similarities and then the differences. Then you move on to the next point. Depending on the length of the essay and the number of points you want to make, a single paragraph can contain the similarities and differences of a feature, but for clarity of presentation you may prefer to allocate two paragraphs to each feature, one for the similarities and the other for the differences.

With this pattern of presentation, signalling the transition between one paragraph and the next clearly is especially important, so that the reader can follow your argument as you move between the two things under discussion. And as with the block version of the 'compare and contrast' essay, don't give your opinion unless the title specifically asks for this.

### The 'to what extent?' essay

Figure 3-5 familiarises you with how to structure your answer to a 'to what extent?' essay question.

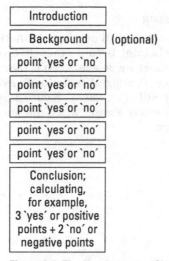

| Introduction |
| Background | (optional)
| point 'yes' or 'no' |
| point 'yes' or 'no' |
| point 'yes' or 'no' |
| point 'yes' or 'no' |
| point 'yes' or 'no' |
| Conclusion; calculating, for example, 3 'yes' or positive points + 2 'no' or negative points |

**Figure 3-5:** The 'to what extent?' essay.

A kind of vagueness is inherent in the question 'to what extent?', and the model in Figure 3-5 reflects this. The only thing you know for certain is that the answer isn't 100 per cent 'yes' or 'no', 'true' or 'false'. You aren't totally agreeing or totally disagreeing with something, you're more likely to be in the range of, say, 70 per cent one way or another.

Your introduction's especially important here in setting up the dilemma, and you may need to add an extra paragraph at the beginning of the body of the essay to add further background information if it's essential to your discussion. The remainder of the essay body presents aspects of the issue one at a time, each paragraph concluding whether this is a 'true' or 'false' feature of the issue.

As with the 'compare and contrast' essay (see the earlier Figures 3-3 and 3-4), you have a choice regarding the order in which you present your points, either blocking all the 'for' or 'agree' points together and then dealing with the 'against' or 'disagree' ones, or dealing with features in an itemised way, alternating between the 'for' and the 'against'. Whichever way you go about the structure, you come to some kind of conclusion, which may be five points for, two points against, for example. Assuming that the points you make are of equal weight, you really just need to count them and see which side wins! Then in your conclusion you can answer 'to what extent?' by showing that you can argue more strongly one way than another, and you can indicate the degree of strength of this argument by the amount of evidence you present.

### The multi-function-word essay

Some tutors set essay titles containing a number of function words. In fact these are quite helpful, because they give you the structure of your essay. The most we've ever seen is five: 'describe (a situation), identify (a problem), suggest (solutions), evaluate (solutions) and recommend/justify (a choice)'. Figure 3-6 presents a solution to structuring your essay answer when the question contains several function words.

| |
|---|
| Introduction |
| Describe |
| Identify |
| Suggest |
| Evaluate |
| Recommend/justify |
| Conclusion |

**Figure 3-6:** The multi-function-word essay.

Presented with this kind of question, you should as always read it very carefully and answer all parts. Skipping over an instruction or somehow merging two isn't satisfactory.

After you write the introduction and conclusion, you should divide the body of the essay into as many parts as there are function words; in an ideal world, each occupies roughly the same amount of space and has a similar word count. The exception is the last part (justify), where, in the light of the information you've previously given, lengthy justification may not be necessary and indeed may be somewhat repetitive.

## Making your story flow

By choosing and sticking to one of the tried-and-tested essay patterns we show you in this chapter, you've already helped your reader to follow what you're saying. The reader's familiar with the shape or structure of your essay, can predict the route your argument's taking, and so is able to concentrate on what exactly you're saying and how well you're saying it. You can make the reader's task even easier if you signpost the route clearly and efficiently.

Crucially, you need to make the transitions from one point to another and from one section to another as clear as possible. A change in direction may be clear in your head, but you have to verbalise it on paper so that it's crystal clear for any reader. Don't assume that what's self-evident for you is also self-evident for others. Remember that a second marker or external examiner may not be quite as familiar with the subject matter as the person who taught it to you, set the essay title and now expects a certain response. So be explicit – put changes in the direction of your argument into words!

In the same way that you use linking words within a paragraph to smooth the flow, similarly you use transition phrases to guide the reader along the main path your essay's following. For instance, in the 'compare and contrast' essay, block model, you benefit from a significant signpost to mark the transition from the comparing section to the contrasting section, such as 'Turning now to features of X and Y that are dissimilar . . .' or 'Having considered what X and Y have in common, I now consider where the similarities end.' A major shift in the direction of your argument calls for a transition signal that draws attention to itself and thus to the moves in your line of reasoning.

For more about using transitional language to signpost within your essay, turn to Chapter 9.

# Planning Around Your Framework

In this chapter you see how the typical academic essay falls into one of a number of basic structural frameworks. While the keywords in the essay title tell you the content to focus on in your essay, the function words indicate the shape it should take. This is an advantage, because the decision's made for you. You don't need to spend time thinking about how to structure your essay, because the framework's normally there in the title. Planning your essay becomes simple.

 After you identify the appropriate shape for your essay, you may want to draw a diagram such as the ones we use to visualise the frameworks. Take a large sheet of paper and draw yourself some boxes to represent the different sections. Brainstorm some ideas into the boxes, and you already have an overview of what your essay's going to look like. This is, of course, going to require a considerable amount of fine-tuning, but the basis is there.

When you come to write much longer assignments, a tremendous amount of thought has to go into the development of ideas and the ordering of material for a single section. But if you have an overall shape in your head to build on, such as the ones used in this chapter, you find breaking a long essay down into smaller, more manageable chunks of writing much easier. Once you break any task down into its component parts it becomes easier to handle and – more importantly – to finish.

# Part II
# Researching, Recording and Reformulating

'It appears to me you have struggled with this essay, Mr. Digwort—I see you started in 1937.'

## In this part . . .

It's always useful to have something to write about, so this part helps you decide on the content of your essay. The chapters cover background reading, both from books or online, as well as how to take top-quality, targeted notes. We devote a whole chapter, too, to a genuinely important issue: Avoiding plagiarism. Chapter 7 says 'Don't!' in no uncertain terms, but it isn't all stern faces. We also provide you with the necessary skills so that you aren't tempted to steal anyone else's writing.

# Chapter 4

# Eyes Down: Academic Reading

## In This Chapter

▶ Finding what you need to read

▶ Reading efficiently and quickly

▶ Analysing what you read

*I*f you want to write, you first have to read. Reading and writing – they go together, don't they? And you have done them since primary school. Your reading and writing skills have been good enough to get you through A levels, so you may assume that they're adequate for university too. The good news is that they can get you through the next three or four years at uni, but not without some polishing and honing, if you want to read and write with confidence and success. This book's about writing skills, but because reading's the basis of your writing, we're going to focus in this chapter on how reading at university is different.

Successful writing at university begins with reading extensively, not just the books on your reading list but also others that tutors may recommend in lectures or ones you come across yourself. This is what makes the whole process so different from what you probably knew at school, when you worked from a single textbook. Now at uni, you're expected to read around your subject for background information and in-depth comment. The seemingly never-ending shelves of the university library beckon, as do online journals and the vast resources of the Internet. Suddenly everything seems overwhelming. How can you read everything available on your subject?

The answer is, of course, that you can't. And nobody expects you to. Only experts – professors and researchers – can claim to have read everything published on a given topic, and even then you may doubt that any of them really have. All you're expected to do is read a reasonable amount of selected literature and then, armed with the knowledge and insights this brings you, write your essays.

This chapter helps you to manage and organise your reading, as well as advising you on the best techniques and strategies for reading literature efficiently and actively – in other words, the what, the how and the how much of reading at university.

When we use the word 'literature' in this context, we don't mean English lit – Shakespeare, Jane Austen and Dickens. (Unless, of course, your degree's in literature!) In an academic context, literature doesn't mean novels, plays and poetry, but all the books and journal articles that researchers and experts in the field have written on a topic. Students studying biochemistry, IT and mathematics may have to do a literature review, and that doesn't mean critiquing *Harry Potter!*

# Reading Academically: How It Differs

You can read the back of the cornflake packet and the menu in your local takeaway, so why should reading at uni be so different? University-level reading stands apart because you're:

- **Reading more – a lot more:** The quantity of reading can be scary. Your reading list alone can have very many titles on it, and each book can be (and probably is!) several hundred pages long. Then your tutor recommends secondary reading as background. Then articles, usually in journals, report and comment on research in your subject. Then more articles that build on the research. And so the list goes on. Will it ever end? You have to be able to see an end, because you're a humble student with a limited amount of time, and other units to read for, each with their own assignments and reading lists.

- **Reading with purpose:** You're reading for a specific reason, not for pleasure or escapism. When you read a novel, for example, you do so for enjoyment or to take your mind off the minutiae of everyday existence. This is what we call passive reading: when you let the story take over and you submit. You get to the end of the story, find out 'whodunnit', and in all probability never open the book again. You forget the details of the storyline. What you remember is the pleasure the novel gave you. Reading for academic purposes, on the other hand, is active reading. You have to be aware of what the texts are telling you, try to evaluate this, and make notes as you go along, especially when you come to important bits of information. You need to remember the content, not the pleasure! And you need to read critically. Once you've gained a basic familiarity with your subject, you're expected to read a variety of texts and analyse their different takes on the issues in question.

✔ **Reading like a flea:** The books you're working with aren't normally written like novels in that you have to begin at the beginning and read through conscientiously until you come to the end, in a straight line. Instead, at uni, you may have to read a couple of chapters to get the information you need. You can read sections of the book, go on to another one, and then return to the first. This isn't going in a straight line, but instead jumping around like a flea! Practically speaking, too, you may have difficulty getting hold of the books you need (see the following section for more on that) so you may be forced to read the recommended literature in whatever order it comes to hand.

# Using Your Reading List

As if you don't have enough to contend with – getting up in time for lectures, feeding yourself on a pittance, wondering whether to attend tonight's 'toga and tofu' party – your tutor's given you a dauntingly long list of books to read for your course, and you've no idea where to start. Never fear, help's at hand.

## Knowing which books to read

Your tutor – the expert – has sifted through the available literature and made a judicious choice of key texts to guide you in your reading, taking into account whether you're in your first year or your third, and your familiarity with the topic. The chosen texts should be accessible to the average student, and normally, if you restrict your reading to the titles on the list, you gain sufficient background knowledge to undertake your assignment.

The books back up what the lectures have covered, perhaps present things in a different way, give you further examples and generally pad out what the tutor's been saying. So if you don't quite get something in a lecture, perhaps you will understand more when a book explains it in a slightly different way and you can read at your own pace in the quiet of your own room or the library.

But even though each and every book on the list is useful and relevant, you don't need to read them all. The content of a number of titles may well overlap considerably, and while some books are indispensable reading (your 'set books'), others are of secondary importance.

Hopefully you have clear guidance on distinctions between the relevance of different books. If you don't, you should ask. Your tutor will be happy to indicate the books that are essential reading and those that are of slightly lesser importance to the course at the moment. Ask for a three-star, two-star and one-star rating, so you're clear which to focus on. Remind your tutor that, with the other units you're taking, you may not have the time to devote every waking hour to their particular baby, so you do need to know the most important titles. Ask at the end of a lecture, or send your tutor an email, and find out which titles are the key ones. Then, when time's short, you can focus on the content of the core texts. Any others you can dip into are a bonus.

If you don't know where to start, go for a general title that seems to give an overview of your subject. Choose the one that's the most recent.

If you're one of those people who likes to have your own, personal, pristine copy of a book, don't rush out and buy everything on your reading list. Most of us have only a limited amount of cash available for books, so you have to be savvy. Some of the books on the list may not be indispensable. Don't go throwing your money away!

## Finding the books on your list

The obvious places to look are the university library and the bookshop. No problem, surely? Wrong!

✏ Problem 1. The copy in the library is out.

✏ Problem 2. You can't afford to buy your own copy.

What do you do? Don't panic, we have some ideas.

### Delving deeper at the library

Depending on the number of students on your course and the number of copies of the key texts in the university library, at first getting hold of a popular book may well seem impossible. But this happens all the time and to most students. After all, you can't expect the library to hold an infinite number of copies of a single title, however essential it may be. So the library has various systems for sharing access fairly:

✏ **Reserving your copy:** You can ask for a book to be put on hold for you. The library then informs you when it's available. The drawback is that this takes time – a week say or even more if the student who has it doesn't return it promptly – and you may not have that amount of time.

✏ **Using the library's 'remove at your peril' title:** Look to see if the book you want is in a 'reserved' or 'short loan' section. This section holds key titles that students can't take out. The advantage is that you have access to the text you need, but on the other hand you can't take it home to read in the comfort of your room. In fact, you may only have access to it for a limited number of hours. This can be a blessing in disguise, because it makes you focus on what's really essential.

✔ **Making copies:** You're allowed to photocopy – not entire books, but up to 10 per cent of any publication – for your own personal use, if your finances permit. Photocopying one or two key pages shouldn't break the bank.

Get to know your way around your university library. What system does it use for classifying books? The system may not seem immediately logical to you, and books you need may be shelved in different places, so familiarising yourself with the main areas where you're likely to find books for your discipline is worthwhile. Find out how the electronic cataloguing system works, get a diagram of the layout of the library resources, and off you go!

### *Purchasing your own copy cheaply*

If you really find that you can't do without your own personal copy of a particular title, you don't have to pay the full cover price:

✔ **Buying second-hand:** Your university bookshop may have a second-hand section, which you should browse through, and often last year's students on the unit sell their course books. At the beginning of the year, in particular, you find lists of books for sale posted on walls in the department, in the students' union building and available online, once you start networking. Get in there quickly if you spot a bargain.

You can buy second-hand through sites such as Amazon and Abebooks, and get books pretty quickly and cheaply. Check comments from previous buyers and the star rating to see how efficient the seller is at delivering.

✔ **Going for shared ownership:** If all else fails, go to the university bookshop and buy a copy. Tutors let the bookshop have a copy of their reading lists before term starts to make sure that the list contains books that are still in print and that copies of the books are on the shelves for students who want to buy them. Chances are that if the library copy's in great demand, your classmates are having the same difficulty as you in locating a copy, so buy the book with a friend (or two) so that you can share it around between you. (Choose your friends carefully!) You can probably sell the book next year to the following cohort of students on your unit and so recoup something of the initial outlay.

Don't do what some students have been known to do: buy a book from the bookshop, use it overnight, and then take it back for a refund the following day saying that they picked up the wrong one and – oh dear – the one they want isn't there. This is dishonest. People who work in bookshops, especially university ones, are just trying to earn an honest crust like other working people.

# Moving Beyond the Reading List: Searching for Literature

Sometimes you need more than your reading list delivers. Perhaps your tutor isn't helpful in recommending what to read or you're researching some aspect of your course that may be off the beaten track. How do you find relevant texts? So you stride up and down the library scanning titles and hoping one jumps out? Well, you can do that, but we have some quicker techniques.

## Using the library catalogue

Look out for authors whose names appear more than once on your reading list and, when you get hold of a key textbook, look carefully at the references at the end and note the frequently occurring names. Then go online to your university library and use the catalogue to look up other books by these authors.

You can also do a keyword search to find books on your subject, but be careful what you search for. Use the search tool wisely and think carefully about the keywords you put in. For example, say you're studying English literature and your assignment's about women in Shakespeare. When one of the authors of this book, Mary, typed 'Shakespeare' into her university library catalogue, the search pulled up 2,506 titles! So you need to refine your choice. When Mary typed in 'Shakespeare + women' she got 27 results, a far more manageable number.

But hang on, what exactly is your assignment about? Is it asking you to write about the women characters in Shakespeare's plays, or is it about Shakespeare's attitude to women? In his plays or in his poetry? Go back to your essay title, pay careful attention to the exact wording, and make sure you know what you're looking for. For example, Mary found that 'Shakespeare's women' resulted in 6 hits, while 'Shakespeare + feminism' gave 8. 'Feminism in Shakespeare' gave 1 title only; 'Shakespeare + gender' 14. 'Feminist criticism of Shakespeare' indicated 4 books on this subject. And so on. These are all different areas of study or different takes on the same area. Which applies to your essay?

Clarify in your own mind what your assignment or research is about and then choose carefully the keywords you use to search for the books you need, thinking laterally about different ways of expressing the ideas in the keywords. Then you can deepen your search by looking in the database for:

- ✔ Titles of books by the same author
- ✔ Titles of books nearby on the same shelves

This may sound painstaking, but it's easier to do online than to trudge up and down the stacks physically looking for books – and remember that the ones you want may not even be there! By working from the catalogue, you know what's available, even if it's temporarily on loan to someone else.

Eventually, certain titles or authors' names keep popping up, so these are the ones you need to look at in greater detail. On your narrowed-down list, check for:

- ✔ **Contents:** The library catalogue should have some sort of summary of a book's contents – even a table of contents – so that you can gauge just how useful the book's going to be to you.

- ✔ **Date of publication:** Check when the book was published. This may be critical in helping you decide how useful it's going to be to you. For example, if you're studying the teaching of modern languages, you probably want the most up-to-date material, especially if you're researching the use of technology in language teaching!

When you get the book between your hands, have a look at the blurb, flip through the book, look at the table of contents if you haven't done so already, and look at the index at the back to get a feel for what the book contains. Is it appealing? Does it seem to be the right book for you?

## Calling on the experts

Among the librarians at the university, you will almost certainly find one, even two, who are dedicated to your subject. These specialists are extremely useful to know, and they are able to guide you through your book list and make sure that you consult the right books.

In freshers' week or early on in the course, you may have an opportunity to enrol on a guided tour around the library to locate the areas where you can find many of the books you're looking for, and also to discover all about the services your library can provide, such as putting books on hold. This is when you get to meet your subject specialist librarian. Make a note of his or her name so that you can you can ask to see the same person next time. As a rule, book lists don't change radically from year to year, so the specialist librarian has a good idea which titles have been in demand in previous years and have proved useful to students who did the units you're doing now. They specialist librarians are good to talk to and from their experience can help you to make wise choices.

Specialist librarians are also pretty knowledgeable about online resources. For example, they may be able to suggest search engines other than Google (yes, believe it or not other, specialist search engines are used in the academic world, and librarians know what they are and how to use them). Flip to Chapter 5 for more on researching online.

# Using Articles from Journals

Some students seem to shy away from using journal articles (sometimes referred to as 'papers'). Maybe something about the name puts them off. But if you think of journals as magazines, you have nothing to be afraid of. They're just magazines on academic subjects. Unfortunately, though, they don't come with glossy photos! They do, admittedly, often look dull with their dense text and lack of visuals (apart from the odd bar chart), but when you realise what a rich source they are, you don't miss the pictures. You can always reward yourself with a glossy mag when your work's done.

Read on to find out just what makes journals so special and how to use them.

## Why journals can be more useful than books

Don't limit yourself to books. Journal articles are a rich source of information and may even be a better source than books. Here are some sound reasons for turning to academic journals rather than books.

✔ **Abstracts:** Journals' abstracts are amazingly useful. An _abstract_ is a summary of the contents of an article and its findings, which comes at the beginning, after the title and name(s) of the author(s). It may be a third of a page (or less) in length. Read this and you know whether the article's worth reading in detail. The abstract of a journal article describes the question the researcher's trying to answer, what he or she does to answer it, and the conclusion. You then don't have to read the whole lot to find out whether it's going to be useful to you. This a wonderful timesaver!

But I hear you ask 'How is this better than looking at the blurb on the back cover of a book?' A blurb is extremely helpful in telling you what the book's about, but it doesn't summarise the content, does it? This is where the journal article has an advantage.

✔ **Accessibility:** Access to books is restricted, in that the library may have only a couple of copies, and they may be out when you need them. The online journal, however, is always there. Online means available all the time. All the students on your course can have access to the online journal article, but you can't all use the same copy of the book at the same time, even if it's in a reserve collection and you can't take it out.

✔ **Currency:** No, we don't mean foreign money, we mean how current or up to date a journal is. Academic journals vary in frequency of publication but tend to be quarterly so a new part's published four times a year. This means that the articles in the latest issue are as up to date as you can get. In fast-moving fields such as anything to do with technology, having access to the latest thinking may be crucial. A book's a much bigger undertaking and may take a couple of years in the writing. After all, you need a lot of ideas to fill a book! An article, on the other hand, takes less time out of an author's life to write and can get published more quickly than a book. In the academic world, therefore, journals are at the cutting edge of thought and opinion in your field, and you should include them in your reading and research.

✔ **Quality:** One thing that makes academic journals special is that they're normally peer reviewed. This means that a writer can't just write any old thing and have it published. Other experts in the field read the articles and edit the content, so that the journal meets certain scholarly standards. In other words, you can trust the content. It's not something whacky. Some journal articles may even be 'blind' peer reviewed, which means that the reviewers of an article don't know who wrote it. In this way, previous knowledge of the author (or lack of it!) doesn't sway them and they can be truly honest and objective about the content. This what makes the academic journal different from general interest magazines and newspaper articles. Because these are published daily, weekly or monthly, there is tremendous pressure on journalists to churn out material quickly and, understandably, it can happen that they don't have time to check their facts. Academic journals, on the other hand, may only be published once or twice a year, because what is important here is that the information is correct. Great care is taken to review and check content so that data is accurate and argument justified.

### *Reading journals: Online or print*

Journals may be in paper form, or online or both. If you're happier working from the printed original rather than the online version of your journal article, that's fine. But bear one important thing in mind. With the ever-growing wealth of literature in academia, many university libraries are having storage problems. Naturally they have to keep paper copies of journals that were printed before online versions existed, but now that they have a choice between the two and storage space is limited, keeping their archives digital is a sensible approach. As literature proliferates, you may have to become accustomed to researching and reading online. The paper version may not be an option unless you make a copy yourself.

Using online journals offers definite advantages. Once you get familiar with the way the indexing and links function, locating useful-sounding material's a lot easier. You need to get into the habit of determining what your keywords are and using these as the basis of your search. Chapter 5 helps you out if you want to find out more about using keywords. If you do a search on key-words, finding articles on the same topic is a relatively simple matter – so much simpler online than physically searching out the journals on the library shelves.

Enthusiastic surfing can lead to losing your train of thought or for-getting previous discoveries. You want to retrace your online foot-steps to an article you hit on a while ago and you can't remember where it was. Keep a note with an old-fashioned pen or pencil of journal names, volumes and so on, so that you can find them again.

One thing to check is actual access to online academic journals. You may have online access to some of them only on university premises, and they may not be available off campus. Or you may need a special password or identification number for off-campus access. Without the identification number, the article may not be available or, if it is, you may have to pay for it. Your university has paid for online access to the journal in question so that you don't need to part with your cash unnecessarily. Remember this when you're planning your work and check with your librarians if you aren't sure. You're going to be very annoyed if you go home to your parents for the weekend, envisaging two days of being fed wholesome food and getting your laundry done while you write your assignment, only to find that you can't load the article you so desperately need. Remember to print a copy or take a photocopy of anything really essential. (Then please recycle the paper – lots of universities encourage you to print only what's necessary then dispose of the used paper in a recycling bin.)

Reading the reference to a journal can sometimes be a little confusing until you get the hang of it. Something like *Journal of Animation* 2005 42(3): 267–287 means that once you've located this journal, be it the paper or online version, you need to look for Volume 42, Number 3, and the article you need starts on page 267. 'Volume' refers to all the parts of the journal published in that year (in this case 2005). In this example, you need the third part, Number 3. Usually a journal's published four times a year, but special editions can also happen. The numbering of pages can be confusing at first, because it can start with page 1 in the first part of the given year and continue through all the parts published that year (so the second part doesn't begin at page 1 again, but at, say, page 115).

# Brushing Up Your Reading Techniques

You may wonder what's so special about reading. You do it all the time, don't you? Of course you do, and you don't get to university without the ability to read – and read well. Problems arise at uni, however, when students realise the amount of reading they have to do and the challenges this presents. Not only the sheer volume of reading gets people down, but also trying to absorb all that knowledge. No longer are you reading for pleasure, you're reading for information. You're more aware of the processes involved in reading and choose different techniques to help you digest the material efficiently.

Make yourself comfortable when you settle down to read, but not so comfortable that you can fall asleep! To help your eyes, get the lighting right and, if you wear glasses or contact lenses, make sure that you've had your eyes tested recently so that you're not putting them under any unnecessary strain.

## Reading smartly

This means doing the opposite of what you do if you're reading for pleasure, when you read to find out how a story ends and you want to be surprised by plot, subplot and red herrings along the way. Imagine settling down with a detective novel and flicking straight to the last page to find out how the killer did it. (Some people do this, but to me it somehow spoils the suspense.) No point really in reading the story. With academic reading, however, you know from the start how it ends, and getting there is more important.

Here are some ways of reading smartly:

✔ **Looking at abstracts.** In the earlier section 'Using articles from journals', we tell you that looking at an article's abstract is a quick way of deciding whether the article (which may be 30 pages or more) is worth reading in depth. You find on many databases that you can download just abstracts, and only if the abstract sounds useful do you go on to download the article in its entirety. So when you're doing your research, you can keep a record of the promising abstracts then choose from this list to download those articles that are clearly the most useful.

✔ **Reading first and last paragraphs.** With an article or a chapter in a book, you may need to read the beginning and the end to be sure whether to discard it. Look at the beginning and see what kind of questions the author's going to answer or what aspects of the topic he or she's going to discuss, and then jump right to the end to see how the author answers the questions or summarises the conclusions. Do you need to read how he or she got from A to B? If you do, then go ahead and read what goes between.

✔ **Reading the first sentence of each paragraph.** This should give you a good idea of the content. In Chapter 9 we see that each paragraph has a 'topic sentence' that contains the key idea in the paragraph, and each paragraph should really only have one main idea. Very frequently, the first sentence in a paragraph is that topic sentence. It doesn't have to be, but it often is. So by going through a chapter and reading all the first sentences, you should have a pretty good idea of what the chapter's about and whether you should read it all. You may well find yourself drawn into the chapter, which is a good indication that you're on the right track and something here is speaking to you.

✔ **Scanning through a text for information.** This is what you do when you have questions in your head that demand specific answers. It's a really good technique to use when you're searching for nouns or names of things. Imagine that you're looking for a date, a person, a theory, a keyword, a place or a phrase. Turn the pages and let your eyes run over them until they find what they're looking for. Your eyes don't go straight from top to bottom or from right to left. Instead, they zigzag and take in whole chunks of the page in their own way. Let them do this and trust the process. They can find the information you're looking for. You do this a lot in life and your eyes are used to it. Scanning's what you do when you look for a name in a telephone directory. You know the information you want and you discard the rest.

✔ **Skimming through a text to get the gist.** You do this when you flip through a magazine to see what's in it and then make a choice of what exactly to read in more detail. Do you want to read your horoscope, or what's hot to wear or what Celebrity X is up to? At uni you may have a lot to read and not much time, so you have to skim through the chapter, book or article to get an idea of what it contains and whether it's going to be of any use to you. Include in your skimming any subtitles, subheadings and illustrations. These help enormously in giving you a feel for the content and its usefulness to you in your studies. Then you can go back to the bit that looks good and read only that.

When skimming through something shorter or just a page of text, punctuation (without you realising it) can help. punctuation marks all have meaning and can add to your general understanding of what the text contains and whether it's of any use to you. A series of question marks may suggest that the author is asking rather than answering questions. You want answers! At the same time let your eyes jump over lines in brackets (less important material) and quotations, which are usually there to back up a point. Similarly, look out for words such as 'however', 'in addition', 'nevertheless' and so on which (as we'll see when writing paragraphs in Chapter 9) are like signposts, pointing the reader in the direction the argument is going.

✔ **Using the index.** This is where textbooks are different from novels – the writer knows that the reader probably doesn't read the content from cover to cover but instead needs to fillet the book for the information he or she wants. What are your keywords, key names and key concepts? Look these up in the index at the back and then read the pages indicated.

Indexes are thorough and include any odd mention of the keyword, so each entry can be quite long. To save you looking up every single mention, be smart. If the reference is to just one page, chances are that it's not that important and you can omit looking the reference up if you're pushed for time. But if the reference is to several consecutive pages, then you should certainly read them. And if the reference is in bold, the work's been done for you. Bold means important – read this!

Few of us have brilliant memories, and with the quantity of reading you have to do at uni, expecting your brain to be able to retain everything is unreasonable. In Chapter 6 we have a look in detail at how to make notes. For the moment, all we need to say is that you need to go to the students' union shop and come back with all the things that come in handy for note making: paper, pens, sticky notes, erasers – and, of course, bars of chocolate.

# Reading online

Increasingly what you read is online, not in print form, especially academic journals. Being aware of how reading online and reading print are different is useful so that you can adjust the way you read accordingly.

### Avoiding getting tired

Most students report getting tired more easily when they have to spend long periods reading from the screen and concentrating to take all the information in. Glare and the way shapes of letters look when they're on the screen are involved here. Our advice is to get up and walk away from the computer every so often so that you get a break from it. You can't concentrate indefinitely, and a walk and a stretch make you feel better.

### Preventing eye strain

Similarly, many students feel that their eyes get strained by staring at the screen. Protecting your eyesight from deterioration is important. Depending on what the text in question allows you to do, try changing the size of the print so that you can read it comfortably, and rest your eyes frequently just by looking away from the screen. Then every 15–20 minutes, get up and have a walk.

### Giving yourself time

Academic reading is more time-consuming than reading for pleasure: you have to take in the information the text contains and you have a solid block of writing to digest. But reading online can really slow things down. A lot of people find that they read more slowly from the screen than from a book, so be aware that reading an academic text from a computer screen can take you about 25 per cent longer than reading a similar text in the form of a handout or book. This may be a factor when you're deciding whether to take a print copy of a text that seems useful to you.

You can ease your online reading experience by avoiding certain layouts:

✔ **Texts that are justified.** This means that the lines are stretched to reach the extreme right edge, creating a square block on the page. This creates uneven white space between words and letters, which is much harder on the eye and adds to your tiredness. Unjustified text (like this!) has a ragged right-hand side, because the spaces between words and letters are allowed to be even and natural. This is easier for the eye to take in. If you've got to read a text and it's justified, then it may be best to print it off and give your eyes a break. Your eyes deal with it better without having to cope with screen glare as well.

✔ **Texts in columns (like newspapers).** These can be really annoying! A number of journals in PDF form are like this. If you adjust the size to make the words nice and big for your eyes, the page seems too large for the screen. You have to scroll down the first column, then back up to the top of the second, scroll down the second, and so on throughout the article. If you change the size of the page so that it fits the screen and you don't have to scroll, the words are too small for you to read comfortably. To avoid squinting or scrollitis or both, making a paper copy may be simpler.

Include in your budget a small amount of cash for printing, because some things you just have to have on paper, either because of the important information they contain or because reading them is easier. The important thing is to keep them in an organised way so that you can find them when you need them. You probably have quite a lot of papers anyway in the form of handouts from lectures, so you need a filing system. Start with an A4 ring binder – wide rather than narrow so that you can get lots in – and have one per unit. Use dividers to separate out different lectures or topics, and get into the habit of carefully filing away your documents at the end of every day.

## *Reading faster*

You have an awful lot to read at uni and never enough time to do it all. One solution is to try to read faster. Funnily enough, reading faster may also mean reading better. People tend to think that if you read slowly, you're giving your brain more time to memorise what you're reading, when in fact the opposite's true. If you read too slowly, you often get lost in the details and miss the big picture. So how can you improve your reading speed? We can suggest a variety of strategies.

To feel you've understood the content of a text, you probably have to try out a number of the techniques we describe. You need to be prepared to adapt your strategies according to the difficulty of the content, its relative newness, and how you're feeling at that particular moment. And some days, what you're reading goes in better than on others.

Read, read and read. Practice makes perfect. No short cuts. By reading more and more you increase your speed.

## Sticking to the 80:20 principle

Here's the $64,000 question: how do you know you've read enough? This is a difficult one to answer, but if you've delved into most of the recommended titles, you've probably got enough to base your essay on. And you can't go on reading indefinitely. You have a deadline to meet and at some point the reading has to stop and the writing begin.

A quick rule of thumb in planning your time is the 80:20 principle, which means that you spend 80 per cent of your time on preparation and 20 per cent on the task. So if you have ten hours in total to read for and write an essay, you spend approximately eight hours reading and two writing. This varies from individual to individual and from subject to subject, but if you start with this rough guide, you should get your essay written and handed in on time.

### Training your eyes not to backtrack

You may feel a temptation to let your eyes stray back over the text you've just read, especially when you doubt you've understood everything. Just ploughing on, trusting that everything's going to make sense if you persevere, is hard. In fact going backwards interrupts the flow, so you've got to take a leap of faith that by the time you get to the end of the chapter, the pieces of the jigsaw are going to fall into place. And often they do. If they don't, you may have to reread the chapter. But again, do this quickly, without backtracking. You have a better chance of understanding if you read something twice quickly than once slowly.

 Moving your finger along the line, as you did in primary school, helps you keep moving forwards in the text. If you're a slow reader, do the opposite of what your teachers told you and consciously make your finger go faster than the speed at which you naturally read. Try to make your eyes catch up with your finger! This works for some people.

### Reading not speaking

You don't want to read your book aloud, do you? So don't read the words in your head as if you're speaking. If you do sound the words individually in your head, you're definitely reading too slowly and you have to break this habit. It doesn't help you understand or memorise, it just slows you down. The exception? A line of poetry or a passage of literature can demand that you read it slowly and aloud in order for its depth and beauty truly to resonate with you.

### Reading not memorising

Don't read too slowly, just go with the flow and let the writer's train of thought carry you along. Don't stop to try to memorise anything, because the fact of stopping interferes with the flow and logic of what you're reading. You can always go back later and pick out facts or key points. Relax, go with the flow, read as quickly as you can, and only stop when you get to the end of a section. Then you can pause and think.

### Taking in more words at a time

When you're a child, you concentrate on recognising one letter at a time, then with practice you can take in the whole word in one glance (this is called *fixation*). You gradually speed up to take in two words together, then three, until you take in several words. The fastest readers have fewer fixations per page. In other words, their eyes can take in more words in a single glance than slower readers. You too can do this, but you have to practise.

Look at a page of text, focus on a word and be aware of the words in your peripheral vision that you can also see. You can see words to the left and to the right of the word. You recognise them and understand them. The trick is to move on swiftly from this fixation to the next, maximising the distance between the words at the centre of each fixation so that your eyes jump forward, stretching each fixation to the limit. Forcing yourself on like this eventually pays dividends and speeds up your reading. You have fewer fixations per page and really race through those books!

Sometimes the book you're reading is just too hard. This may happen when concepts are particularly difficult to grasp and you haven't got your head around some new terminology. Don't despair. Have a word with your tutor and maybe he or she can suggest an alternative that presents the ideas in a slightly more accessible fashion. (You never know, a *For Dummies* book on the subject may exist!) You're probably able to access the original book at a later stage, when you're more confident and ready for it. Just don't be put off if it seems too hard to begin with. Remember, too, that a chapter may go into more detail than you actually need, and as long as you understand the main points, the complicated convolutions may not be of any use to you.

### Varying your reading speed

If you persevere with your reading speed, you're gradually able to adapt your speed to the requirements of the task. Be aware of the relative complexity of the content of the text you're reading – if it's a subject you're familiar with and written in a straightforward way, then go for it! Make those eyes speed along the line and down the page, zigzagging as they go. Then you can slow down when the content gets trickier. Efficient readers are in control of their reading speed and adjust it automatically, just as you do with your foot on the accelerator when you're driving.

### Dealing with unfamiliar words

In all probability your subject has a specialist vocabulary that you gradually acquire from lectures and reading. When you're reading, you can come across a term you're not familiar with, so the temptation is to check in a dictionary. The important thing is not to stop to look things up too often, because this interrupts the flow you're hoping to achieve in your reading, which helps in your overall comprehension. But if a word is bothering you and it comes up several times, you probably do have to pause and seek an explanation. Before you reach for a dictionary, look to see if a glossary at the back of the textbook explains how terms are used, especially if they're being used in a special way.

Keep a list of specialist terms and their definitions – these are useful when you're writing essays, and in any case, the act of noting them down helps you to retain them.

## Putting it all together: The SQ3R technique

SQ3R has been around for ages and has helped lots of students, so it may well work for you too. It gives you a clear five-step framework for what to do when reading. Give the technique a go, modify it if need be, and develop your own way of processing the literature mountain.

1. **Survey:** This means skim through the text to get the gist of what it's about (see the earlier section 'Reading smartly'). Don't do any 'proper' reading at this point, but instead notice the structure of the text and observe the use of typography such as *italics* or words written in **bold**. Does the text have any graphics or diagrams? Does it have a 'what this chapter's about' section at the beginning, or a summary of the key points at the end?

2. **Question:** After your initial sweep through, make a list of the questions that you think this text may answer. Does it appear to go over old ground and tell you what you already know, or does it seem to contain new information and ideas? Ask yourself also 'What am I trying to get out of this text?' 'What do I need to know?' Look at the headings and see if they match your needs. If time is short, you can

reject the text at this point if it doesn't appear to offer any new perspective or you have no strong reason to read it (like your tutor's recommended it!). Best to move on and find the right text for you.

3. **Read:** Now read the text using the advice given in the section 'Reading faster', adapting your speed appropriately and being aware of how you're reading. Keep at the front of your mind the questions you wrote down in step 2, and go back to reread sections if you think you may have missed something important or are unsure.

4. **Recall:** Put the text to one side and either say out loud (perhaps into a digital recorder) or note down what you've discovered. Try to answer the questions you want to answer. To avoid plagiarism (turn to Chapter 7 for more on this), use your own words. Don't try to memorise word for word what you've read, but put the ideas into the words that seem the most natural for you. This is, in fact, an important step in the memorisation process, because you're making the ideas your own when you actively turn the writer's words into ones you choose yourself. Don't worry that your words are simpler or less elegant – you can polish them at a later stage. At the moment what counts is that you commit them to memory.

5. **Review:** Do you have the answers to the questions you asked in step 2? Do you need to look elsewhere? Reflect on what you've gained from reading the text and see where you are now.

## *Reading critically*

As well as reading to find information or to follow an argument, another aspect of reading at university level is reading critically. This is the hardest style of reading, because you probably haven't done much of it before. Reading *critically* means that not only do you have to grasp what the author's saying, you have to assess how and how well the writer argues his or her case.

Make a list of questions such as:

✔ What's the writer's main argument?

✔ Does the writer's argument come across as balanced or may it be biased in some way? What evidence supports this?

✔ Are the examples good ones or perhaps a bit obscure?

✔ Does the writer distinguish clearly between facts and opinions?

✔ Do any parts of what the writer says seem to contradict themselves?

✔ How is the writer using language? (Check for terms that he or she may be using with slightly different meanings.)

✔ If the text contains data in the form of statistics, does the writer use all the information or only some?

✔ Does the writer make any assumptions that he or she doesn't back up?

✔ Does the writer agree or disagree with what others have said on the subject or with what your tutor has said? If disagreement exists, which argument seems stronger?

✔ Where is this leading? Can you anticipate what's coming next?

Questions such as these help you to evaluate what you've read and weigh up the importance of this particular text in the bigger context of the unit you're studying. Stop, reflect, and try to get some perspective on your reading.

# Keeping yourself going

Everyone becomes demotivated at times and can't drum up any enthusiasm for studying, especially when some aspect of a course is less interesting than the rest. And this is when reading can be so hard to do, because your mind tends to wander and you can think of a hundred other things you'd prefer to be doing.

Get the book out and tell yourself that this text must contain something interesting – and you're going to find it. You've got to find some sort of hook that catches your interest, because if you have no interest, taking in information and consequently writing your essay is very difficult. Ask yourself if the writer has a different perspective on the topic. What does he or she have to say that's different from what you've read so far? Why has your tutor recommended that you read this particular text? If you can identify what makes this text special, then you may have a way in. Promise yourself some time out or a little treat when you've finished your reading, then grit your teeth and do it. Find one or two little nuggets of information, and that's success. This motivates you to keep going with the next reading task, and gradually the small successes build up, making you feel more positive towards the topic, even though it may not be the most exciting aspect of your course. You never know, you may even get interested in it!

Take a look at Chapter 2 for more on getting started and keeping going.

# Chapter 5

# Researching Online

· · · · · · · · · · · · · · · · · · · · · · · · · · · · · · · · · · · · · · · · · · ·

*In This Chapter*

▶ Recognising the need for caution

▶ Evaluating websites

▶ Knowing where to look for the best resources

· · · · · · · · · · · · · · · · · · · · · · · · · · · · · · · · · · · · · · · · · · ·

*P*rinting presses have been around for more than 500 years. Over that time, the development and growth of publishing have fostered some solid agreements on best practice and good principles. The Internet, in contrast, has had a very short life so far. A few decades of incredible growth have allowed an unbelievable array of resources to develop, but the checks and balances to help keep standards high have not developed as quickly. That's why, in this chapter, we explain that you need to think carefully about the appropriateness and accuracy of online resources.

The best and the worst of research is available on the Internet, and this chapter helps you find your way through the confusing maze of sites that promise you everything. We help you identify the sites that really deliver.

 Use the Internet for your research but don't make it your only source. Use books and other print media as well (see Chapter 4 for more on using printed resources).

## Exercising Caution as You Surf

The Internet's an incredible resource for students, but it's still a new form of information. Often students don't get much support in trying to sift through the vast quantity of available information. The upside of this resource is the almost instant access to data of many types from a diverse range of sources. The downside is the danger of overload and the possibilities of accepting fallacious information as truth.

You need your wits about you and your critical faculties sharpened if you're to make the most of the Internet for your studies.

Although the Internet is (on balance) a wonderful resource, you need to bear in mind its inherent dangers. Don't expect that you can accomplish a careful, thorough search in one quick 30-minute surfing session. For a comprehensive investigation, you need to set aside a good few hours.

You can really easily be overwhelmed with the quantity of apparently relevant information, like searching for a needle in a haystack and finding yourself completely lost in the hay. That's why you need to be a discerning and even suspicious surfer. As we explain in the later section 'Finding Academically Acceptable Websites', before you cram your essay full of info from www.we-know-everything.com, you need to verify the reliability of the source.

One of the best ways of using quality websites is quite simply to stick to those your course tutors recommend. Your course information probably contains a list of online resources, and don't forget that you can always speak to your tutor. Not only can he or she point you in the direction of other useful and reliable sites, but you may also get some expert advice on which sites to avoid like the plague.

# Getting Started: Using Popular Websites

In the course of your research you're likely to log on to some much-loved Internet resources. So here's the lowdown on some of the mainstream sites you may visit.

Bookmark your most commonly accessed web pages, keeping them as 'Favorites' so that you can go to them when you need to rather than having to find them again through your search engine.

## Checking out key websites

Here are some standard sites that most academics agree are suitable for your research:

- ✔ **Google scholar** (`http://scholar.google.co.uk`): Peer-reviewed journal articles and extracts from books, without any of the usual commercial links.

- ✔ **IngentaConnect** (`www.ingentaconnect.com`): You may have to pay for a full article, but you can access abstracts for free and many academic libraries have a subscription.

- ✔ **Internet Public Library (www.ipl.org):** An enormous virtual public library.

- ✔ **Infomine (http://infomine.ucr.edu):** A virtual library of Internet resources for users in universities. Created and maintained by librarians, it's an American site with a wide scope and useful help pages for searching.

- ✔ **Questia (www.questia.com):** Another massive virtual library of books and articles, although you need a subscription for full access.

- ✔ **The British Library (www.bl.uk):** 10,000 pages of information and an endless gallery of images.

If you need particular software such as Acrobat Reader to view items on these sites, this should be freely available (freeware). Be sure to check, because otherwise you may end up paying for a download you don't need.

## Broadening the Net

You probably have a favourite search engine, or at least one that you use habitually. That's not a real problem, but varying your searches once in a while is a good idea in order to find more information. It also forces you to take on board some different viewpoints to the ones you usually look at and might give you some different insights. Here are some other search engines to try, aside from the popular Google, Yahoo!, Ask Jeeves and Lycos:

- ✔ All the Web: www.alltheweb.com

- ✔ Complete Planet: http://aip.completeplanet.com

- ✔ Academic Info (for finding subject guides): www.academic info.net

When you use a search engine, keep your search page intact. When you find something that interests you or shows promise, open it in a new tab or a new window. That way you don't lose your original search page.

## Working with Wikipedia or not?

Before considering the value of online encyclopaedias in academic work, you may want to think about the kinds of references that are recommended for students to use, either in print or other versions. An academic essay usually requires you to provide an in-depth analysis of a fairly narrow topic. You need to take into account key theories and more up-to-date issues of the sort reported in journals. To these ends you may use a print or online dictionary in your essay to confirm some definitions or be clear on the meanings of some words. You don't use such sources any further.

Take the same approach with encyclopaedias and reference texts (both print and online). They may serve a purpose in setting up your area of discussion, but for analysis of complex issues you need to turn to documents published in your field. An encyclopaedia is too generic in whatever format. Your paper may also need to relate to your own experience, and you can't find that in a reference text.

Wikipedia isn't the only site that non-expert users write, but it's the most commonly used and perhaps the most famous.

Even the founder of Wikipedia (Jimmy Wales) recognises that it often isn't an appropriate source for academic work. It's a democratic site that allows any user to add or edit materials, and then fellow users assess the reliability and accuracy of these materials. This results in some problems in terms of bias, subjectivity, error and confusion.

Table 5-1 helps you to sum up what's hot and what's not about online references of this type.

## Table 5-1 Pros and Cons of Wikipedia-style References

| Pros | Cons |
| --- | --- |
| You can establish some useful background information to help contextualise your work. | The information's uneven, reflecting the user group's interests rather than issues of significance. For example, on Wikipedia more information's available on J.R.R. Tolkein's fictitious Middle Earth than on some real nations and actual geographical places. |
| You can make use of the links at the end of articles – these can be more useful than the articles themselves as they are often academic articles. | Some entries and pages are so controversial that they have to be protected, such as those dealing with inflammatory topics like Nazism, unidentified flying objects and Dianetics. This means that only certain users can alter content, to prevent bias, defamatory language and falsities being entered. Although sites do this to improve monitoring, if the site has a political bias or is very one-sided, the checks and balances are also going to be rather unreliable. |

| Pros | Cons |
| --- | --- |
| Searching and reading about the area you're interested in helps you identify alternative keywords that you can use for further searches. | Because you have to check the facts the site presents you with for accuracy, you may not find the effort worth bothering in the first place. |
| You can use the History tab to look at previous incarnations of pages and see the changes that have been made. | Because the site's constantly undergoing revisions, the information's unstable. What the site presents as a fact one day may vanish the next. |
| The sheer size of the Internet means that pretty much all subjects are covered. | If this is your exclusive source, your work is thin, unverified and narrow. |
| You can expose controversies and subjects prone to bias – if this is the subject of your essay, you can weave the arguments into your discussion. | |

Some tutors have started using the composition of wiki-glossaries or other entries as assessments in themselves. This can be a good way to see if students can summarise key points clearly and effectively. However, in order to do this well, you would still need to reply on sound academic sources for your source information.

# Finding Academically Acceptable Websites

As well as the online resources your tutor recommends and the popular sites we outline in the earlier section 'Getting Started: Using Popular Websites', you're bound to widen your net and look at other sites. But how trustworthy are these other resources? Anyone anywhere can post information on the Internet, and you can easily find yourself looking at ideas or facts that are incorrect, from a dubious source, or just very outdated.

Therefore you *must* verify your information and ensure that it's reliable and acceptable for use in your essay. In the following s ections we give you a crash course in analysing sources.

Do look at the options for changing the way in which you view the information. You can enlarge text or change the layout, and this can make reading the text a more pleasant task.

## *Recognising scholarly sites*

To start you off, Table 5-2 outlines some of the key things you're looking for when assessing whether a site's academic.

| Table 5-2 | Scholarly versus Popular Website Features | |
|---|---|---|
| *Feature of Site* | *Scholarly Quality* | *Popular Quality* |
| General look and feel | More text than images; generally earnest and often lacking humour | Lots of images; probably more attractive than an academic site; adverts and pop-ups |
| Images | Charts, graphs, models | Photographs and animations |
| Language | Uses jargon where necessary; formal language | Popular, informal language, often colloquial |
| Structure of writing | Formal; usually makes use of abstracts; lists bibliography | Informal; sometimes even lacks paragraphs |
| References and citations | Lots of references to recognisable sources | Lacking or rather sketchy |
| Editorial role | Reviewed by expert peers and has a stringent application procedure | Possibly reviewed by an editor, but not always |
| Target audience | Academics, students and researchers | The interested general public |

## *Determining sources and authors*

If you come across an unfamiliar site, you can start by looking closely at who owns and runs the site, and who writes material for it.

### *Examining the address*

Look at the domain address. The final letters help you see whether the site's academic. The source of a website is really useful in establishing the authority of the information. Table 5-3 shows the most common web address endings and what they mean.

| Table 5-3 | Decoding Web Addresses | |
|---|---|---|
| *Nature of Site* | *UK Address Ends . . .* | *US Address Ends . . .* |
| Academic | .ac.uk | .edu |
| Commercial | .org.uk | .org |
| | .net | .net |
| | .co.uk | .com |
| Not-for-profit or commercial | .org | .org |
| | .net | .net |
| Personal web page | .net | .net |
| Governmental | .gov.uk | .gov |
| | | .us |
| Corporate | | .info |

Of course, the domain name's only going to give you so much information. Loads of commercial sites have started using .org, previously a sign of a non-profit organisation, and so you need other measures of quality as well.

### Categorising the site

Start by discovering what kind of website it is, because this influences the type (and quality) of information presented:

✔ Is it sponsored by some kind of corporation? This could increase the bias and subjectivity.

✔ Is it a blog? If so, how can you check the suitability of the authors? These sites usually emphasise opinion (sometimes to the detriment of fact).

✔ Is it a vanity site? Has someone merely established a site without worrying about the quality in general?

✔ Is it an index that links to other sites and content? How can you be sure that the recommendations are good?

✔ Is it trying to advocate a particular point of view? This is definitely not a balanced site.

✔ Is it trying to persuade you to buy something (is it an e-commerce site)?

You can also look at links to and from the sites. Are the sites endorsed by or connected with other good sites? Do they link to excellent quality sites or just a random bunch of addresses?

### Considering media sites

Sites that large publishing groups, television channels and national radio stations run are generally well established and subject to a fair amount of scrutiny. They report information and often have really useful archive pages with stories and images from a couple of decades at least.

For academic papers, you should stick to the quality press (what used to be the broadsheet papers) unless you're trying to show how the media dilutes and changes ideas. The quality press tends to provide in-depth coverage and detail in its reporting, although because it targets a specific audience, the political stance affects the quality of the work.

You need to be careful about the subjectivity of the national press in the UK (as in other countries). Be aware that the *Guardian* is left-leaning, *The Times* and the *Daily Telegraph* are right-leaning. *The Independent* aims to be a centrist paper. Many people accuse the BBC of having left-wing sympathies, despite its constant claims for impartiality. Make your own mind up!

### Analysing authors

You need to check that the people producing the writing actually know what they're talking about. When you picked up this book, you probably looked to see who wrote it and checked whether we were talking about essay writing with any authority. Having found that we're both tutors, you rightly inferred that we've spent ages helping students improve their writing and should have lots of ideas and experience.

You also probably know this range of books and are satisfied that the quality's great, otherwise it wouldn't endure and be so popular. Putting these things together, you rightly assumed that the publishers wouldn't risk messing up their series by asking people to write their books who aren't able to make a good job of it and so the authors must be okay.

All of this is critical analysis of the authors and the source. You need to apply the same judgement to the websites you visit. We don't recommend that you necessarily spend ages looking up every writer's qualifications, but you can certainly take a peek at any biographies or info in the 'About us' section. You can also run a search on the authors to see whether they have any other publications on related topics, for example. And you may even be able to contact them through the 'Contact us' section on the website.

## Scoping the scope

The *scope* is the extent of the site. You can measure scope in time, geography, area or extent. You can sometimes find sites with lots of exclusions due to copyright or limited time periods (such as only going back one or two years, so missing key information).

You can also quickly gain a sense of the depth of the information through looking at the balance of text to pictures on the page. Generally, academic sites are dominated by text, hopefully broken up into paragraphs and comfortable to view. If all you get is pictures and advertisements, the site's unlikely to fulfil a solid research brief. (Obviously this is different if your research topic is visual advertising or graphics of some sort.)

## Matching up primary and secondary sources

Understanding the context is important for secondary sources. For example, the most common secondary source you come across on a daily basis is the news as presented on television, radio and through the newspapers.

Say a story's breaking about a film actor winning an award and making a speech. The full draft of the speech is the primary source. These are the words the actor actually spoke; a film of it probably exists, so you can listen to the recording and hear the nuances of speech as well as reading the transcription.

However, the sources you're most likely to encounter are the reports of the speech, which are secondary sources. You catch sight of the tearful celebrity on the front page of a paper on a newsstand, or hear a snippet of the celebrity thanking his or her agent on the radio as you pop into a café to pick up a latte. You aren't likely to trawl websites searching for the full speech.

We trust the media to let us know something unusual or interesting. If the actor uses the speech to slam the Government or confess a crime, direct reports of the words are splattered all over the television and newspapers. In such a circumstance you're more likely to check out the primary source, wanting to see what the actor actually said, rather than allowing the media to edit it for you. Here, you're less likely to rely on a secondary source, because you want to judge for yourself.

Take the same approach with academically inclined websites. If something's odd, important or really interesting, you need to try and get to the primary source to check the interpretations for accuracy and fairness.

## Being wary of bias

If you still can't be sure about the level of bias from the authorship, you need to evaluate the content yourself. Look carefully at the language and see whether you're being subtly (or unsubtly) persuaded to agree with the authors. Review the advertising (if any) on the site and decide whether it may be affecting the content.

A biased site is capable of presenting very carefully selected information and facts. You may find that the facts are accurate and conclude that the site's unbiased. Remember, however, that the facts may not be causing the difficulties, which may be stemming from the selection of some information and the omission of other data.

Look out for definite information. Academics are generally cautious in their recommendations because they're aware that people are different (often needing diverse advice) and that people can argue against facts – they need verification. Sites that use definite vocabulary such as *always, never, none, all* and so on may be lacking in the kinds of nuance you really need.

## Assuring accuracy

You may think that having to check the truth of what you've so carefully already researched is a real bore, but you need to know that the information's reliable. Like all academic work, seek out the citations and references to the key points being raised. Are they properly listed?

You may have to research further and check both secondary and primary sources. *Secondary sources* are those that present an interpretation of facts, while *primary sources* originate the information. Sometimes a secondary source is an inaccurate version of the primary information – see the nearby sidebar 'Matching up primary and secondary sources' for more. You need to ensure that the site distinguishes between primary and secondary data in the first place.

## Checking currency

Websites come and go, and finding dates on some pages can be difficult. For many types of information, you need to know when things were written or posted if you're to be sure that the information hasn't been superseded.

Some documents include the date that information was collated (such as on national or regional government web pages). Other data needs a great deal of updating, and a date should show when the page was last updated. The website should also give you access to previous archived pages.

You can also get a sense of the currency of sites by checking that their links to other pages still work.

Websites are great for the latest info, but not always for the oldest. If you're trawling an online archive, find out what date the work starts, because you may need earlier information in print form.

## Completing your checklist

In addition to those we present in the previous sections, here are some additional questions that help you decide whether you want to use a website as a reference:

- ✔ Does the site ask you to register? If so, it should have a privacy statement and let you know the kind of user data it collects. Only sign up if you're relaxed about providing such information.

- ✔ Is the site designed in a well-organised manner, giving a sense of professional quality? Is the navigation effective and logical?

- ✔ How wide-ranging is the content? Is it really too narrow, or does it represent decent coverage of the topics being discussed?

- ✔ What is the quality of the writing and presentation? Check for accurate spelling and errors in language that may betray the lack of a scholarly approach.

- ✔ Are you able to reference the pages? Either the name of the author or a link to an organisation should be clearly visible, if possible with a way to contact the authors with queries.

- ✔ Do you have any evidence that other experts in the field have verified or approved the work the site presents? Is it peer reviewed or endorsed by a national or credible international agency? Do you have evidence of any independent evaluation?

- ✔ Are bibliographic sources presented? What is the quality of these references?

A wide range of measures tell you whether a source is going to be worth using. As you develop the skills of critically evaluating what you find, you're able to sort out the good, the bad and the ugly.

## Killer librarians?

In 2001 a North American student died while taking part in a clinical trial at Johns Hopkins University. Before the trial, the research scientists looked up the side effects of the trial drugs they were trialling, using electronic resources that only went back around 40 years. Because they didn't review the print archive that showed the side effects from earlier studies, they allowed a student with asthma to participate, and this resulted in her death.

Some people blame the librarians for not cataloguing and digitising the earlier research. Others blame the scientists for their lack of research. Others still find fault with the committee who agreed the project – should they have demanded a more thorough literature review?

Your essay isn't likely to have ramifications of this nature, but this story does flag up the limitations of some electronic resources.

## *Searching with keywords and other terms*

How best to search depends on what you are looking for and how much detail you already have. It really helps if you think about synonyms for your main terms before you start searching. If you're looking for information about what people do in their free time, you should think about the range of keywords you might use. As well as 'leisure' you might use any of these: spare time, spare moments, pastime, hobby, vacant time, time on one's hands; holiday, relaxation, rest, take one's time, repose, idle, loose end etc.

You need to think broadly so you don't limit your responses and you are probably already very adept at using keywords to search on the internet in a flexible and imaginative manner. Think about a time when you were trying to organize night out at the movies, but you couldn't remember the exact title of the film. You may have input the name of one of the stars, or the director. Perhaps you even put in 'film about Australia' or whatever, which would throw up a review of the movie. You might have used the specific cinema if you knew roughly where it was showing and you will have mixed up different search terms until you found what you needed.

In many ways, your academic research is the same. You might know that you need a reference to the work of a theorist but you could end up drawing a blank if the details aren't spot on. So, you should use your strategies for working around the gaps in the information and getting to the point you need.

# Chapter 6

# Note Taking and Organising Your Material

## In This Chapter

▶ Assembling your note-taking kit

▶ Getting your notes in order

▶ Finding techniques that work for you

*T*aking notes during lectures or making notes as you read? This chapter focuses on the latter: on *annotating* (making notes on the text) and writing up notes on a blank piece of paper. You're concentrating on writing an essay and are selecting relevant information from books you've found and handouts you've been given as a basis for what you're going to write. This isn't the same as sitting in a lecture and taking down notes of what the tutor's delivering on that particular occasion, although you may well find that a lot of the tips and suggestions we give you in this chapter are also useful for note taking in general when you're sitting in a lecture hall.

'Why make notes anyway? Isn't my memory enough?' we hear you wonder. Unfortunately not. Few people have the mental brilliance or brain capacity to remember in detail everything they read or listen to, and hence we all depend on some form of notes to trigger our memory and stimulate a train of thought. But more than that, the act of note taking helps you to make sense of what you're studying and aids your mental processes. Note taking helps you to understand the material, and as such, it's a vital step in the preparation for your essay. Later on, when you have another essay to write on a similar topic or you're revising for your exams, you may be glad you made clear, helpful notes.

When you make notes, they aren't for anybody else. You pick out what's significant for you, for your essay, and hence the system you develop has to be memorable, easy to use and tailored to your needs. You aren't tested on the quality of your notes, but on what you do with them. If nobody else understands your system, that really doesn't matter, as long as it works for you and helps you deliver an essay you can be proud of. Therefore, our suggestions in this chapter are just that – suggestions. Use them to develop your own method of signalling the important bits, summarising content and adding questions and comments.

# Preparing to Take Notes

As with any job, you need the right tools, so, before you begin, make sure that you have everything you need and a sensible storage system in place to help you organise the notes you make.

## Stocking up on supplies

Some people find that they can't work unless they have exactly the right pens or paper. Make yourself comfortable, with your favourite tools readily to hand, and you're setting yourself up for success from the start.

Here are some stationery essentials for successful note taking:

- Pens and pencils
- Rubbers ('erasers', for any concerned American readers)
- Highlighter pens in different colours
- Ordinary pens in different colours
- Sticky notes (little ones, in different colours)
- Paper clips
- Paper (A3 and A4)
- A4 files
- Dividers
- Hole punch

Colour coding can be useful, so bear this in mind when you go shopping for stationery and equipment.

## Creating a filing system

Paper and notebooks come in all shapes and sizes, so buy what feels right for you. Generally, being able to move papers around in your A4 file is helpful, so a pad of looseleaf sheets is a flexible choice. Lined, unlined, squared . . . choose whichever type of paper inspires you and makes you want to write on it. You may even find that plain white is boring and go for another colour. These choices are all in your own best interests, to give you pleasure and satisfaction while you're writing – the better you feel about the whole process, the more likely you are to do a good job.

Though you can be totally self-indulgent when making notes, and can write your first draft on bright green or pink paper if you wish, never hand in work on any other colour than white. Your tutor won't be amused!

If you haven't already worked out your system, get an A4 file for each unit you're studying, with a set of coloured dividers. Use these to separate out your notes for each subsection of the course, and keep one section labelled 'Assignments'. Tutors often set essays right at the start of a course even though the hand-in date may be months ahead, so be ready with a section in your file for any information relating to your essay, and keep it all stored there. When the time comes to start writing, you feel you have a head start if you look in the 'Assignments' section of your file and find lots of odd ideas, references to books and comments.

Number the pages in your notebook or file so that you can cross-reference. This is especially important if you happen to be writing in a bound notebook that doesn't allow you to reorder the pages. If you're using a ring binder, accidents do happen, and pages fall out, so numbers really are a good idea!

If you're planning a very long essay for which you bring together lots of information for inclusion and comment, take a separate A4 file for collating your notes and divide it into appropriate sections, for example for the introduction, background, list of references and so on.

## Working with index cards

Index cards are an alternative to notebooks and pads of looseleaf paper. Some people like the portability of cards, and they do fit into pockets and bags so easily. You probably need to work out a numbering system so you can put them back into order if you drop them. You can also refer to the number of the card when you are making a plan for your essay. It also makes it easy to cross-reference your cards and link ideas together.

The temptation with index cards can be to fill the card entirely with your notes, and then you have no blank space to accommodate later links, references and more ideas. Try to stick to just a single idea per card, and remember that index cards come in different sizes. The very smallest (13 x 8 centimetres, or 5 x 3 inches) may be a bit too small for notes. A size to consider is approximately 15 x 10 centimetres (or 6 x 4 inches), which is big enough to write a fair amount on, yet still small enough for your pocket.

If you go for index cards, do buy a box to keep them in, with dividers, so that you can keep notes for different courses and units nicely separated. You can even get pastel-coloured index cards, which can be useful if you want to colour code your notes.

# Annotating: Marking Up Texts in a Useful Manner

Often, note taking begins as you read the material: you may want to flag up an interesting point, jot down a question the text raises in your mind or signal a quotation you want to use. In the early stages of your note taking, you're likely to want to make notes on the text itself. Here are some ideas that you can you use as you annotate.

## Writing in your books

One of the first things to ask yourself is whether you actually want to write in your books. Some people never do this, because they see it as defacing texts. Certainly don't write in library books or any that aren't yours! This may seem obvious, but a surprising number of library books do get written in, and this is just not acceptable. Borrowing a book and finding that a previous user's added comments is really annoying. And another person's notes may not be particularly helpful, more often than not acting as a distraction Don't even write in pencil and rub out your comments later, as this can damage the book, especially if several people do this. If you start feeling the need to annotate a page, it's probably a good indication that you should make a photocopy.

By all means write in books that you've bought yourself – they're yours, after all. But if you're considering selling them on at the end of the year, remember that you get more money for books that are in good condition, and pause before you scribble all over them. You have alternatives. Write your ideas and comments on sticky notes, for instance, which you can easily remove when you're done.

# What good notes can do for you

Here's a list of compelling reasons to create comprehensive, organised notes. Good notes:

✔ **Help you feel in control:** So when you're writing your essay or preparing for exams, you're confident and in a positive frame of mind.

✔ **Give you a solid basis for your research and thinking:** Notes can help you to see connections. Reading a solid block of text is one thing, but seeing how the ideas hang together is quite another. If you start experimenting with highlighting in different colours and even moving away from the text to mind mapping or some kind of diagrammatic representation of content, this stimulates your brain to perceive things in different ways, perhaps giving you insights that the solid block of text on its own may not.

✔ **Bring you closer to the text:** Notes help you internalise the course content so that it doesn't seem to be 'that stuff my tutor's telling me' but rather 'what I've found out and am continuing to discover'. By interacting with the text, you're making it your own, and when you look back at it later, you've picked out the key bits you need to focus on. Your eyes can skim over these highlighted phrases and comments, bringing them back into the front of your mind so much more quickly than if you're presented with virgin text.

✔ **Build up your list of references:** By keeping track as you go of key information about your sources, such as the author's name, title of book and page number, you save yourself from accidental plagiarism (see Chapter 7) and ensure that writing your bibliography's a doddle (see Chapter 14).

# *Working with PowerPoint handouts*

Tutors have their own preferences for using PowerPoint and print-outs of slides. Some hand out the photocopies at the start of the lecture, some at the end, some put them online, others don't use them at all. The slides can be a good summary of the content of the lecture and, depending on what the teacher's chosen to include, you should be able to annotate them with your own notes and comments.

If you know that you're getting the handout at the end of the lecture, this doesn't mean you shouldn't make your own notes. The tutor's chosen to wait until the end to give you the handout in order to make you concentrate and encourage you to make your own notes. What you should do in this case is spend a bit of time as soon after the lecture as possible marrying the two together, adding your own notes to the handout so that you have a single glorious document containing what your teacher's written in the slides and your own understanding of what the lecture covered. This is the best of both worlds. You've then got a firm basis to work from when you're looking back for ideas for your essay.

If you like to work on your PC, and if your tutor makes the PowerPoint presentation available online, you can perhaps customise or annotate the slides. You can space out the lines or create areas for adding your own comments. Online or on paper, you're interacting with the content of the lecture and getting to grips with what it's all about.

## Finding your own mark-up system

So what's the style going to be? If you've only got a pencil, you can still develop a meaningful style with a system of underlining once, twice or three times, or using squiggly rather than straight lines, or circling words. Added to this you can put an asterisk by a phrase that you comment on in the margin, or maybe use an asterisk to emphasise something of supreme importance to you.

Whatever way you choose is right – no set-in-stone so-called correct way of underlining or marking up text exists. If a particular method works for you, that's the best way. If your friend does it differently, fine. (This doesn't mean, however, that you can't compare methods and pick up ideas from one another.)

If you find you want to highlight or underline absolutely everything, something's going wrong! Texts do have key paragraphs where every sentence seems meaningful. But not every paragraph or sentence is like this, so if you do find yourself tending to annotate everything, stand back a while and ask yourself if you're being sufficiently critical. If something's really that important, you can always come back to it later. Just don't go overboard with the highlighter. Sometimes you find that when you're new to the subject, you want to underline or highlight absolutely everything; then as you begin to take command of the subject, you interact more sparingly.

## Colour coding

Many students use highlighter pens in a random way, and that's fine. You can take this a stage further and use different colours more meaningfully. Here are some ideas:

✔ Use one colour to indicate the main idea in an argument, another to indicate evidence for that idea.

✔ Go through a text and highlight in the same colour the topic sentence in each paragraph (the sentence that makes the central point; see Chapter 9). When you come back to the article, you can follow the gist very easily.

Highlighting the topic sentences in a chapter of your textbook and then reading them is an extremely useful technique to use on the evening before an exam, when you have a short time to revise. And it's good for triggering thoughts when you're settling down to write your essay.

✔ Have a single colour for your own ideas as opposed to someone else's. Then you can easily see which points refer to the content you've read and which were the questions and thoughts running through your mind as you were reading. You can more easily look back for the bits in pink (or whatever colour you've chosen to represent your thoughts). These are the questions you need to answer in order to take your work on to the next stage.

✔ Highlight quotations to remind you that these are just that – quotations – and not your own words. This guards against plagiarism (see Chapter 7) by reminding you:

• To paraphrase or somehow express the idea in your own words when you come to writing up your essay

• That you have to acknowledge the author in what you write and in the list of references (see Chapter 14)

With the best will in the world, planning can and does go wrong. What happens is that you find yourself working against the clock and, in the pressure to finish, phrases from your notes find themselves word for word in your final version. Only they're not your words, they're someone else's. You don't have the time to go back and find where the sentence came from – you may even forget the sentence isn't your own – and you include the sentence in your essay without acknowledgement of authorship. Then your tutor accuses you of plagiarism. If only you'd highlighted the sentence in the first place!

# Making a Page of Notes

A point comes when you can't write in the margins of a book or handout any longer, and you have to take a sheet of paper and start writing notes down on that. If you haven't done much of this before, it can be a bit scary, but you just have to take the plunge. Read on to get some pointers on ways to structure your notes, what to write and how to jot things down speedily.

If your notes look messy, don't worry. What you do with them is what counts.

## Selecting what's important for you

Self-discipline is good here. You may be dreadfully tempted to have your pencil poised from the start and jot down everything you think may be of some use. This isn't a good habit! Here's why:

- You tend to make a note of every single detail. Note taking isn't copying word for word. Not every detail may be relevant, and you can end up with too many pieces of information. Then you can't see the wood for the trees.

- As you get more and more tired (and/or bored!) you can easily slip into copying chunks word for word from the original. These chunks oh so easily find themselves in your essay. Then what happens? You're accused of plagiarism (see Chapter 7).

So what should you do?

Don't touch those pens! Well, not straight away. Read the chapter or the section you need (sitting on your hands if your fingers are itching to scribble away, and turning the page with your nose if you have to). When you've read a chunk, close your book, close your eyes, and think for a few minutes. Then pick up your pen and write down the answers to the following questions without looking back at the text:

- What's the main point or argument in what I just read?

- How does the text prove this?

- What examples does it give?

- Is this directly relevant to my essay? In what way?

Once you've done this, you're allowed (phew!) to open your book again and look back for the odd quote or detail you need.

Why do your note taking this way? Good question. Even better answers:

- By making yourself think about what you've read in this way, you're forcing yourself to recall and evaluate it. You're internalising the content rather than just copying out bits.

This is helpful not only for the immediate purposes of writing your essay; it also forms part of the process of memorising for any exams you have to take.

✔ You're avoiding plagiarism (see Chapter 7). You're making yourself use your own words from the start.

## Laying out your notes

The key to useful note taking is to allow yourself plenty of white space so that you can add further notes and comments as you go along. Most people still seem to use paper for making notes, so draw up a page with a margin on both sides (quite a wide one on the right) so that you can accommodate the extras. Should you be making notes on your PC, slipping in further scraps of information or thoughts as they come to you is easy, but a piece of paper doesn't offer this flexibility, and from the start you have to build in some white space for additional notes. One way of organising the layout of your page is as follows:

✔ **Top of the page:** Put clearly the source (name of book, lecture, date).

✔ **Left-hand margin:** Use for numbers, names of sections, sub-sections (these should be clearly visible).

✔ **Wide right-hand margin:** Jot down your thoughts and questions after the lecture or when you've done the reading.

✔ **Middle section:** Use for the notes themselves.

✔ **Section at the bottom:** Include a summary or links.

Draw up a few pages in this format, try it out and see how it helps you. You may be surprised how useful you find being organised in this way.

## Drawing and making diagrams

Thinking visually helps a large number of people, so, if they incorporate simple drawings or diagrams into their notes, this helps them sort out information and thus remember it better. You may be one of those people. Lots of other people who don't normally describe themselves as particularly visual can help themselves to think by drawing spidergrams or mind maps.

Figure 6-1 is an example of the kind of map you may draw if you're making notes from a chapter of a book. We've taken Chapter 2 from this book as a basis, so you can flip between the diagram and the actual text. Notice that not every single section of the chapter is represented in the diagram, because the imaginary student's selecting the parts that are of particular relevance to his or her situation and adding comments. Notice also that some things that perhaps weren't obvious before seem to stand out now. In this case, the student needs to go shopping!

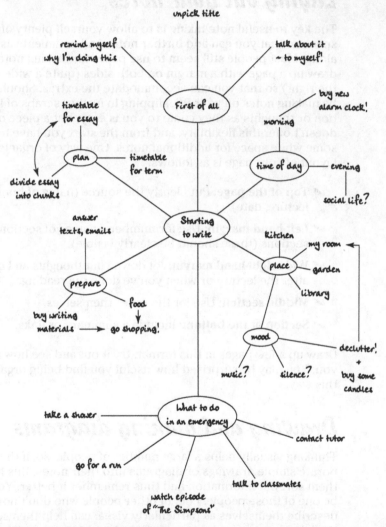

**Figure 6-1:** Example of a mind map.

Now compare Figure 6-1 with Figure 6-2, which is a more traditional linear presentation of the same notes, and see which one appeals to you more. This really is a question of your own personal preference. You may find connections easier to see in the first diagram because the linear train of thought from the original text is broken up into a more circular display with keywords in the bubbles.

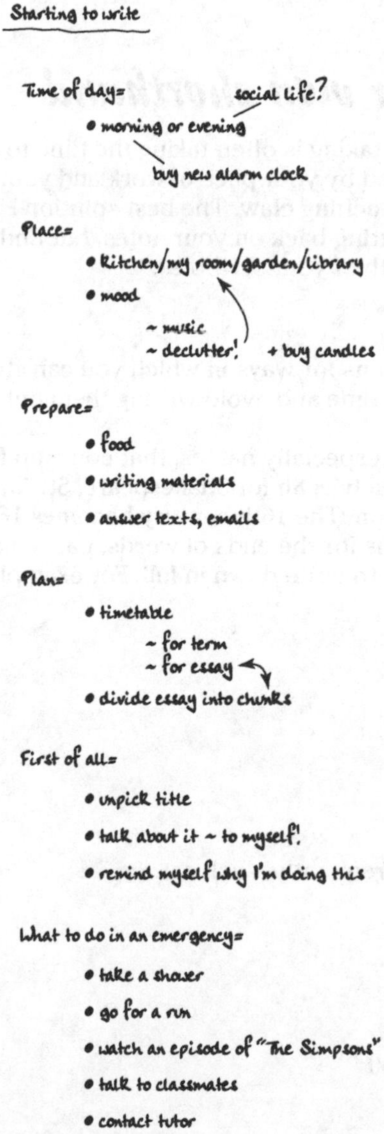

Starting to write

Time of day=          social life?
    • morning or evening
             buy new alarm clock

Place=
    • kitchen/my room/garden/library
    • mood
        ~ music
        ~ declutter!   + buy candles

Prepare=
    • food
    • writing materials
    • answer texts, emails

Plan=
    • timetable
        ~ for term
        ~ for essay
    • divide essay into chunks

First of all=
    • unpick title
    • talk about it ~ to myself!
    • remind myself why I'm doing this

What to do in an emergency=
    • take a shower
    • go for a run
    • watch an episode of "The Simpsons"
    • talk to classmates
    • contact tutor

**Figure 6-2:** Example of linear notes.

If you're using a PC, you can use functions in the drawing menus that enable you to draw maps and diagrams on the screen, so you don't have to use pen and paper if you don't want to. Try googling 'mind maps' and you'll see examples that will give you ideas of how to draw them. If you really get into this way of working there is software that you can buy, for example Tony Buzan's Mind Maps. But there's no need to part with your precious cash if you don't want to.

## Creating your own shorthand

The hardest bit of note taking is often taking the time to write by hand – you get frustrated by your pace of work and your hand soon resembles a rigid, aching claw. The best solution is to write less. We don't mean cutting back on your notes, but finding short-cuts to reduce the length of your scribbles.

### Using abbreviations

Here are some suggestions for ways in which you can shorten words so that you save time and avoid writing them out in full.

You can reduce words, especially names, that come up frequently to a couple of letters, such as Sh for Shakespeare, Str for Stratford, Ldn for London and so on. The 16th century becomes 16c. Then start using abbreviations for the ends of words, particularly longer ones that can take time to write down in full. For example:

> ing becomes g
>
> ment becomes mt
>
> tion becomes tn
>
> ive becomes v
>
> ness becomes ns

Other words come up frequently, such as:

> diff (different)
>
> sev (several)
>
> char (character)
>
> soc (social, society)

So in your notes the sentence 'Flaubert offers in his novels a demonstration of his literary values. The distortion of his characters in their hypothetical reality contributes to the coherence of *Madame Bovary* as a work of art" could become 'F offers in novs a demonstratn of his lit values. The distortn of his chars in thr hypothetcl realty contribs to the cohrnc of MB as a wk of art'.

Once you get into your unit, the same key vocabulary keeps coming up, so you can have an abbreviation for each keyword and thus save a few nanoseconds of time here and there.

## Omitting letters

You can also miss out vowels (a, e, i, o, u) when you're taking notes, because the consonants can be enough to indicate what the word is. The context clarifies any possible confusion. For example:

> U dnt hv to wrt the wrds in fll.

Use texting abbreviations if they come easily to you. But don't forget to revert to Standard English spelling for the write-up!

You can't shorten every word. Spell short words such as prepositions and conjunctions (for example, in, at and to) in full, because they're so very short to begin with.

## Ditching accuracy

Don't worry about the spelling when you're making notes. You can correct spellings (and your spellchecker can help!) when you come to write the essay proper.

Take a look at this:

> The thoery is taht you can jbumle the letrets in a wrod, and as lnog as the fsirt and the lsat lertets ramein in pacle tehn the wrod wlil siltl be rabealde. (The theory is that you can jumble the letters in a word, and as long as the first and the last letters remain in place then the word will still be readable.)

You're probably not going to write a sentence like the one above in which the letters in the words are jumbled to such an extreme extent. But I think you get the message. A few misspellings in your notes aren't going to render your notes indecipherable. And they're only for you anyway, not for anyone else, so no one's judging you.

### *Incorporating symbols*

Get into the habit of using symbols to help you write efficiently. Table 6-1 has some common symbols, and you may also look at your computer keyboard and mobile phone texting for inspiration.

| Table 6-1 | Symbols That Help You Abbreviate |
|-----------|-----------------------------------|
| *Symbol* | *Meaning* |
| < | Smaller than |
| > | Bigger than |
| + | In addition, or positive |
| − | Negative |
| = | Same as |
| ≠ | Different from |
| ♀ | Woman/female |
| ♂ | Man/male |
| ∴ | Therefore |
| ☺ | Whenever you're happy! |

You may want make a list of some other symbols you can use. The important thing is that you have your own list that you stick to – no matter if other people can't understand your symbols, as long as you can.

# Stopping the Notes and Starting to Write

Enough's enough. At some point note taking has to stop and essay writing proper starts. You can let making notes go on for ever, especially now that so much information's available through the Internet.

The temptation is to throw away your notes when you've handed your essay in. And if your notes are a mess, then the bin's probably the best place for them. But if you end up with notes that are still readable, don't tear them up. Notes from lectures and course books are helpful in the revision process if you have an exam at the end of the semester. They may be useful when you come to write another essay, because they're a record not only of the content of your essay but of the writing process itself and what you went through in the production of that essay. You can recall how you managed and organised your notes and be able to assess what worked for you and whether you can improve on any aspects of your note making. You never know, you may even be proud of your notes!

## Knowing when to move on

In Chapter 4's sidebar 'Sticking to the 80:20 principle', we advise that a good rule of thumb is to spend 80 per cent of your time on reading and note taking. So, for a short essay, if you have approximately ten hours available to research and write up your essay, you have only eight hours to read and make notes. The note-taking phase has to be efficient, therefore, and you've got to be focused. Keep asking yourself:

✔ Is this the exact information I need?

✔ How is it helping me?

✔ Can something else help me better?

Keep an eye on the clock and when you reach the time to stop and begin the writing-up process, do so. Stop! Your tutor sees the finished product, not your notes. They're a very important part of the process, but not what you're assessed on.

If you feel that you haven't made the most of the time you've allowed yourself for making notes, or if you think you can do things differently, don't despair. This is all part of developing your skills, and if you take the time to reflect on what you can do or organise better, you can make it right next time around.

## Turning your notes into a plan

Somehow you have to create order from your notes. You need to organise your ideas into a plan that helps you write a logical, clear essay.

## Weeding out ideas

Sometimes you feel you've got so much information inside your head that it's going to burst! On other occasions you don't seem to have absorbed enough. But, whatever the state of your head, you've got to get cracking. Whether you have a mountain of stuff or a molehill, go ahead and spew it out!

You can only write one thing at a time, so as the ideas jostle each other to come out of your pen or fingers, they may be sorting themselves into some kind of order. If not, don't worry, just scribble them down. If you really do have too many, you need to:

✔ Look back at the essay title and ask yourself whether each of these points really relates to your argument; if not, weed them out.

✔ Categorise the points into really essential, less essential and not essential; weed out the latter.

Once you've pared down the number of points, they may seem more manageable.

Don't throw away the notes that contain the less essential points, because in the finishing stages of the process you may be able to squeeze the ideas in somewhere appropriate.

## Growing ideas

Don't feel despondent if your initial brainstorming doesn't seem to produce a lot of points. Next to each point write *three* bullet points or lines branching off from there. Even if, for the moment, you can't think of anything to put by each bullet point or line, this reminds you that you have to say more about this point – the development *does* come eventually. The branches tell you to find three things to say. When you've got those three things, you've got a paragraph. Often, once you get the first, this triggers other things in your head, and before you know it you have a point to include in your essay with three ways of developing it. This may not happen immediately, so give yourself a little time. Go away and make yourself a cup of coffee or leave the essay until the morning. If you're still really stuck, compare notes with a friend and see whether you've got a blind spot somewhere.

The other reason ideas may seem thin sometimes is because you're taking the reader too much for granted. You may need to explain what you want to say more fully. *You* may understand what you mean, but it may not be obvious to the reader. Your mantra has to be 'explain' all the way through. Don't make leaps in your argument and don't assume that your reader's following you; make your points clear.

Whichever situation you find yourself in, and you may well be in a combination of predicaments with too many ideas for one part of your essay and too few for another, you have to get the points down on paper so that you can start organising them. If you haven't done so already, you need to develop your own individual method of doing this with the tools that you find work for you.

## Organising ideas into a plan

Whichever method you employ for getting the ideas out, the end product's an essay plan. You may modify this slightly as you go along, but generally once this is in place you have the framework you need to produce the essay itself.

Whatever the layout of your brainstorming, at this stage you structure the ideas you've put down and produce a linear plan for your assignment. You now have to use the colours, linking lines, arrows or whatever you've chosen to cluster together your points to form your argument. So everything in, for example, red goes in the first part of your essay. Put the red ideas into clusters, grouping them logically and then subdividing clusters further if necessary. This gives you headings, subheadings and further subheadings if need be. You end up with something like Figure 6-3.

Your essay probably doesn't fit perfectly into the model above, but the diagram should give you an idea of what the plan can look like.

As you organise your ideas into a structure, be sure to use one of the essay frameworks we show you in Chapter 3.

When you've got your essay plan, you've already done a large part of the work. The framework isn't a straitjacket, however, and you *can* make small modifications as you go along. But knowing that your ideas are organised and you have a plan gives you reassurance that you know what you're doing and where you're going.

Section 1: Arguments for

Main point
- development
- further development
- further development

Second point
- development
- further development
- further development

Third point
- development
- further development
- further development + rounding off this section

Heading
Subheading
Minor heading
Minor heading
Minor heading
Subheading
Minor heading
Minor heading
Minor heading
Subheading
Minor heading
Minor heading
Minor heading

**Figure 6-3:** Organising your structure.

# Chapter 7

# Avoiding Plagiarism

● ● ● ● ● ● ● ● ● ● ● ● ● ● ● ● ● ● ● ● ● ● ● ● ● ● ● ● ● ● ● ● ●

## *In This Chapter*

▶ Knowing what constitutes plagiarism

▶ Realising why plagiarism happens

▶ Summarising and paraphrasing to avoid plagiarism

● ● ● ● ● ● ● ● ● ● ● ● ● ● ● ● ● ● ● ● ● ● ● ● ● ● ● ● ● ● ● ● ●

*'W*hat's all the fuss about plagiarism? Why can't I just cut and paste a few words from what someone's written? Aren't they the experts? How can I, a mere student, say something better than an expert can? Nobody's going to know if I copy a few bits from elsewhere anyway . . .'

These are thoughts that may go through your head at some time in your university career, probably at moments when the pressure gets to you, either because you're feeling out of your depth or a deadline's looming. These are the times when you're tempted to take desperate measures and *plagiarise* – take someone else's words or ideas and pass them off as your own. You think that a little 'lifting' of sentences may conceal the gaps in your knowledge or speed up the writing process. Everyone's tempted to plagiarise at some point, but you mustn't. Plagiarising can have serious consequences for your university career.

This chapter helps you to understand why you may want to plagiarise and how to guard against doing so. We also show you techniques so that you can use your own words and feel confident about doing so.

## *Understanding Plagiarism*

Cheating isn't a new crime: it's been going on since time immemorial. It's just that the Internet with its 'copy and paste' feature makes it so quick and simple to do. And as the ease with which we can copy something over into our own documents has grown, so our attitude to misuse of this facility has hardened. You don't go into someone's house and steal their belongings, do you? That's theft. Similarly, you shouldn't enter someone's mind and steal their thoughts. Plagiarism is theft of intellectual property and is a crime as much as any other.

## *Falling into the copycat trap*

For students at university, unattributed copying can happen for various reasons:

- ✔ **Plagiarising unintentionally:** This is when you don't mean to copy, but somehow you do. An example is when you note down a sentence from a book and omit to put quotation marks around it and record where you got it from and who wrote it. When you come back later to look at your notes, you forget that the words aren't actually yours. As a result, you use them unchanged and unacknowledged in your essay. Your tutor recognises the sentence and accuses you of plagiarism.

- ✔ **Taking shortcuts:** You're coming up against a deadline, and in your panic to finish on time, you find yourself lifting phrases, if not whole chunks, from a book or article, thinking that the most important thing is to meet the deadline. Well, you may meet the deadline, but you may also find yourself with 0% for the essay if your tutor spots the plagiarism.

- ✔ **Thinking you can get away with it:** You may find an obscure passage in a book or on a page on the Internet, and it seems to say precisely what you need to say at that moment. You feel confident that your tutor doesn't know the original and that you can slip it in unnoticed. You're taking a big risk here, which comes from underestimating just how good tutors are at spotting these little 'lifts'. (Skip to the later section 'Seeing how tutors catch you out' for more on how eagle-eyed tutors are.)

- ✔ **Believing the author says it best:** You're struggling to find a way to rephrase the author's perfect, concise, clear wording. Anything you write seems somehow inferior. So you just plonk the author's words into your essay and hope no one notices. But of course they do!

In foreign academic cultures, copying the work of others can be seen as honouring the author of the original. You're saying that the writer's expressed the ideas so perfectly that you can't (as a humble student) express them better than the expert. To change them is disrespectful and even arrogant on your part, so you copy them faithfully out of respect and humility. Unfortunately, British universities see things another way, and although your own words may seem inadequate or second best, these are what you must use. This is something that, if you come from a different academic background, you may have to think long and hard about and even talk over with your tutor, because you're having to make quite a shift in the way you look at writing.

The later section 'Keeping on the Straight and Narrow' helps you avoid these routes into plagiarism and the ensuing slapped wrist.

## Seeing how tutors catch you out

Believe it or not, your tutors understand the pressures on you to plagiarise, but at the same time are extremely alert to the possibility of it happening – so don't underestimate them! Tutors have a good eye and ear for what students can produce, and have a sixth sense developed over years of marking students' scripts. They also have technology to help them.

If you cheat, your tutor is going to catch you. Here's how:

✓ **Spotting a shift in voice:** If you plagiarise, especially using a long chunk of plagiarised text, the 'voice' of the original author can come through. The words may sound too polished, too slick, and the vocabulary or sentence structure may be different – whatever it is, something doesn't fit with your voice, and this gives the game away. Sorry to have to say this, but the section is probably going to sound too good for a student! And you have to be terrifically clever to weave it into your text. Poor linking can betray you. Your tutor has a nose for these things and, like a sniffer dog, pursues anything that smells suspicious, so be warned.

✓ **Recognising your words:** Tutors are experts in their field and they've read so much that they're likely to spot something they've read before. A little red warning light goes on in the tutor's head saying that a line or a couple of lines are familiar; the tutor then stops, considers, and actively searches out the original if he or she suspects that what you've written is from a published work and you haven't acknowledged it. Tutors know their key texts very well, and the lesser-known texts pretty well too! You may read a text for the first time and think that it fits perfectly with what you want to say in your essay, so you copy it, forgetting that hundreds of people (including your tutor) may have accessed that same text many times before. What's new and original for you may have gone round the block dozens of times already. So stop that finger before you hit copy and paste. Are you really sure that no one else has ever read this text but you? Are you sure your tutor hasn't?

✔ **Catching you by doing some online detective work:** Just as technology makes copying and pasting and therefore plagiarising easier for you, so tutors can more easily identify your sources too. Your tutor can simply Google a phrase or two and see whether you lifted it from an online source. More than that, much more sophisticated technology has been developed and will continue to be improved that can identify plagiarism, not just by students from online sources but by students from other students' work. In the early days, when online resources were something of a novelty, no doubt some students did get away with plagiarism. But technology has caught up and now, frankly, it just isn't worth the risk. If you're caught, you pay the penalty.

## Considering the consequences

Be under no illusions: universities take cases of plagiarism very, very seriously. In your first year, you may not be fully aware of what you're doing and your tutor may be lenient with you. If it's your first offence, and depending on how much you've plagiarised (plagiarising a sentence and plagiarising a whole essay are different degrees of offence), you may be allowed to resubmit with a number of points deducted from your grade, or you may receive 0%. You need to have a good chat with someone about what you did and gain from the experience so that you don't do it again.

Repeated or very extensive plagiarism, however, can have a significant effect on your degree, to the extent that you may not get one. You can be dismissed from your university if you're proven seriously and significantly to have tried to pass off another person's work as your own. Thinking about this, surely you're better to submit your own imperfect ramblings and get a third-class degree than to try to beat the system by plagiarising and ending up with nothing, aren't you?

## Keeping on the Straight and Narrow

In the previous section, we show you how serious and foolish plagiarising is. Here are some pointers to follow so that you avoid being put in a position where it can happen:

✔ **Keeping track of quotes:** When you're making notes, don't forget to put quotation marks around all the phrases and sentences that you take word for word from the text you're reading. Or highlight them in a colour that means you know immediately that the words you've written aren't yours. When you come back to read your notes, which may be several weeks later, when you may have forgotten, you can see immediately that anything in quotation marks or highlighted doesn't belong to you. If you want to use a quote, you have to acknowledge the origin. Chapter 6 has plenty more useful hints on effective note taking.

Also keep a note of all the information you need to acknowledge the author, such as name(s), title, date of publication, place of publication and publisher, and include page numbers so that you can find the quote again if need be. You're expected to provide a full bibliography at the end of your work, and you can save time by noting all this information right from the start. Flip to Chapter 14 for more on referencing.

✔ **Managing your time:** For some students, plagiarism is an act of desperation when they're running out of time. The problem boils down to time management, which is difficult for everyone with a busy life, but is particularly important when you're faced with getting all your essays in on time. And you face so many distractions when you're at university! Your first year in particular – when you have such a lot of new friends and, above all, freedom – can be tough if your parents or teachers have always managed your time for you. Don't think too badly of yourself if you mess up and don't leave yourself enough time to write your essay properly. Check out Chapter 2, which offers advice on managing your time.

Don't plagiarise, but write everything in your own words, as you should do. You may hand in your work a couple of days late and incur a late-submission penalty, but that's better than 0% isn't it? And your conscience is clear. Tell your tutor about the difficulties you're having. They're all part of the development process.

✔ **Having confidence in your own interpretation:** What your tutor wants to see is evidence that you've read the original, thought about it, attempted to express the content in your own way, and used it to answer the question you were set. In other words, your tutor's looking for evidence of knowledge, not for evidence of parroting! Unless you're providing a short and relevant direct quotation, you have to use your own words, inadequate and unpolished as they may seem. The following section, 'Writing in Your Own Words', can help you build confidence in your abilities.

✔ **Imagining getting caught:** Take a moment to imagine how being caught plagiarising feels. It's embarrassing to say the least. Do you really want to face your tutor and be accused of copying? Have a little respect for your tutors. They know what to look for and have honed their detective skills. They *will* catch you out and they *will* challenge you with proof of what you've done. The situation's unpleasant for all concerned, and the only person who suffers is you. So please don't put yourself through it.

# Counting the costs of copying

Think that your university's rules on plagiarism are pedantic and overly strict? Think again. Your uni's trying to prepare you for the big bad world where intellectual property theft is a very serious business. Take a look at these real-life examples of the consequences of plagiarism:

✔ Joe Biden, Vice-President of the United States to Barack Obama, was found to have copied a section of a speech made by the British Labour politician Neil Kinnock, without attribution. Some words were different, but the framework of the paragraph was the same. Rather embarrassing for Mr Biden – and his speechwriter was perhaps out of a job!

✔ The late George Harrison of the Beatles was accused of copying the melody of a song originally recorded by the Chiffons, 'He's so Fine', when he released his song 'My Sweet Lord'. The court case went on for years, trying to establish whether the similarities between the two melodies were intentional or accidental. The lawyers involved must have laughed all the way to the bank! Harrison eventually lost the case, even though the copying was ruled to be subconscious.

✔ Raj Persaud, a celebrity psychiatrist who has appeared regularly on television shows in Britain, was accused of plagiarising the works of others in one of his books. The General Medical Council suspended him from practising as a doctor for a short time. Though he was afterwards reinstated, will his media career recover from this blot on his record?

In the fields of politics, music and medicine, therefore, plagiarism really matters and you can be taken to court or another professional body and charged with this offence. It costs in terms of reputation, time and money, and can have an effect on your job. It isn't something that you only have to bother about while you're at university.

# Writing in Your Own Words

As well as avoiding plagiarism, expressing an idea in words different from the original is important in your development, because by doing this you internalise knowledge and make it your own. But no one pretends that finding your own words is always easy. If it were, it would be no big deal and people would plagiarise far less frequently.

Thankfully, we have some useful tricks up our sleeves to make your essay writing easier. The following sections show you how to paraphrase and how to summarise – techniques that help you to express ideas in your own words.

The important thing is to have a strategy for analysing and paring down a text so that you can reduce it to the key points that are critical to the thrust of your essay and then express these in your own way. And as you do this, you need to avoid using direct quotations from the original unless absolutely essential (see Chapter 12 for more on when to use quotations).

## Paraphrasing

When you *paraphrase,* you rewrite text so that it conveys the same ideas but in words different from the original – using synonyms (words that mean the same as those they replace) and reworking the structure of a sentence. What you end up with is a text that's usually longer than the original, because the first author has in all probability been more succinct than you can be. But you're not going to have to paraphrase an entire text, you're just taking little pieces from here and there and meshing them together.

To help you get the hang of paraphrasing, we work with chunks of text from Figure 7-1.

### Knowing what you can't paraphrase

You can't paraphrase absolutely every single word, and you're foolish to try to do so. Proper names such as job titles, names of people and places, dates and many numbers all resist paraphrasing; you risk sounding ridiculous. Take the first sentence from the text in Figure 7-1.

> New research shows that cleaners are some of the happiest workers in Britain, along with child carers, medical secretaries, hairdressers and petrol pump attendants.

> ### Service workers are the happiest staff
>
> New research shows that cleaners are some of the happiest workers in Britain, along with child carers, medical secretaries, hairdressers and petrol pump attendants.
>
> The study of 35,000 employees found that the highest levels of job satisfaction were among those providing personal service, even if the pay is poor. There are highly paid professional and managerial staff who enjoy excellent pay and conditions, but many of these appear to hate their jobs. Civil servants lie almost at the bottom of the league table, with solicitors and various engineers and scientists not far behind.
>
> Michael Rose of Bath University, who led the study, said a key element of job satisfaction was the potential to work part-time and unsupervised. A cleaner's job may not appeal to all, but it has hidden perks. 'You can trim your hours and you don't have a supervisor breathing down your neck all the time. You can sit in the boss's chair . . . if you feel like it,' he said. Petrol pump attendants, too, had a choice of working part-time shifts with relatively little direct supervision. One explanation offered for the high job satisfaction rate of medical secretaries, who are at the top of the league with 75% of them happy in their job, is that they are 'doing something useful'. Seeing that you are playing a key role in the delivery of healthcare is very satisfying, despite the low pay scale of £8,000 – £15,000.
>
> The study divides overall satisfaction into *Material satisfaction* such as money, promotion and security, and *Quality satisfaction*, which involves the job, relations with the boss and hours. Taxation experts and prison officers score high marks for material satisfaction. The profile of carpenters and ambulance staff is the opposite: high on quality and low on material satisfaction.
>
> The report strongly warns against the rapid growth of telephone call centres, noting that telephone staff register some of the lowest levels of job satisfaction. It also gives a warning that many computer and communications occupations also record 'poor to dismal' levels of job satisfaction.

**Figure 7-1:** Example of paraphrasing text.

Do you want to paraphrase 'cleaners' by using the term 'cleanliness engineers' or 'sanitation officers'? You may want to say 'people who look after children' instead of 'child carers', or 'administrative staff in doctors' surgeries' for 'medical secretaries', but quite frankly the effort becomes a bit silly. Common sense tells you that you have to use the specific job titles.

Similarly, you may want to substitute 'the UK' for 'Britain', but some people understand the former to mean England, Wales, Scotland and Northern Ireland, while others take the latter to mean only England, Wales and Scotland *without* Northern Ireland. The accurate area may be crucial to interpreting the data. So do be careful and think before you make a simple substitution such as this.

Further on in the text, numbers such as 35,000, 75% and £8,000–£15,000 transfer into your paraphrased version as they stand, and meddling with the author's name and affiliation, 'Michael Rose of Bath University', is disrespectful, although standard practice in academic writing is to refer to an author by the family name only – Rose. Likewise, you shouldn't tamper with the names of the sections of his study, 'material satisfaction' and 'quality satisfaction'.

You have to look to other words in the text for places to paraphrase and seek alternative ways of constructing your sentences.

### Looking for synonyms

Look again at the first sentence of Figure 7-1 and ask yourself what other words come to mind that express the same ideas. These are some possibilities:

| | |
|---|---|
| New | fresh, recent |
| research | a study, a survey, an investigation |
| shows | reveals, demonstrates |
| some of | among |
| happiest | most satisfied, most contented |
| workers | employees |
| along with | together with |

 A thesaurus comes in very handy when you're searching for synonyms. Use the one in your word-processing software or an actual book. If you're not sure of a possible synonym, do check by cross-referencing with what a dictionary says about the word.

A simple word-for-word transfer then gives you:

> A recent study reveals that cleaners are among the most satisfied employees in Britain, together with child carers, medical secretaries, hairdressers and petrol pump attendants.

The sentence is already beginning to look different from the original, but it doesn't *feel* that different until you start playing around with it even further and use alternative forms of words, as we show you in the next section.

### Using other parts of speech

By different parts of speech we mean the different forms a word can take depending on its function in the sentence. So 'employee' (noun) is from the 'employ' (verb) family of words, which give us 'employer' (also a noun), 'employable' (adjective), 'employed' (adjective and past participle), 'employment' (another noun) and so on.

By exploring the various parts of speech belonging to a word in the sentence that you want to paraphrase, you're very likely to find ways to say the sentence differently. If you play around with the synonyms and the other parts of speech, you can come up with something that begins to sound quite a bit different from the original. Your sentence may then become:

> British cleaners, child carers, medical secretaries, hairdressers and petrol pump attendants have been studied recently and found to be among those most satisfied by their jobs.

The key change here revolves around the substitution of the verb 'study' for the noun 'study' and restructuring your sentence around this change. So you've worked at the sentence and turned it around into something that's *nearly* yours.

Although the alternative words are yours, the basic idea isn't and can never be. However well you paraphrase, you aren't finished until you acknowledge the source. So you have to follow the paraphrase with the in-text reference (family name of author, date). You then give full details of the publication in the list of references at the end of your essay. Only when you've done all of this can you lean back and tell yourself that you *haven't* plagiarised but instead you've rightfully acknowledged the author of the original. Chapter 14 gives you the lowdown on how to acknowledge your sources.

If you're having difficulty finding other ways of expressing an idea, try saying it out loud. Imagine that you have to explain the idea to someone who doesn't have your background knowledge. How can you break the idea down and convey the message in a simple way? When just thinking about it silently in your head doesn't provide you with alternatives, actually talking out loud to an imaginary person often does.

## Summarising

Looking back at Figure 7-1 in the earlier section 'Paraphrasing', you're highly unlikely to need to paraphrase the entire thing. More often you feel a need to paraphrase a sentence or very short section. What you probably need to do with a text like the one above, a paragraph, a chapter of a book, or a journal article is to summarise it in whole or in part. While paraphrasing results in a version that's similar in length to the original text and often even longer, *summarising* means a drastic reduction in length. Read on to find out how.

### Knowing how summarising works

Three words typify a summary:

- ✔ **Succinct,** because you use a minimum number of words to convey the maximum of meaning.

- ✔ **Selective,** because you include only the essential information.

- ✔ **Short,** because it reduces the original to its essence. How short? No answer exists to this question, because it depends on what your purposes are. A summary can be of any length, even a single line; for example, a summary of this book may be 'a book about how to write essays at university'.

Table 7-1 outlines some dos and don'ts for summarising.

| Table 7-1 | Rules for Summarising |
|---|---|
| *Summaries Should* | *Summaries Shouldn't* |
| Give a general outline of the content of the original | Paraphrase the entire text |
| Be written objectively | Go into detail unless essential |
| Be written in your words, the way you express yourself when you're writing | Include your ideas or comments, only the author's |

By the way, your summarising skills come in useful if you ever have to write an abstract for an academic paper or an executive summary for a business report. The techniques we're showing you here stand you in good stead for the future.

### Summarising techniques

Follow these steps for effective summarising:

1. If you've got a text in front of you that you need to whittle down to its essence, the first thing to do if it's a single paragraph is go through it underlining or highlighting the key phrases or ideas, or, if it's a series of sentences, the topic

sentences (the sentences that sum up the main point of each paragraph; see Chapter 9).

2. Express the selected keywords or topic sentences in your own words by using your paraphrasing skills of looking for synonyms and exploring other parts of speech.

3. Try to join together the words you come up with in Step 2 into a coherent sentence or set of sentences. In your summary, you may have to juggle with the order in which the information appears in the original, in order for it to flow.

4. Add linking words to bring out the meaning where necessary.

When you've done this, you may have something that's still too long for your purposes, in which case you have to eliminate anything of secondary importance. You don't need any details or examples. Check for repetition of any kind and deal with it. Choose your words carefully and try to convey the main ideas in the minimum number of words.

If you again use Figure 7-1 in the earlier section 'Paraphrasing', you can see how this summarising technique works in practice. The topic sentences, in the words of the text, are:

New research shows that cleaners are some of the happiest workers in Britain.

The study of 35,000 employees found that the highest levels of job satisfaction were among those providing personal service, even if the pay is poor.

Michael Rose of Bath University, who led the study, said a key element of job satisfaction was the potential to work part-time and unsupervised.

One explanation offered for the high job satisfaction rate of medical secretaries, who are at the top of the league with 75% of them happy in their job, is that they are 'doing something useful'.

The study divides overall satisfaction into *material satisfaction* such as money, promotion and security, and *quality satisfaction*, which involves the job, relations with the boss and hours.

The report strongly warns against the rapid growth of telephone call centres.

Put these into your own words, and you may get something like:

> A recent study has shown that service workers in Britain have the greatest job satisfaction.

> Of the 35,000 people interviewed, the service workers were more satisfied in their work despite poor salaries.

> Michael Rose from Bath University identified being able to work part-time and lack of supervision as important for job satisfaction.

> The most content were medical secretaries, who named the usefulness of their work as key.

> Both material satisfaction, for example financial, and quality satisfaction, for example environmental, were studied.

> Fast-growing telephone call centres are a cause for concern.

Depending on the context in which you're writing, you may further manipulate the text by stripping out information that you don't feel is significant, like this:

> In a recent study into job satisfaction in Britain, Michael Rose of Bath University identified service workers as having the highest job satisfaction despite poor salaries. He saw reasons for this as including the possibility of working part-time, lack of supervision and the usefulness of the work.

The only thing left to do is to give the summary an academic feel. You don't mention first names or where authors are based unless that's essential, so you refer to the writer simply as Rose. You also tighten up by being more precise about the date of the research. Full details of the study then appear in the list of references at the end of your essay. In addition, a linking device such as 'according to' is common in academic writing to emphasise the fact that you're referring to the work of someone else, and it helps to join your summarising sentence(s) smoothly to what precedes it.

> According to Rose (2001), check service workers have the highest job satisfaction in Britain despite poor salaries. He identified the possibility of working part-time, lack of supervision and the usefulness of their work as reasons for their contentment.

This is, of course, not the only way to summarise the text, and you probably have ideas of your own about how to express the key ideas. For instance, if in your essay you're going to discuss at length the situation of telephone call centre staff, then you reintroduce this point and reweight your summary by eliminating reference to the reasons for contentment among the happiest workers, because this is less important to what you go on to say.

> According to Rose (2001), whereas service workers, despite poor salaries, have the highest job satisfaction in Britain, the fast-growing telephone call centres are a cause for concern.

Why not pick up a book and have a go at summarising (and paraphrasing; see the earlier section). As with many other things in life, practice makes perfect and the best way to get to grips with something is by doing it rather than by reading about doing it. You can quote me on that.

# Part III
# Mastering Language and Style

## In this part . . .

Concerned that your command of language might not be up to the job of writing essays? Fret no more. These three chapters provide a quick brush-up in the basics of essay language use, ensuring that you can structure and punctuate sentences and paragraphs properly and accurately.

We also draw back the veil on the mysteries of academic 'voice' so that your writing has the necessary formal, academic tone.

# Chapter 8

# Writing with Confidence: Brushing Up Your Grammar

• • • • • • • • • • • • • • • • • • • • • • • • • • • • • • • • • • • • • • • • • • • •

## In This Chapter

▶ Using punctuation correctly

▶ Considering when to use capitals

▶ Understanding the different parts of speech

• • • • • • • • • • • • • • • • • • • • • • • • • • • • • • • • • • • • • • • • • • • •

*M*any people applying to university worry about not having been taught much grammar at school. Many are concerned about the quality of their written English, hoping it's appropriate for university study.

You may find that writing throws you into a panic and you keep putting it off until the last possible moment, only to find that your work is a real rush. Or perhaps you manage to sit down and try to get words on paper a little earlier, but this doesn't help because false start after false start ends up resigned to the wastepaper basket.

English grammar is simpler than you may think. This chapter outlines the key elements of writing that you need to understand, focusing on the typical concerns of undergraduate students writing essays.

We have room in this section only for a general overview of some grammar basics. For a more thorough discussion of how to improve your writing, take a look at *English Grammar For Dummies* (Wiley) by Lesley J. Ward and Geraldine Woods.

# Punctuating Properly

You need to punctuate your work in order to make clear what you're trying to say.

Try reading your work aloud. Where you need to take a breath, you need punctuation. This is a useful way to spot the odd missing comma, but don't let your breathing dictate your punctuation. You're aiming for work that the reader can understand, and punctuation is about clarity of ideas.

## Apostrophes

Even some really good writers struggle with correct use of the apostrophe. You need to get to grips with it, however, because apostrophe errors send a message of carelessness.

You use an apostrophe for contractions, where the apostrophe stands for one or more missing letter and must be used in the place where the letter(s) should go.

> cannot – can not – can't
>
> it is or it has – it's
>
> they have – they've

While you need to understand about contractions, you shouldn't use them in your essays at all.

You also use an apostrophe to demonstrate possession. You need to be careful about where you place the apostrophe. With ordinary nouns (singular or plural) its use is quite straightforward because you simply add *'s* to the word:

> Elizabeth's toy
>
> Bob's coat
>
> winter's storms
>
> a bicycle's bell

One exception to this is when the noun is plural and ends in an s already. In these cases, you place the apostrophe after the s:

> a girls' school
>
> nurses' ideas
>
> ladies' toilets

The other exception with possessives is the word *its*. Annoyingly, but definitely, the possessive use of *its* must never have an apostrophe. The only time *its* has an apostrophe is when you're using a contraction of *it is*.

> The oven reached its top temperature.
>
> The cat licked its paw.
>
> The book had a stain on its cover.

You may be tempted to use an apostrophe in plurals such as *the 1970's*. Don't, this is only acceptable (but not standard) in American English. The correct form is *the 1970s*.

## *Brackets*

Round brackets like this ( ) are more generally used in normal text (there's a word about square brackets in the section on ellipses). Round brackets are also known as *parentheses*, which comes from the Greek meaning 'to put or place something'. We mention the origin of the word as it's also the key to correct use. Parentheses are for non-essential, additional information that pops up during a sentence. This information you include in brackets should be subordinate to the rest of the sentence and should be an elaboration, illustration or explanation.

In less formal types of writing, brackets can be used for isolating a kind of *aside*, or personal comment from the author to the reader, but it's not really appropriate in academic writing.

In essays, the most common use of brackets is to place references and sources in sentences to show where ideas have come from originally.

Your sentence should read properly and fully with or without the part that's in brackets. You shouldn't require the part in brackets in order to understand the sentence.

Always check both the beginning and end of your section in brackets. It's very confusing for the reader if sentences have symbols (like brackets mysteriously appearing but never being closed (just like I have done here). See how confusing that can be.

Always use capitals, commas and the usually conventions of punctuation within the brackets. When you punctuate information in and either side of brackets, remember that you need to *place* the part in brackets within the main sentence:

Silver birch trees are often used in public spaces due to their height (and white bark).

Parts of 'The Wasteland' were written when Eliot was recuperating in Margate (Ackroyd, 1984), where Vivien was also staying.

Municipal planting needs voracious, hardy growers (such as Vinca Major) rather than delicate, subtle plants.

Brackets are also used for referring to a numbered lists, or a model, diagram or appendix:

The main results (1-4) are in the key table (final Figures').

In general, other than for references, try and keep brackets to a minimum, only using them when really necessary.

### Commas and full stops

Commas and full stops are the kinds of punctuation you use most frequently. You probably remember the golden rule for full stops: every sentence ends with one. Commas, however, aren't essential to a sentence. You use them to separate ideas and objects, and usually for three main purposes in student essays:

- ✔ **Lists:** I prefer mangoes, grapes, pears and bananas.

- ✔ **Joining:** Nectarines are suitable, while peaches are too furry.

- ✔ **Adding in an aside:** Fresh fruit salad, once at room temperature, should be served with single or double cream.

You can also use commas in place of repeating some key words in a sentence, but using more sentences is often easier. Here, the comma replaces the repetition of 'are better served in':

Some fruit salads are better served in a bowl; others, in a long glass.

Typically, students fail to use full stops and commas to show where sentences begin and end. This can result in *run-on sentences* (sentences that you should split into two separate sentences) or incomplete sentences that aren't fully formed.

This is a run-on sentence:

The popularity of allotments has increased people growing their own vegetables are developing communities where sharing produce has helped break down stereotype and prejudice.

It should read:

> The popularity of allotments has increased. People growing their own vegetables are developing communities where sharing produce has helped break down stereotype and prejudice.

Here are incomplete sentences, with incorrect punctuation:

> Council schemes for recycling food and garden waste into rich compost. A decrease in the quantity of rubbish being sent to landfill.

This is what the student meant:

> Council schemes for recycling food and garden waste into rich compost have decreased the quantity of rubbish being sent to landfill.

### Colons and semi-colons

A colon indicates that what follows is an explanation of what precedes it, usually a general notion followed by a specific point.

> People enjoy pop music more than jazz: they prefer catchy melodies.

Semi-colons usually replace full stops where sentences are very closely linked. Semi-colons usually have full sentences both before and after to avoid the whole paragraph becoming fragmented. Use them sparingly.

Long dashes (also called *em dashes*) differ from hyphens. A hyphen is short and is used within compound words, such as cross-reference; up-to-date; twenty-five. You will notice there's no space either side of the hyphen. Long dashes do sometimes have spaces either side however (this depends on what your university style guide recommends).

You can use em dashes in the same way as round or square brackets but they should be used very sparingly indeed. You need them to separate a part of your sentence that interrupts the flow. Since they do interrupt your writing, try not to use then at all otherwise you'll end up with a disjointed style. If you really think you need them, ensure you don't have more than one pair in a paragraph.

In fiction, some authors use dashes at the end of sentences in a stylistic fashion, sometimes singly. In academic essays, the only real use you may have would be to amplify or explain an idea and you should always stick to pairs.

> The 1870 Education Act was passed – despite the concern of some politicians – and resulted in the establishment of the first state system of schooling.

> Since the Disability Discrimination Act, wheelchair users have been more likely to visit galleries – according to the DCMS – as they have been guaranteed better access.

### Ellipses

Ellipses are demonstrated by three dots enclosed in brackets – either square or rounded. They look like this (...) or this [...]

These really have only one function in academic writing and that's to demonstrate where parts of a quotation or transcription have been left out in your essay. Here, the quotation would be too long and so I have left out the parts that aren't relevant:

> Since the end of the Cold War a new consensus seems to have emerged [...] more skilled workers will make the economy more productive.' (Brighouse, 2006:27)

Sometimes you use them for clarity. The author might have used 'it' in their sentence and you might need to reiterate the name so the reader can understand. This arises because when you quote someone, you're taking what they're saying out of its original context and some of the meaning could be lost.

For example, the original could read:

> 'The Latin name for the foxglove is *digitalis*. It can be grown in shady areas. It comes in a range of colours including various shades of pink, yellow and creamy white.'

You might not want the first two sentences, but if you quote the last one verbatim, it won't be clear what you're talking about so you need to insert the noun in place of the pronoun:

> '[Digitalis] comes in a range of colours including various shades of pink, yellow and creamy white.'

### Question and exclamation marks

Question marks fall at the end of direct questions, and you should really use them in academic writing only when they're part of quotations from texts or interview data. If your essay's full of questions, you undermine what you're saying. Your examiner wants to know your answers, not just read a further list of questions.

Exclamation marks are almost always inappropriate in academic writing.

# Capitalising Correctly

Getting capital letters wrong betrays a failure to take care with written work. You probably know that you need to capitalise the letter I as a pronoun, and proper nouns, but you should also be aware that you need capital letters for these cases:

- ✔ Brand names
- ✔ Days and months (but not seasons)
- ✔ Historical periods (like the Middle Ages)
- ✔ Initial word of each sentence and of titles
- ✔ Each keyword in a title (such as: *Pulp Fiction*, or *A Tale of Two Cities*)
- ✔ Roman numerals
- ✔ Names of countries, nationalities and languages
- ✔ Proper nouns

You don't usually need capital letters for generic terms, such as *conservative views.* This is different from direct reference to an individual person linked to a specific party, so you would need a capital for this: *the foremost Conservative in the UK.* Here you are using capitals for specifics and lower case for generics.

Of course, like many aspects of language, some arguments still abound about different terms, for example, newspapers tend to write about the *second world war* but might also say *World War II* which looks inconsistent. They each have a style guide from their editors to follow. These aren't usually published, but the Economist's Style Guide is available and is widely accepted as a definitive guide to good writing. You can access it at: http://www.economist.com/research/styleguide/.

You're a student and not a journalist and so you ought to also check with your university (and your tutor if possible), but also look at well-known style guide for help. If you're in doubt and still can't get a definitive answer from your tutor, then the most important thing to remember is that you should be consistent.

# Using Different Parts of Speech

In this section we explore the eight parts of speech that you use in your writing.

## Verbs

Each sentence needs a verb and a subject. The *verb* is the action, and the *subject* is the thing being acted on. The most common error in essay writing with verbs is when the verbs don't agree with the subject, usually because of confusion around plural and singular forms of the subject.

Take a look at this sentence:

> All the teachers is agreed about playtime.

Can you see the problem? The subject is plural, but the sentence uses the singular form of the verb. In the correct sentence the subject and verb are both plural:

> All the teachers *are* agreed about playtime.

Now look at this sentence:

> The cat were drinking milk.

Wrong again. This time, the subject is singular, but the verb is plural. Here's the right phrasing, with both verb and subject singular:

> The cat *was* drinking milk.

Often, students fall into the trap of thinking that the noun immediately in front of the main verb in your sentence must be the subject of that verb. For example:

> Many types of literature is to be studied on the course.

The writer has mistaken the noun 'literature' for the subject of the verb 'to be' (is). Actually, the noun that attaches to that verb is 'types'. The types are studied. And because 'types' is plural, the verb form needs to be too. Here's the correct version:

> Many types of literature *are* to be studied on the course.

Now that reads better, doesn't it? Bear this in mind as you work with longer sentences, because the distance between the verb and its subject can be much greater and can possibly lead into error.

Some dialects and accents use spoken verb forms that are incorrect if written. Avoid writing 'He like to go for a swim'. It should be 'He likes to go for a swim', even though in speech the former may be acceptable.

Another common verb error concerns tenses. You need to be consistent in your use of tenses to avoid confusing your reader, so stick to either past or predominantly present tenses in a paragraph.

Here's an incorrect and confusing sentence:

> She shows a drop in understanding and so was tested for hearing loss.

Can you see that the first verb (she shows) is in the present and the second (was tested) is in the past? Now here's the correct version, in which both verbs are in the past tense:

> She showed a drop in understanding and so was tested for hearing loss.

Generally, when students construct long and complex sentences, the tenses tend to go awry. Stick to shorter sentences and you're less likely to make errors.

Consult the section in Chapter 10 on using active and passive verbs in your essay

## Nouns

Nouns are names of people, animals, places: any kinds of things (concrete nouns) and ideas (abstract nouns).

In terms of what you need to watch out for in your essays, keep an eye on plurals because their spelling can be irregular – you don't always just add an 's'.

| | |
|---|---|
| house | houses |
| theory | theories |
| thesis | theses |
| child | children |
| criterion | criteria |
| focus | foci |
| curriculum | curricula |

If in doubt consult a dictionary.

The other issue is gender. Some nouns have gender-specific forms such as actor/actress or waiter/waitress. These are not currently in favour. The masculine form is preferred and applied as gender neutral, but you should check with your tutors whether you should use a particular convention.

This is absolutely vital if your essay is actually about gender issues. If you don't attend to this aspect, it shows a complete lack of understanding rather than merely a little insensitivity.

## Pronouns

A pronoun can replace a noun and help your sentences become less wordy. Lots of types exist, but the main thing to keep in mind is that the pronouns must agree with the verbs in your sentence. You're more likely to use *her, them, theirs, that, many* and so on than *I, me, your, myself* as academic writing isn't usually about your own life.

A pronoun refers to a noun or takes a noun's place. For clarity, you need to be careful to use the correct pronoun, or your reader might not know to what you are referring. So, if your noun is singular, for example, so should your pronoun be singular:

> 'A student using the library should always produce his or her ticket.'

> (not 'their' ticket, because you have used the singular form of student.)

If you wrote:

> 'Students using the library' you would use the plural form:

> 'Students using the library need to produce their tickets'

Singular pronouns include: anybody, each, nobody, a person, someone, everybody etc.

You'll find that it will simplify your wording if you use pronouns, but they need to make sense.

> Roses make great fragrant screens in gardens. Roses can be different colours. The rose comes in a dazzling array of shapes and styles. The rose is now more disease resistant than ever before.

It would be better to replace the word *roses* with the pronoun *they* from time to time. See that the word rose needs to be replaced with the pronoun *it*. When you use pronouns they need to agree and so you are replacing a singular noun word with a singular pronoun and a plural noun with a plural pronoun.

> Roses make great fragrant screens in gardens. They can be different colours. The rose comes in a dazzling array of shapes and styles. It is now more disease resistant than ever before.

Be really clear what the pronoun is referring to in the sentence:

> Young people like museums as they are great.
>
> (What, or who are great – museums or young people?)
>
> We visited the castle and the library and the class really liked it.
>
> (Which did they like?)

Keep the same voice when you use pronouns. If you are using the third person (such as she, he, it or they etc) stick with it throughout the passage and don't switch, say, to the first person (I, me).

This is wrong:

> A child should bring their reading book to class so don't forget yours.

Either of these would be correct (depending on the context):

> A child should bring their reading book to class and not forget it.
>
> You should bring your reading book to class - don't forget it!

## Keeping up with the times?

Because of its role as an international language, English is changing and rules that were once hard and fast are no longer so rigid. Generally, you're best to be somewhat conservative in academic writing. In the case of relative pronouns, 'who' is usually reserved for referring to people and 'which' for things. 'That' is used for things and for people too, especially in informal settings.

But some users of English are comfortable with a phrase such as 'the person which . . .' rather than 'the person who . . .' This may shock the purists but may indicate a future change in acceptability.

If you're in a muddle about relative clauses, the very best thing you can do is to consult a good grammar book that explains all the intricacies at length. May we suggest our sister publication, *English Grammar For Dummies?*

In academic writing when students are striving to achieve a good effect by composing lengthier sentences, one of the commonest errors is sentences like this:

> Poetry has many verse forms, one of them is the sonnet.

In this sentence, 'them' should read 'which', so:

> Poetry has many verse forms, one of which is the sonnet.

This is the way to join the two parts of the sentence happily. Otherwise they are two separate sentences.

Check what 'it' refers to in a sentence. The reference may be perfectly obvious to you but not to anyone else. For example:

> The iron hit the floor and it was damaged.
>
> (What was damaged – the iron or the floor?)
>
> The girl trod on the cat's tail by mistake and she was upset.
>
> (Who was upset – the cat or the girl?)

# Adjectives

Adjectives describe nouns and they usually come before the noun they're modifying. Adjectives often take modifying words before them (such as less or very).

You can use adjectives in absolute, comparative or superlative forms. Table 8-1 helps you see what these forms look like.

| Table 8-1 | Adjective Forms | |
| --- | --- | --- |
| *Absolute* | *Comparative* | *Superlative* |
| weak | weaker | weakest |
| good | better | best |
| vital | more vital | most vital |
| effective | more effective | most effective |

In your essays, using the superlative makes your work sound over-dramatic and results in claims that you're unlikely to be able to support with evidence.

Adjectives should add something to your English and shouldn't distract the reader from what you're trying to say. In academic writing you want to sound assertive and clear and so the absolute form is likely to be advisable. Adverbs like 'very' and 'really' before an adjective are usually unnecessary and so comparative forms are best avoided.

# Adverbs

Two main types of adverbs are likely to crop up in your essays. Conjunctive adverbs (*also, however, furthermore* and so on) join phrases together, while other adverbs indicate when, where or how something has happened. In this case, the words often end in *-ly* and you can place them in different positions in the sentence.

> The research paper *clearly* demonstrates the point.

> The data were presented *ambiguously*.

 Don't split an infinitive with an adverb. 'To boldly go' is okay for television shows but not academic research. In a university setting, the space vessel has to *go boldly*.

 Don't push the reader towards agreeing with you through persuasive language rather than the evidence. Words such as *obviously, clearly* and *plainly* can come across as rather patronising.

# Prepositions and conjunctions

You link words together in a sentence using prepositions and conjunctions:

- ✔ Prepositions link nouns to the other words. *On, over, beneath, among, above, about, towards* and *without* are all prepositions. They indicate relationships of objects in time, space or with logic.

- ✔ Conjunctions link the phrases themselves. *And, for, after, if* and *either* are all conjunctions (although you may find some of the same words listed as adverbs or prepositions in some cases).

## Placing prepositions

Preposition placement is controversial. In the past, academics advising on writing style considered it inappropriate to end any sentence with words such as *with, into* or *of*. Trying to avoid this has tied some writers and speakers into knots. If you are forced into a really ridiculous sentence, you're better off using the preposition at the end; but avoid doing so if you can, because your writing reads better with firmer endings to sentences.

Table 8-2 gives examples of sentences ending in a preposition, and alternative structures. See which sound better to you.

| Table 8-2 | Preposition Placement |
|---|---|
| *Preposition at the End* | *Alternative Structuring* |
| Teachers decide who the programme is directed at. | Teachers decide to whom the programme is directed. |
| Children with autism know what it is like having no one to play with. | Children with autism know what it is like having to play alone. |
| Exam grades can affect the higher and lower groups and the children between. | Exam grades can affect all groups: higher, middle and lower. |

The alternatives are slightly stronger in each case. You may feel that the first example sounds overly formal. It is correct, however, and being a little formal is often better rather than running the risk of a pedantic tutor marking you down.

Perhaps more important is the correct use of prepositions. These errors are now quite common in speech, but should not appear in academic writing:

Wrong versions: Could of / should of / bored of

Correct formation: Could have / should have / bored with

### Sorting out conjunctions

A conjunction joins the parts of a sentence together. These seven *coordinating conjunctions* coordinate sentences, connecting ideas, showing the relationship between them clearly:

And

For

But

So

Yet

Nor

Or

These words are great for connecting ideas, but you should avoid starting sentences with coordinating conjunctions.

Examples of coordinating conjunctions in sentences include:

> Turner's sketchbooks show an obsession with colour and an accomplished drawing style.

> Children with dyslexia have access to a dictionary, but sometimes this does not help.

Other conjunctions are known as *subordinating conjunctions* as they portray a different emphasis on the parts of the sentence.

> Since
>
> Because
>
> If
>
> Unless
>
> Whether
>
> Although

The sentences have a slight shift in emphasis as a result. The first one now shows that colour is more important than sketching and the second emphasises the uselessness of standard dictionaries:

> Since Turner's sketchbooks have many studies in colour, his accomplished drawing style seems less important.

> Although they have access to the dictionary, their dyslexia renders it pointless.

## Interjections

You can ignore interjections in academic writing because they're about emotion and feeling. For transcripts of interviews or similar data you may need them, but these exclamations are more for fiction than essays.

An interjection is an exclamation. Here they are italicised so you can identify them easily:

> *Wow*! What a great essay I have written.

> I read it and I thought, *Hello*! what's that all about?

> This theorist is being very controversial, *eh*?

> *Hey*, I have a great idea about socialism

# Writing when English isn't your first language

If English is not your first language your first place to go is the support service at our university. They should provide classes (usually known as 'English for Academic Purposes') that you can pursue alongside your studies, or better still, complete before you start your course.

Many guides exist that will help you with tricky words and will explain grammar in more specific detail than we have space for in this essay writing guide.

If you find vocabulary difficult, find a dictionary with a specific sections on prepositions and use this as your guide. Some are written especially for people who have additional languages and these could be a real help and so a worthwhile investment.

Do remember that people who have English as their first (or only) language also find they struggle with many aspects of their writing and so don't be downhearted if you are finding it difficult. Ask your course tutor where you can get help and you may be surprised at the range of support that's available.

# Chapter 9

# Penning the Perfect Paragraph

• • • • • • • • • • • • • • • • • • • • • • • • • • • • • • • • • • • • •

*In This Chapter*

▶ Constructing coherent paragraphs

▶ Thinking about sentences

▶ Making sure that your essay flows

• • • • • • • • • • • • • • • • • • • • • • • • • • • • • • • • • • • • •

*P*aragraphs are collections of related thoughts grouped together to help ideas develop coherently and logically. Being able to structure your essay into neat and clear paragraphs shows careful thinking, and by linking the paragraphs together effectively you present a sound and plausible argument.

 Many of the points in this chapter are about coherence. Make sure that you know what *coherence* means – your work is coherent when it's logical and follows a clear way of developing that makes sense and doesn't contradict itself or confuse the reader.

## Understanding Paragraphs

Paragraphs are the building blocks of your essay. They're collections of sentences all dealing with the same idea. Each paragraph is made up of a group of sentences that together form a kind of conceptual and practical unit. Readers anticipate that when they start reading your new paragraph, they can see the presentation of a new idea together with support and evidence for that new idea.

Read on for some more essential facts about paragraphs.

### Thinking about types of paragraph

Table 9-1 shows you the different types and purposes of paragraphs and the key words you can use to make clear what you're trying to achieve.

| Table 9-1 | Types of Paragraph | |
|---|---|---|
| *Type of Paragraph* | *Purpose of Paragraph* | *Key Words to Use* |
| Defining | To explain an object, process or idea | X is defined as; Y is a sort of . . . |
| Describing | To say what something or someone is like | Use words to describe size, properties, location etc. or use an analogy (X is like Y) |
| Evaluating | To judge or assess | Good, useful, relevant, poor, weak, inaccurate |
| Classifying | To group things into categories | Belongs to; is part of; is related to; is a sort of |
| Selecting an option | To say which of several options is preferable | In my view; I think that; in my opinion; it seems to me; I believe that |
| Comparing | To show the similarities and differences | X is similar to y; however; in contrast; both of these; differs from; unlike |
| Explaining | To say why, how, who or what | The cause of X is; because of; due to; as a result of; consequently; therefore |

If you're writing a paragraph that's about selecting an option, you *must* support your views with reference to evidence and research.

## *Looking at the do's and don'ts*

Well-written paragraphs are:

✔ A way of dividing up your writing into topics or key points – they allow you to build your argument bit by bit.

✔ Clear and thorough – each paragraph should be balanced, with enough information to back up the points you make and no irrelevancies.

✔ Full of appropriate evidence – when you're writing a supporting paragraph, this should contain sufficient exemplars to reinforce the point you're making.

✔ Logical and sequential – you shouldn't jump around with your ideas; they should build from one to the other. You're aiming for coherence, where the argument flows and the essence of what you're saying is unambiguous. You connect to the preceding and following paragraphs, following up the points that you've made and laying the way for the ideas that follow. Paragraphs fit coherently into the whole.

In academic writing you need to make your paragraphs substantial, but not too long. We can't say exactly how many sentences make up a paragraph, but a rough rule is to aim for a minimum of three sentences and a maximum of about seven or eight sentences. The number also depends on what you're writing about, the length of your sentences, and the point you've reached in your essay.

Try to break up each page with no fewer than two and no more than about five paragraphs. Too many paragraphs betray a lack of attention to the development of the argument, whereas too few paragraphs show that you haven't thought much about the structure of your ideas.

Now that you know what you're aiming for when writing a paragraph, be sure to avoid the common mistakes. Work that has poorly constructed paragraphs falls into two main styles:

✔ **Too many paragraphs:** Each sentence is a paragraph. An essay like this lacks coherence because it doesn't develop ideas, just acts like a sort of long-winded list. You don't ensure a logical progression, and the essay reads like jerky, disjointed bullet points rather than a flowing argument. You need to group your sentences into paragraphs, connecting up those that deal with specific points.

✔ **Too few paragraphs:** These essays end up being one really long uninterrupted jumble, which often lacks logic. A page that's all one paragraph can be daunting to read, and you can easily get lost as you're reading. You need to find the natural breaks in the ideas to see where to make the writing into more manageable paragraphs.

Table 9-2 illustrates what your page looks like with too many paragraphs, too few, and appropriate division of the text.

| Table 9-2 | Viewing Paragraphs on the Page | |
| --- | --- | --- |
| *Too Many Paragraphs* | *Too Few Paragraphs* | *Reasonable Number of Paragraphs* |
| Xy xyxy yy xyxy xy.<br><br>Xyx yxyy xyy xyxy xyxy xy xyyxyxyxyx.<br><br>Xyyx yxyx yx yxy.<br><br>Xy yx y yxy.<br><br>Xyxyyx yxyx yyxyxyy xxyx xyxy xyyx.<br><br>Xyxy yxyyxy xyyxy xyyx yxyx.<br><br>Xy xyx yyx yxyy xyx yyx.<br><br>Xyxyy xyxyx xy xyyx. | Rtyy ut yutyutur rtyyut yuty utur rtyyuty utyut ur rtyyuty utyutur rtyy utyuty utur rtyyu-tyutyutur rty yutyu tyutur rtyyu tyut yutur rty yutyuty ut ur rtyy utyutyu tur rtyyut yutyutur rty yutyu tyu tur rty yuty uty utur rtyy ut yutyu tur rtyy utyut yutur rtyy utyu tyutur rtyy utyut yutur rty rt rty tyyr trt uuty. | Rtyyut yuty utur rtyy ut yut yutur rtyy utyuty.<br><br>Rty yuty utyutur rtyyu tyut yutur rtyyut yuty utur rty yutyutyutur rtyy utyut.<br><br>Rtyy utyu tyutur rtyyut yuty utur rtyy utyu tyut.<br><br>Rtyyu tyut yutur rtyyut yuty utur rt yyutyu tyu tur rtyy utyu. |

 You sometimes can't see the wood for the trees when you're writing, and so you can slip into the bad habit of forgetting about paragraphs. One good way to check how you're writing is to distance yourself physically from your work. Either on screen or with a paper copy, step away from your work and look at it from a short distance. (Time you stood up and stretched your legs anyway!) Which of the columns in Table 9-2 does your page resemble? It should, of course, be the one on the right. If it doesn't, you know what you need to do: either break your text down or join up sentences to form paragraphs.

# Structuring a Paragraph

Even though each paragraph is about a different idea, you follow the same process as you write each paragraph, and use the same structure.

## Following the process

The following steps take you through penning your paragraph, from organising your thoughts to checking the final product. Once you get the hang of effectively structured paragraphs, these steps come easily and you're able to reduce the time you spend. For now, however, follow these steps and you'll find you have clearer, more logical paragraphs.

1. **Think about the exact question that you're addressing in this paragraph and consider the best approach to answering it well.**

   Which is the key part of the question and which facts and thoughts provide the answer? Consider whether you need further evidence to support your answer to the question. If so, where can you find the information? Try to show how the area's important within your broader topic.

2. **Jot down the key question for the paragraph and the answers to the questions in Step 1.**

   You can do this straight onto the computer or in a notebook, whichever suits you best. If you do it straight onto the computer, remember that you're not writing your essay, you're just writing notes, so you can write messages to yourself, like 'need more info on this – govt website?' What you're doing is giving yourself a list of things you need to research.

3. **Using the list of what you need to research, focus on gathering the information you need for the paragraph.**

   Don't forget that you're still trying to answer the key question you've identified. Collect all the information together.

4. **Think about your own views on the pieces of information you've gathered.**

   What do you think of what you've discovered? Why is the area important? Look over the facts and information again – what's going to help you make your case?

5. **Reorder the information, facts and ideas so that they make the most sense.**

   Leave out what you don't yet need. You should really only have examples that answer the question you identified in Step 1. Other information is for a different paragraph (you can use it later, so don't try to cram it in where it's not going to help).

6. **Put the paragraph together.**

   Different parts of the paragraph have varied functions. You need to turn the question you identified at the start into a statement – the opening sentence for the paragraph (and it's usually the topic sentence; see the section 'Penning a topic sentence'). You then move on to the details that support and develop your opener, giving details, facts and examples in your supporting sentences (see the section 'Writing supporting sentences'). You end with the closing sentence.

7. **Read through what you've written.**

   Check that your paragraph starts by stating the main topic then goes on to support the statement and round off neatly.

8. **Repeat the process until you get the hang of doing this less mechanically.**

   You find that, after a while, paragraphs come more naturally and you can write and research without referring to this list.

## Penning a topic sentence

You can't assume that your reader's going to guess the subject of your paragraph: you have to make clear what you're writing about. Therefore, you need to articulate the key notion or idea of each paragraph in one clear sentence. This is known as the *topic* or *main* sentence. It's usually at the start of the paragraph but it can be in the middle or at the end. The topic sentence should be simple, clear and solid.

Stick to having the topic sentence at the start of the paragraph if you have any doubts about where it should go.

In each paragraph, the topic sentence acts as kind of signpost. You direct your reader through your essay via the topic sentences. If they're sufficiently well crafted, your reader should have an overview of your work by reading the topic sentences alone.

Your topic sentence summarises the main idea of your paragraph and shows the reader what your paragraph's about. Keep to one idea per paragraph; for further ideas you need new paragraphs. Also, ensure that your topic sentence is relevant to the overall thesis and not off the point.

Take a look at these two short paragraphs. Read the first one and decide what you think it's about. The second paragraph is the same expect for the addition of a topic sentence. (Don't read the second one until you've read and thought about the first.)

Many children have had their opportunities curbed at a relatively young age as a result of the loaded cultural references. Even where the vocabulary is wide and numerical skills can be shown, some of the ways that questions are worded make them inaccessible.

Tests for intelligence are controversial because they can have far-reaching consequences. Many children have had their opportunities curbed at a relatively young age as a result of the loaded cultural references. Even where the vocabulary is wide and numerical skills can be shown, some of the ways that questions are worded make them inaccessible.

Which paragraph makes more sense? Can you see how helpful the topic sentence is, and how it improves the writing?

Repeat the topic sentence as a subheading for each paragraph while you're writing and redrafting. You need to delete these sub-headings in the final draft, but in the meantime you have a title for each paragraph and you can check the flow of your work as well as the relevance of what's in each paragraph.

## *Writing supporting sentences*

The rest of the sentences in the paragraph expand and develop the idea of the topic sentence (see the previous section), using evidence and exemplars. You present explanations, elaborations, examples and evidence, and you show the details that support your topic sentence. You state what you mean more fully, perhaps providing distinctions between subtly linked concepts or making definitions more explicit.

While your topic sentence sets the scene, your supporting sentences develop the ideas and provide detail.

The supporting sentences may involve more discussion of the area or they can develop your ideas in a range of different ways such as by:

- ✔ Discussing the words in the topic sentence in detail, perhaps giving definitions
- ✔ Drawing comparisons or explaining cause and effect
- ✔ Giving your opinion or view of the topic (you must always accompany this with other evidence or facts)
- ✔ Illustrating the topic sentence with details
- ✔ Outlining the history or background of the topic
- ✔ Presenting statistics or figures
- ✔ Providing examples of the topic

As you write further paragraphs, you can unravel and analyse your points in increasing detail.

In your topic sentence and the supporting sentences, you should discuss the same issue, first introducing it and then breaking it down and analysing it. Don't confuse the reader by introducing new ideas in the same paragraph.

# Considering sentence length

Each paragraph comprises two or more sentences of various lengths. In this section, we think about how long you make your sentences.

## Writing short sentences

Conveying complexities in short sentences is generally difficult, but having short sentences in your work is useful for the sake of balance and readability.

Different types of sentences exist, such as those that ask questions (interrogative, including rhetorical), those that forcefully state something (explanatory) and those that command (imperative). None of these has a particular place in academic work, but they're commonplace in other forms of writing.

You need to use *declarative* sentences predominantly (or exclusively), because these state arguments and facts.

Don't overuse short sentences. A series of short sentences produces a staccato effect and can be unpleasant to read. How does this sound?

> You should always proofread your essay. You should check your spelling carefully. You should not be too reliant on your spellchecker. It may not be able to distinguish between similar words. It will identify most errors so you can rectify them. You need a dictionary as well. You need to check words yourself. You need to be sure your spelling is accurate.

It's not very comfortable to read, is it? It doesn't flow at all. Compare it with the version you see in a moment.

Sometimes, having many short sentences leads to repetition of the keywords because you have to introduce concepts again. If you find that this happens frequently, see whether replacing the full stop with a comma works better.

### Writing long sentences

You can easily lose the meaning when sentences are too long and complicated. You should write long sentences with complex construction only if you're an expert writer! Not many of us are, so you're best to keep things pretty straightforward. Chop up your longer sentences to make the meaning clear.

An example of the kind of sentence you should avoid is one with too many simple conjunctions such as 'and', 'so', 'but' and 'because'.

> You should always proofread your essay and check your spelling carefully but you should not be too reliant on your spellchecker because it may not be able to distinguish between similar words but it will identify most errors so you can rectify them but you do need a dictionary as well and check words yourself so you can be sure your spelling is accurate.

One way of rewriting this in a more academic style is:

> Although you should always proofread your essay and check your spelling carefully, you should not be too reliant on your spellchecker because it may not be able to distinguish between similar words. Nevertheless, it will identify most errors in order for you to rectify them. You do, however, need a dictionary as well in order to check the words yourself. In this way you can be sure your spelling is accurate.

 When you do use a long sentence, think about where you site your main point. If you conceal your key idea in the middle of the sentence, you may find it difficult to make your point clearly. You can place the key point at either the start or the end. Placing it at the start allows the rest of the sentence to consist of extra, explanatory information. This is easier to read and understand than a sentence that puts the information at the start and ends up with the idea. Look at these examples:

> *The West Wing* is an effective political television drama, considering its pithy screenplay, superlative acting and innovative camera work.

> Considering the realistic dialogue, convincing acting and careful pace, the most effective political comedy of the decade is *The Thick of It*.

Both of these position the emphasis of the main point well, but with the second one you need to read to the end to find out what's actually being said.

The number of clauses a sentence contains determines its simplicity. A clause is a collection of (related) words including a subject (sometimes implicit rather than explicit) and a predicate (which tells you something about the subject).

Sentences with more verbs are usually easier to read.

### *Mixing short and long sentences*

If short sentences can sound choppy and long sentences muddled, what should you aim for? The answer is variety. A paragraph containing sentences of different lengths is usually more interesting for the reader, and it shows the control you have over your language. If you have a short and pithy sentence following a series of longer sentences, you make a good impact. Similarly, if you introduce an idea with a short sentence, you're likely to have a clear and fresh start that you can then go on to elaborate.

In the following paragraph the number of words in each sentence is indicated. You can see that the paragraph contains a couple of short sentences (7 and 9 words) as well as a very long one (45 words). The others are in between.

> A subtle way of making your writing feel interesting to read is to use variety in the length of your sentences. *(21 words)* Use a relatively short sentence from time to time. *(9 words)* Then go on to include a much longer sentence if you feel that it is the best way to express your ideas at this point in your essay, if it is appropriate, and if you are totally in control of the structure of your sentence. *(45 words)* We include the word count for each sentence in this paragraph to show you how it works. *(17 words)* Do you see how mixing lengths works? *(7 words)*

Just a moment's reflection on the different styles demonstrates that a livelier approach is always going to be to use a mixture of different styles. A paragraph with sentences of different lengths is more interesting to read than a list of bullet point ideas, where you use lots of short sentences, and is easier to understand than long, wordy phrases that never seem to end.

Getting the balance right is achieved by reading and rereading both your work and that of academics, in journals and books. Often, key texts on your courses are chosen because they are well written. The choice of texts reflects the tutor's tastes to a certain extent, because most key academic ideas taught on undergraduate degrees are presented in a range of sources.

Ask your tutor to point out which books are written in a good academic style, offering a useful model for your own writing development. You're after clear writing with a mix of different-length sentences and sensible use of technical language that's still readable.

# Ensuring Coherence and Logical Flow

Coherence is tricky to pin down because it's about the flow of an argument. If your reader has to reread sections or flick back to earlier passages to get the meaning clear, your work lacks coherence. Something's happened to upset the logical flow of ideas: perhaps you've omitted a step; maybe you've included irrelevant and confusing repetition; possibly the reader's searching for missing evidence or has spotted a contradiction.

Use the suggestions in this section to ensure coherence and a logical flow in your essay.

You're looking for flowing language and a coherent argument that develops smoothly without leaping around or repeating itself.

## Ordering sentences within the paragraph for coherence

Once you have a clear topic sentence (see the earlier section 'Penning a topic sentence'), you need to develop your ideas. This is an outline of the kind of development you can make:

1. Explain your thinking about the topic sentence, perhaps clarifying any ambiguities.

2. Present any exemplar or illustration.

3. Give any required explanation of the examples.

4. Round this section off and show how you're moving to the next topic.

Think about how your paragraphs are stacking up as you go. Here are some questions to apply to your work to help you keep an eye on how it's flowing:

- ✔ In each paragraph, do all the supporting sentences relate to the topic sentence? Ensure that you keep the content relevant.

- ✔ If you have sentences that don't match up, are they vital to your essay? If they are, you need a new paragraph; if they aren't, you can leave them out altogether.

- ✔ Can you divide up your paragraph further by theme? Can you establish new paragraphs to allow you to explore ideas more thoroughly? If you find two ideas vying for space in one paragraph, split the paragraph.

- ✔ Do your sentences link forwards to the next paragraph and idea? Do your sentences link backwards, following on from the previous paragraph and idea? In both cases you need to ensure that the links between sentences are clear and solid. Create additional linking sentences if you need to.

- ✔ Are you moving from better known or easily understood to less obvious and more complex ideas? This is the best tactic. The opposite way of writing results in you throwing your reader in at the deep end, presenting unfamiliar ideas from the start, which can be confusing.

- ✔ Are you sure that the topic's crystal clear? Your main idea should be the central subject of the paragraph. Check that nothing in your writing creates confusion for the reader about what constitutes the main subject of the paragraph.

 You're aiming to present a logical development of ideas, and sometimes you can help the reader through repetition of the keywords in the paragraph. This is a surprising tip, becaue tutors normally want you to avoid repeating the same words. In this case, you're making things absolutely clear. Doing so helps when you have complicated ideas and long sentences. Don't do it too often, though – just when you're stuck on a way to get an idea really clear. For example:

> Literature in the field of education presents a wide range of definitions of giftedness. Gifted children are therefore difficult to identify clearly, as there is no single clear definition of giftedness. Giftedness is described by the UK government as being above the normal level for academic subjects such as mathematics and science. The gifted child will be ahead of their peers in terms of their conceptual understanding and ability to pick up new ideas.

## *Making the language flow*

You're after flowing work, concisely written. Here's a checklist to help you remember what's what in producing good, flowing sentences:

- ✔ Your work is cut down to the minimum required to make sense.

- ✔ You use the finest words for the purpose (using a thesaurus where appropriate).

- ✔ You use a variety of words (rather than repeating the same word in one sentence and/or adjacent sentences).

- ✔ Your ideas link to one another and follow on clearly.

- ✔ You use a mix of long and short sentences to enhance meaning (see the earlier section 'Considering sentence length').

Check your grammar (Chapter 8 can help with this). Often, student essays become incoherent for a simple reason such as a shift in tenses or subject–verb agreement part way through a paragraph. This has the effect of forcing the reader to go over what he or she has read and pretty much guess what the writer was trying to say. The reader may be unable to work out what you mean or may come to a different conclusion than the one you intend.

Also check that you've kept your language simple. Many students use complex words because they're trying to impress. The problem with this tactic is that students often use the words inaccurately, shifting the meaning of a sentence. Chapter 10 takes you through which words to use when writing in an academic style.

Another concern is that the convolutions that writers go through to avoid repetition may result in very poorly expressed ideas. It is better if you use some repetition to increase the clarity of your writing, but only from time to time.

## *Signposting your sentences and paragraphs*

To help the reader follow your argument, you need to use transitional language that signposts your moves between sentences and paragraphs.

## What's transitional language?

Transitional words are specific words that signal to your reader that you're shifting emphasis, or support an idea that you've presented. Table 9-3 outlines some key transitional words.

| Table 9-3 | Using Transitional Language |
|---|---|
| *Purpose of Words* | *Possible Language* |
| To reinforce ideas | also; in addition; additionally; indeed; as well as; for example; to reinforce this idea; in confirmation of; to verify; moreover; furthermore; in fact; therefore |
| To exemplify | for example; as demonstrated; for instance |
| To show order | First; second; third; finally; then; next; following that; initially; ultimately; transitionally |
| To shift ideas | although; but; instead; yet; alternatively; on the other hand; in spite of; nevertheless; however; in contrast; though; alternatively; conversely; otherwise; instead |
| To concede a point | Naturally; despite; while; although; granted; despite; notwithstanding; of course |
| To conclude a section | finally; ultimately; in conclusion; accordingly; thus; therefore; so; consequently; as a result of; hence; finally; and so; in view of |

Think carefully about the words you use to indicate what you're about to say, because the right words improve the clarity of your writing.

Use the words that best match the overall tone of your writing; don't suddenly shift your language because you've picked some words from Table 9-3 that sound more impressive to you than others.

# Checking for coherence and flow

Your topic sentences help you get a sense of how your work should flow. For the purpose of checking the flow of your argument, take a look at the *document map* or *outline view*, which is a particular way you can view your essay on your computer. Different software packages have their own ways of doing this and their own names for the outline view, but here follow instructions for looking at your document in this way if you use MS Word, which is the most common package in universities:

1. Select each of your topic sentences and turn them into 'headings' (it's a temporary change you're making for this exercise).

2. You do this by applying the 'heading' style, which you can find in the 'formatting'menu;

3. The computer now knows which parts of your text are headings and when you click on 'outline view' it will display only the headings, leaving you with a summary of the outline of the essay.

Once you have accessed this outline of your essay, you can view your essay through the document map facility, listing each heading and the subheadings, giving you an outline of your essay. You can review the logic and flow of your ideas and pick up where you may have repeated an idea or jumped forwards or backwards.

 You should also try to spot your own errors, but this can be really difficult because you may well predict what you know you wanted to say rather than actually reading the words on the page. If you want a second opinion, ask a critical friend to cast his or her eye over your work and let you know where it jumps around or becomes confusing. Getting together with some other students who are on the same or similar courses can be really helpful. Reading one another's work can help you to see where you can make improvements.

Another way to see how well your language flows is to use a readability test, usually available as part of your existing computer software. In MS Office, for example, look on the Word Options tab, click 'Proofing', select 'Check grammar with spelling' and choose the 'readability statistics box. The two most common readability tests are the Flesch Reading Ease test and the Flesch–Kincaid Grade Level test. They both work by checking the word length and sentence length in your work, and they give a score from 1 to 100. A higher result in the Flesch Reading Ease test, or a low score in the Flesch–Kincaid Grade Level test indicates more readable work. If you run the test on your work and get a poor score, that may be an indication that you've used over-long phrases or badly constructed sentences.

An easier version of this would be to use the SMOG method. It stands for Simplified Measure of Gobbledygook and is a (simple and free) formula you can use if you don't have access to the software. Here's the method:

1. Find a passage of your essay;
2. Mark out ten consecutive sentences;
3. Within these sentences, underline the words with three or more syllables;
4. Total up this number of words;
5. Multiply the answer by 3;
6. Choose, from the top row of numbers, that which is closest to your answer and find its square root from the lower list (in italics);

    1, 4, 9, 16, 25, 36, 49, 64, 81, 100, 121, 144, 169

    *1, 2, 3, 4, 5, 6, 7, 8, 9, 10, 11, 12, 13*

7. Add 8 to your total and you have the readability level.

You are after a number lower than 10 if possible as this is optimum for most readers, usually indicating clarity.

Don't just run the test and make changes until you get a good score. The tests help to alert you to overuse of jargon and sentences of strange lengths, but they can't tell you if your content makes any sense or your argument's coherent.

# Chapter 10

# Writing in the Academic Style

........................................

## In This Chapter

▶ Striking the right tone in your writing

▶ Adopting a formal style

▶ Avoiding bias

▶ Cutting out waffle and vagueness

........................................

*W*hen you pick up your pen (or your mouse) to write an academic piece, your aim is for your reader (your tutor) to take your writing seriously. In order to achieve that, you need to speak to your tutor in his or her own language: you need to follow the conventions of academic writing.

In this chapter we help you polish your academic style. We show you how to write an essay that gets the balance right between being easy and clear to read on the one hand while maintaining straightforward discussion of some complex issues on the other. We help you to be precise and specific rather than vague and general, and formal without being stuffy and stilted.

 The greater number of recommended academic sources you read, the more familiar and comfortable you become with the style you need to adopt. So, if you're serious about improving your writing, you can benefit from increasing your reading.

## Adopting the Right Tone of Voice

The balance is a tricky one to manage, but you need to come across as firm and confident without being overbearing and letting your reader think that you aren't open to the persuasion of compelling evidence.

## Remembering your audience

Think about what you can assume and what you need to explain. Don't waste words describing basic ideas that you covered in session one of your course. In particular, don't quote the lecturer's PowerPoint presentations or handouts. That comes across as lazy and rather patronising. Lectures are springboards from which you can take up references and ideas and undertake your own research.

Quoting your tutor's published work is flattering and often helpful (at least he or she probably agrees with the ideas), but take care to reference really well. Plagiarising from your tutor is just about the worst academic crime you can commit (and easily the most stupid).

## Being modest

You don't need to denigrate your work or talk about it as if it's worthless, but you do need to realise that your ideas are only part of a much larger whole.

One way to be clear about the role of your work in the bigger picture is to be careful with the language you use to describe it. You can describe other people's work that you've consulted as vital, useful, critical, groundbreaking and so on, but you can't describe your own work in such terms.

You can say that you hope your work can contribute to the development of an idea in your field, but don't go beyond this modest claim.

## Being cautious

Academic writing errs on the side of caution. Good scholarly work should accept that others' ideas, projects and investigations may possibly turn up different results or present a challenge to your ideas. With this in mind, not many studies can claim to have the full and final answer to any specific question.

Simultaneously, scholars need to have some conviction about what they're researching. Being too tentative has little point because this undermines the value of what you say.

In order to help you present your views with the right balance of commitment and caution, take a look at Table 10-1, which gives you ideas of words you can use.

| Table 10-1 | Using Cautious or Committed Language |
| --- | --- |
| *Being Cautious* | *Being Committed* |
| **Vocabulary:** arguably; potentially; possibly; seemingly; apparently | *Verbs that show commitment to an idea or viewpoint:* I think; I advocate; I feel; what I mean is; I understand that; I believe; X or Y should/must |
| **Verbs:** I imagine; I suppose; I hypothesise; I project that; X or Y may/could | *Expressing your view:* it seems to me that; from my perspective; in my opinion |
| | *Showing firm agreement:* certainly; plainly; clearly; undoubtedly; never; always |

Check whether you've struck the right balance in your essay by using highlighter pens to mark your use of these words. Use two different colours (or use underlining and circling or whatever you like) and then evaluate the frequency of the different kinds of language. They should be about even. If you have too many forceful words, your writing sounds arrogant, but if you're too tentative, you sound ineffectual and feeble.

You can also check through your essay for parts of the verb 'to be' (for example 'it is' and 'they are') that trip all too quickly off the tongue and may make you sound too sure of yourself. You're often better to say 'this may be so', 'this may show that . . .', 'this can indicate that . . .' and thus allow for further academic debate on the subject.

## Be careful with your attitude

When writing, you need to take care to get your ideas across appropriately. You're aiming for reason, logic, argument and coherence, not personal experience and colourful, singing language.

You want to show that you've read and understood a range of authors and views and that you've synthesised what they've said, adding your own opinion. You don't, however, want to come across as someone who knows everything and is unwilling to absorb and consider new ideas.

You're aiming for confident and knowledgeable, not too arrogant or too humble.

Don't be pompous. A fine line exists between using the right word (which may be the correct one in a specialised context) and using an arcane one for show. Whoops! 'Arcane' is just the kind of word that you should think twice about. It means 'secret, showy and mysterious'. How many people use it nowadays? When we use it here, do we sound like we're showing off? See the following section for more on choosing your language carefully.

# Writing in a Formal Style

In general, academic essays are formal in nature and so are impersonal, but they should also be straightforward to read and interesting. As we show you in this section, formal doesn't mean writing in a stilted, technical fashion, but it does mean taking care with the language you choose to use.

All of the points in this section about formal language refer to the main body of your essay. If you're incorporating material from another source – reporting speech, including dialogue from a film or interview, using a reflective journal that you kept for a particular assignment – you use the format of the source, which is likely to be informal.

## Using 'I' in your essay

Whether using the personal pronoun in your essay is appropriate depends on your discipline and the nature of your essay. For example, if you're writing a narrative on your own educational biography, you can't possibly complete the exercise without using 'I'. However, that's a very specific task and is an unusual requirement on a degree course. Usually tutors are after a balanced and objective review of some clear ideas, and they prefer to read the response to the title with reference to experienced theorists rather than the views of students, however carefully considered.

The style of writing should be appropriate to what you're writing about and, since academic writing is generally formal, the personal pronoun is usually discouraged.

Unless you've been asked to use 'I' in your essay, avoid using it where possible. Assume that you're not expected to do so.

Here's an example of inappropriate use of a personal style:

> In this essay I am going to show how Intelligence Quotient (IQ) tests are constructed and explain their origins and development, because they are important. Using journal articles I have read, I will then describe the early pioneers of IQ testing and bring in modern controversies about these tests. I will show how they are not used well in schools and I think we should have more training about them as they are not really understood, which is something I picked up on during my school experience.

Now here's a more suitable, formal and academic paragraph:

> This essay will explore the origins and nature of Intelligence Quotient (IQ) tests, explaining their importance in education. The early pioneers of IQ testing will be discussed initially, followed by an examination of recent and current controversies. As well as published research, the discussion will draw on anecdotal evidence from teachers, demonstrating some misconceptions about IQ and the effect of IQ testing not being discussed during teacher education.

Your tutor should help you get a sense of what's acceptable in terms of how personal you should be in your writing. For scientific disciplines, for example, you're expected to use an impersonal style. You don't find a lab report saying 'I lit a wooden splint and plunged it vertically into the glistening glass vessel in order to ascertain the presence of gases'.

In contrast, if you're writing a narrative about your childhood to help you evaluate some contemporary children's experiences, you shouldn't use an impersonal style. The purpose is to express some emotion and feeling, so an active, personal style is more direct, easier to read and better for engaging the reader.

## *Active or passive?*

You need to understand about active and passive language. Take a look at Table 10-2, which lays out some active and passive sentences.

| Table 10-2 | Active Versus Passive Sentences |
|---|---|
| *Active Phrasing* | *Passive Phrasing* |
| Armstrong walked on the moon in 1969. | The surface of the moon was first visited in 1969. |
| The cat chased the dog. | The dog was chased by the cat. |
| The US people elected Obama in 2008. | In 2008, Obama was elected. |

In the left-hand column you see *active* sentences where the person or thing performing the action comes first in the sentence. The second column shows *passive* versions: the person performing the action comes second or is omitted. (Obama is the object in the last case, and the US people are those performing the action.) This omission makes passive sentences more impersonal.

Which version you use depends on what you're writing about. The second one reads as rather stiff and artificial, but if your focus is on the date or the place, it's clearer than the first version, where the person is the key.

You find that guides to writing want you to eliminate the passive way of writing because the active way is more engaging. In academic writing the preference is for impersonal writing, and you need to be sure that your active writing doesn't get too personal. If it does, your work's more about opinion than facts.

The key is to keep an impersonal style while using active verbs where you can. Table 10-3 gives you some examples that you may come across in your essay writing.

| Table 10-3 | Essay Writing Using Passive and Active |
|---|---|
| *Passive Constructions* | *Active Constructions* |
| Studies of this kind are to be discussed . . . | These studies merit discussion . . . |
| Findings were acquired by . . . | Findings come from . . . |
| This is shown through comparative techniques . . . | Artists will demonstrate this through comparing different techniques . . . |
| Methods were considered more effective than . . . | Methods proved more effective than . . . |

| Passive Constructions | Active Constructions |
|---|---|
| It was found that . . . | I find that . . . |
| The main drawbacks have been ignored by doctors . . . | Doctors have failed to consider drawbacks . . . |

# Avoiding overstatements

Your academic essay is a considered, well-researched, careful discussion and the language you use should reflect this approach. If you really must emphasise something, use a different word (or add in 'very') but avoid exaggerating, by minimising superlatives and words like 'massively', 'unbelievably' and so on.

Here are some non-academic, informal overstatements that shouldn't find their way into your essay:

> amazing
>
> awesome
>
> crazy
>
> gigantic
>
> great
>
> super
>
> terrific

Rather than resorting to words like these, if you're presenting some really significant facts, think about inserting a diagram or table for visual impact.

Keep your writing neutral. Try not to sound angry or overexcited, and don't get dewy eyed or sentimental. Avoid apologising for your work, and try stay grounded, dodging passages where you go off on flights of fancy. Have faith in the evidence and ideas you've gathered. Confidence should make your argument strong, without you having to use flowery, overblown language.

# Expanding contractions

In speech we tend to use contractions (like 'we're' instead of 'we are') unless we're trying to emphasise a point for effect, as in: 'Do not put your fingers in the socket.' And we use contractions in our informal writing. This book's written in an informal, chatty manner, and so we've used contractions throughout. But when we're working on academic papers and reports, we don't use contractions at all.

Table 10-4 shows you some common contractions and how you write them out in full.

| Table 10-4 | Contractions and Words in Full |
|---|---|
| *Contracted Words* | *Words in Full* |
| Can't | Cannot |
| Doesn't | Does not |
| Don't | Do not |
| Isn't | Is not |
| Shouldn't | Should not |
| We'll | We will |

At the proofreading stage, a useful and quick way to check for contractions is to use the 'search' function. Look up each contraction in the table just above this paragraph and also look up any others you might have used. Jump through the document and replace the contractions with the full versions. An even quicker technique is to use the 'search and replace' function, where you only have to type in the full word once.

Take care with this however, as you shouldn't replace contractions from direct quotations or dialogue. It wouldn't be a great to end your 'Gone With the Wind' essay if you replaced the contraction. 'Frankly, my dear, I do not give a damn' just doesn't have the same effect.

## Keeping your eyes peeled for clichés

Clichés are phrases that are overused. They're exhausted and tend to be meaningless and pointless. And they're often informal in tone, so they're doubly inappropriate for academic essays.

Identifying clichés is not always easy, because the phrases were once clever, witty and interesting, but have become part of how we speak and write every day.

The word cliché is French and refers to a printing or moulding technique for producing repeated images.

Clichés are lacking in imagination and apply in so many different circumstances that their generality makes them imprecise and open to misinterpretation. Many of the clichés that you should avoid don't crop up in academic writing anyway, but beware of the trendy, journalistic phrases that have entered the language from business and politics.

These phrases aren't really slang, but they're overused, or hackneyed and should be avoided as well. These are clichés. What happens with clichés is that they become tired and then lose their meaning, becoming a sort of padding. You can spot this in speech when people say things like:

> at the end of the day...
>
> I must say / I have to say...sticks out like a sore thumb
>
> the winds of change / sands of time
>
> the writing's on the wall
>
> calm before the storm

One good way to try and avoid cliches is to be very aware of anytime that you are trying to draw a comparison or conjour up an image. It tends to be at these times that these clichés sneak into writing.

The following paragraph is an extract from the entry on clichés in the *Economist Style Guide* (first published 1986; 2005:34):

> At this moment in time, with all due respect, let me take this window of opportunity to share with you a few clichés that some people may find particularly irritating. Basically, I would have to begin by kick-starting the economy, on a level-playing field, of course, and then, going forward, I would want to give 110 per cent to the creation of a global footprint before cherry-picking the co-workers to empower the underprivileged, motivate the on-train team and craft an exciting public space, not forgetting that, if the infrastructure is not to find itself between a rock and a hard place, at the end of the day we shall have to get networking and engage in some blue-sky thinking to push the envelope way beyond even our usual out-of-the-box metrics.

Don't worry if that makes no real sense to you – that's the point! The passage uses a lot of words, all of them recognisable, but none of them really saying anything.

Some common clichés found in student essays, with preferred alternatives, include:

| *Cliché* | *Alternative* |
| --- | --- |
| In today's society / these days | Today |
| Pros and cons | Advantages and disadvantages |
| To the best of my knowledge | (Nothing- just leave out) |
| The youth of today | Young people |
| The bottom line | Ultimately |
| By and large | Generally |

Student essays are clearer when they are free of cliché. For example:

> In this day and age, the effectiveness of garden design is measured through its creators touching base regularly with the end-users from everyday life. It must be a give and take process with people from all walks of life leaving no stone unturned to impact their ideas on the development of a garden which in the bitter end, meets everyone's needs.

Would read better as follows:

> The effectiveness of garden design is currently measured through regular communication between creators and users from everyday life. People from different backgrounds should be consulted for thorough discussion if people's needs are ultimately to be met.

## Steering clear of slang

The point of slang is to reinforce group identity and give members a sense of belonging. It's not that hard to spot if you try to imagine someone outside of the group trying to decipher what you're saying. The language that teenagers use is often incomprehensible to people of different generations, for example, or think of language that only pertains to a certain group of employees such as soldiers or librarians.

It's fine to use this in speech because the people with whom you're chatting can ask you for clarification if they're confused. In an essay, the marker can't check with you and so might not be clear what you actually mean.

In academic work, we're not thinking for a minute that you're starting your essay 'Waassuup! Yo, my essay's gonna blow you away.' Of course not. You may use phrases such as *the bottom line* or *one thing is certain,* but these are also slang, although not as obviously bad as waassuup.

Slang can come in and out of fashion and can cross over to become part of generally accepted language. The word or phrase is still likely to be informal, however, and therefore inappropriate for an academic essay. The word 'cool' for example, meaning 'trendy' or 'good', is a slang word that in the 1960s was only really used by teenagers and young people. It's now in the common vernacular and used by people of all ages. It's still not an academic word (unless you are actually describing a temperature).

Spot the slang phrases and words in the extracts below:

It is understandable that some prisoners would be gutted to learn that the education courses were being slashed. They would be bored out of their minds and it would be like a bubble had burst. Time heals all wounds and they would get over it though.

Global warming is the kind of thing that people get really wound up about, but no one can prove it.

Did you spot the slang? Better alternatives supplied in brackets.

Gutted (deeply disappointed)

Slashed (cut drastically)

bored out of their minds (bored)

a bubble had burst (it would be a dramatic change)

Time heals all wounds (this is cliché as well as slang and so I would suggest something like, 'in time they would become used to . . .')

get over it though (recover)

people get really wound up about (upsets people / worries people/ makes people anxious)

# Using a wide range of language

One way to please your tutor is to vary the words you use and show the extent of your vocabulary. To come across as an accomplished writer, you need to avoid repetition, which is using the same old words time and time again, and instead make use of *synonyms* (words that mean the same). You can also play around with nouns and verbs from the same word family.

Think of the verb 'go down'. Synonyms include 'fall', 'decrease', 'decline', 'drop', 'sink', even 'plummet'. Each has its own nuances of meaning and may be more applicable in certain situations, but the following may give you an idea of how a bit of variety can lend more interest to your text.

> The number of students doing university degrees in chemistry is going down. The number is going down because the number of students taking chemistry at A level is going down. The Ministry of Education is investigating why the numbers are going down and hopes to stop them going down by attracting more chemistry teachers.

Or:

> The number of students doing university degrees in chemistry is falling. This decrease is because of the drop in students taking the subject at A level. The Ministry of Education is investigating the fall in numbers and hopes to halt the decline by attracting more teachers of the subject.

Notice how the second sentence avoids the repetition of 'going down' in the first example by using a variety of synonyms and by changing the sentence structure so that nouns (decrease, drop, fall, decline) are used in place of the verb. The word 'chemistry', which is mentioned three times in the first text, occurs only once in the second, as the word 'subject' refers to it instead.

 If you feel that you're weak in the vocabulary department, then use the dictionary and/or thesaurus features in your word-processing software. They may not carry enough detail for your purposes, however, so you should equip yourself with a more substantial and detailed reference book. Costly? Not necessarily, but you may want to put it on your Christmas list.

## Using the right specialist words

Each specialist field has its own vocabulary, and words used in the real world may have a slightly narrower or modified meaning within that field. In addition, some terms are used only within the field and rarely in the outside world. Think of this as a secret language that only the initiated employ. This is often termed 'jargon', and every walk of life has it, from brain surgeons to car salespeople. (Apologies for offending any car salespeople.) It allows users to communicate more quickly and efficiently than if they ramble about what they want to say. The more you're exposed to jargon, the more you start using it yourself.

If you *are* using jargon, check that you've got the right word! Students often use jargon without fully grasping its meaning. Jargon may sound pretentious and make students seem rather silly, especially when they've misunderstood the words, which isn't unusual. You really do come across as a bit dim if you pretend to know the insider language of your area of study but get it wrong! A specialist dictionary probably exists for your field of study, and you should use it. Otherwise, note carefully the terminology that the books and journals on your reading list use, and employ the specialised vocabulary that they do.

Sometimes you find that different experts use terms in dissimilar ways. You should make clear what you mean by a given term and define it in order to show that you know what you're talking about, thus avoiding any possible misinterpretation. You're as well to say something like 'The term X is used here to mean Y, as used by Smith (2001).' By referring to the expert, Smith, and the work (published in 2001; see Chapter 14 for more about the list of references) you're making perfectly clear what you're talking about.

Also be sure to understand that some words that you use in everyday language, such as 'criticise' have a different meaning in academic circles. You may think about how your sister criticised you for something you said or did, but in your essays a criticism is a more formal weighing up of pros and cons. Being critical of your siblings is about showing disapproval, but in scholarly work you're looking for reasons and potential gaps in logic.

Don't overdo the jargon. You can't avoid the words and phrases that get your ideas across to people who understand your area of study, but that's not the same as peppering your writing with deliberately complex words in order to impress.

## *Minimising your use of long words*

Academic essays use a mix of simple and more complex vocabulary. In academic work, you're unlikely to be able to avoid long and unfamiliar words, because of the technical nature of the subject under discussion (see the previous section for more on jargon). Since you need to reply on complex words for the technical aspects of your argument, you should really try to make the rest of your work easy to understand by using shorter, simpler words.

Long or unusual words can make a passage seem complex. Short and common words are easier to read and leave the reader with a simple, clear effect.

You need to use your judgement. Table 10-5 gives some examples of words that you can simplify:

| Table 10-5 | Substituting Long for Short |
|---|---|
| *Long Words* | *Shorter Equivalents* |
| Ameliorate | Improve |
| Commencement | Start |
| Utilise | Use |

Can you see that the short words are more commonly used and read better?

Where you aren't sure of the meaning of a long word, you're always best to avoid it entirely. Here are some (real) examples of students misusing long words, with the presumed correct word in brackets:

It is better to have an idiosyllabic approach than a traditional one. (idiosyncratic?)

The children's behaviour was far from exemplified on the visit. (exemplary?)

The origination of the idea was from the eighteenth century. (origin?)

Passing the test is manifold. (mandatory?)

He created a paradox that is used to this day. (paradigm?)

Rote learning incumbents pupils with ideas. (inculcates?)

Know what a word means when you use it. In the examples, some of the errors aren't even real words, but most are and so a spell check doesn't identify the problem. Don't force your reader to guess what you mean.

## Substituting phrasal verbs

Something to look out for in your writing is the use of *phrasal verbs*, which are verbs expressed in two or more words rather than one. People use these a lot when they're speaking, so phrasal verbs often sound colloquial and out of place in an academic essay. When you write, you can often use an alternative single word that's slightly more formal, and this may lend a more serious tone to your essay.

For example, look for 'carry out' an investigation and replace it with 'conduct'. Similarly, instead of 'look into' a question, write 'investigate'. Table 10-6 gives you some more examples.

| Table 10-6 | Phrasal Verbs and Their More Formal Equivalents |
|---|---|
| *Phrasal Verbs* | *Equivalents* |
| bring up (a question) | raise |
| come about | happen |
| get rid of | eliminate |
| put up with | tolerate |
| turn down | reject |

Can you see how the words in the right-hand column have a slightly heavier feel to them? As you read around your subject, you come into contact with a wide range of verbs like these. Perhaps they don't slip readily off your tongue, but, as you become more familiar with them, they begin to come more frequently to your pen (or fingers).

The more you read academic texts, the more easily you pick up these formal words, and before long you're using them like an expert. As with everything else in life, practice makes perfect (well, a lot better, anyway).

## *Never using formatting or punctuation for effect*

The purpose of punctuation is for clarity, not to shock or surprise the reader. Similarly, the recommended formatting of an academic essay is designed to make the work easy to read and assess. You shouldn't deviate from the conventions in order to achieve a dramatic effect. Doing so makes your writing seem journalistic and reduces its academic impact.

Your facts, figures, ideas and argument should be persuasive without you having to force a particular emphasis into your sentences. When authors do this a lot, they're almost shouting in your ear and gesticulating wildly. The reader feels that the author has no confidence that the words can speak for themselves.

Here are some examples of what *not* to do:

- ✔ Using bold for emphasis: Local councils have a **responsibility** to care for their elderly populations.

- ✔ Using italics for emphasis: The council-run bus services are appalling and *very* expensive.

- ✔ Using different fonts and font sizes for emphasis: On every street corner there is **graffiti** and **litter**.

- ✔ Using exclamation marks for emphasis: The leaflets from the council are not even available in Braille!

- ✔ Using capital letters for emphasis: I have NO IDEA how the councillors managed to get elected.

# Remaining Objective

In academic writing you are aiming to present evidence and evaluate it as clearly as you can. You are not asked to write about personal beliefs or prejudices. In our everyday language we tend to show how we feel about certain things, ideas and people and in informal conversation this is fine. In academic writing, it is not fine. Even where you are asked for your views and opinions, these should be linked to the evidence you are evaluating and not to some long-held, unquestioned belief. Be careful with your language and try to eradicate bias coming through from the words you select. You'll find that reading the prescribed texts set out by your course tutors will lead you into the kinds of language you should be using.

Some of the texts may be older or from another culture. For example books from the USA may use 'handicapped' to describe people with disabilities. This word is not really used in the UK and is considered offensive. It is being phased out in the USA now, but even in texts from 2006, you could find it used commonly.

## Avoiding biased language

Make sure that you use politically correct terminology. Fashions in language do change over time, but you should definitely avoid gender-biased language (*mankind, fireman, air hostess*) and use gender-neutral terms instead (*humanity, firefighter, flight attendant*).

The same is true of racist language, homophobic language and loaded language used to describe people with disabilities. In general, prefer the second list to the first:

| Biased, loaded language | Better wording |
|---|---|
| Dyslexics | Children with dyslexia |
| Handicapped | Person with disability |
| Spastic | Person with muscular dystrophy |
| Blacks and whites | Black people/White people |
| Hispanics | Be specific, i.e. Cubans / Colombians |
| Hearing impaired | people prefer Deaf or deaf (you'll need to check) |
| Autistic | People with autism |

*What you're aiming for is to be objective, rather than personal. The emphasis of your writing should be on information, evidence and facts, rather than your personal opinions.*

Language is dynamic. African Caribbean people in the UK were known as Afro-Caribbeans, for example, but this has fallen out of favour. Children who are cared for by the state are sometimes known as Looked After Children now, but some prefer to be referred to as Children in Care. Some people object to being called lesbian or gay and others object to being called homosexual. Check with your tutor if in doubt about the terms to use and those to avoid.

When you are comparing minority groups with the rest of the population, avoid the word 'normal' as it implies that the minority is abnormal. When you think about it, none of us is really 'normal'; we all have our quirks and differences.

Use the pronouns 'he' and 'she' with care (flick to Chapter 8 for more on pronouns). Don't assume that 'he' is the doctor and 'she' is the nurse! Misunderstandings can occur over which person a pronoun refers to, especially when you're writing about several different people, so do check that your reader's clear who 'he' or 'she' is in each case.

An example we've seen in several books about teaching is that the writer explains from the start that 'she' refers to the teacher and 'he' to the student throughout the book. Nothing politically incorrect or devious is implied here, It's just a practical solution to a tricky language issue in the interests of clarity.

# Being Clear, Concise and Precise

Many students fall into the trap of assuming that writing in a formal academic style must be dry and complicated. They fill their essays with convoluted phrases, extended sentences and meaningless waffle. Instead of achieving the desired effect of impressing the reader, they end up with a complicated, confusing, woolly essay.

For your reader to appreciate your argument, your writing needs to be clear, simple and to the point.

## Being specific

In an academic essay, a succinct, authoritative nature characterises good writing. Neither of those factors can exist if you fill your work with generalisations. Use specific language throughout and refer directly to evidence and theory rather than making broad assumptions.

In addition, don't be vague. For example, 'We interviewed some people' doesn't cut the mustard in a uni essay – change it to 'We interviewed ten people' or whatever number's appropriate.

## Cutting out unnecessary fluff

We all tend to use extraneous words in speech, and that can be quite irritating, but in writing the issue's more significant. Essays have word limits, and you shouldn't waste your allowance on words that don't say anything much.

In order to get your ideas across, use the words you need and no more.

### Untangling your language

Here are some language mishaps you may encounter:

- **Tautologies – repeating what you've already said**: Reverse backwards; myself personally; ways and means (only one word from each of these phrases is required).

- **Pleonasms – using excess words:** A new innovation; a young newborn; please repeat that again (remove *new, young* and *again*).

- **Redundancies – more of something than you need:** Please also bring it as well; it's incredibly unbelievable; they invented it when it was original (get rid of *as well, incredibly* and *when it was original*).

Tautologies are particularly common in students' essays. Table 10-7 outlines some that are frequently used in common usage by many people in general (just kidding!).

| Table 10-7 | Shedding Light on Tautologies |
|---|---|
| *Tautology* | *Why It's Wrong* |
| Revert back | To revert means *to go back* |
| The final results/end results | Results are always as a consequence, so they're 'final' or 'end'. You may have interim findings, but take care with *results*. |
| Very/quite/extremely unique | It's either unique or it's not. Unique means one of a kind. |
| Past history | You can't have any other type of history. You can use ancient or modern, but they're both past. |
| Join together | By joining, you are coming together. |
| Rough estimate | You can't have a precise estimate. |
| Regular routine | Irregular routine isn't routine at all. Routine has to be regular to be routine. |
| Consensus of opinion | Consensus means an agreement or compromise and implies opinion. |
| Difficult problem | Difficult's a synonym of problematic and so they're the same thing. |
| Advance warning | You can only warn someone of something before the event. If it's during or after, you're describing or commenting. |

Once you become aware of common language tangles, you may notice that you have favourites – combinations of words that you tend to use frequently. We all have a pattern in our use of language. We favour certain words, and the way we string our words together can be different from the way our friend does, although we're both speaking the same language. So you may have some 'tics' that identify you as a speaker and also as a writer. You need to be aware of what you put down on paper, because some of these idiosyncrasies may not be appropriate to academic writing. Tautologies are one, and once you are aware of them, be on your guard. Keeping a note of your own tics is a good idea so that when you're writing another essay you have a checklist of what to look out for.

## *Avoiding padding*

Check for words that are superfluous and that you can eliminate without changing the meaning. Adjectives or intensifiers often fall into this category – words such as 'brilliant', 'definitely', 'literally' and the much overused 'really'. These words tend to make your text sound colloquial and add nothing in an academic context. Make a (black)list of them and go through your essay with a fine-tooth comb eliminating them.

Each word in your essay should be there for a good reason. Padding and bulking out your essay don't qualify as good reasons!

In general, you should prefer one word to two. Take a look at Table 10-8 for examples of long-winded wording matched with simpler alternatives.

| Table 10-8 | Condensing Text |
|---|---|
| *Unnecessarily Wordy* | *Simple* |
| Research has been done that shows | Research shows |
| Strategies or ways of helping could exist that would help children by | Strategies can help children by |
| On a continuous basis | Continually |
| Most people generally are of the belief that | People think |
| In 50 years of existence from now | In 50 years |
| In his book *Offices,* published in 2001, the author Brent says | Brent says (2001) |
| It can maybe have an impact on the results, causing | It could cause |
| In view of the reasons that | Because of |
| Statistics can be shown to demonstrate and explain that | Statistics explain |
| What I am going to show when I write this essay is | I will show |
| It appears that there are some concerns about the writing | Concerns exist about the writing |
| The way in which | How |

Leave out unnecessary preamble as well. You don't even need to state that you are going to demonstrate something 'in this essay'. We know it's in your essay – we're reading it already We can't think of a single occasion when these phrases are helpful:

It is important to say, in addition . . .

It may be considered that . . .

It could be recalled that . . .

It is interesting to consider that . . .

These words can add character to speech, but they're out of place in formal academic writing.

The earlier section 'Substituting phrasal verbs' can also help you write more concisely.

### *Forgetting fillers*

*Fillers* are unnecessary words that are appropriate in conversation but extraneous in written language. Basically, what we're talking about is the kind of extra sort of words, you know, that don't add anything to the meaning, but kind of make the whole thing sound just a bit more, you know, friendly. Okay, you get the idea!

Rewriting that long sentence to cut out the fillers, it would look like this:

> Basically, what we're talking about is the kind of extra sort of words, you know, that don't add anything to the meaning, but kind of make the whole thing sound just a bit more , you know, friendly.

You can see how much more succinct our wording is without these filler words.

Table 10-9 lays out some of the words you should avoid as much as possible.

| Table 10-9 | Common Fillers to Avoid |
|---|---|
| *Where They Appear* | *Fillers* |
| Anywhere | just; even; basically; well; really; a lot; pretty (meaning quite); sort of; kind of |
| At the start of a sentence | well; anyway; like, you know; right; okay; so |
| At the end of a sentence | if you see what I mean; like; right; if you get me |

### Condensing text using the 'Who does what?' technique

One way to reduce extra words is to use the *Who does what* technique:

1. **Start with the subject.** Ask yourself who's doing something in your sentence, and write that down.

2. **Move on to the verb.** What is the subject *doing?*

3. **Find the other subject.** *What* is the subject doing?

This method makes you reduce words. Table 10-10 shows you the technique in action.

| Table 10-10 | The Who Does What Technique |
| --- | --- |
| *Original Sentence* | *Sentence Following Who Does What Technique* |
| The method is widely used by psychologists and is known as the psychological digit-span test. (15 words) | Psychologists refer to this commonly-used measure as the digit-span test. (11 words) |
| The theory was introduced by Piaget and is called cognitive dissonance. (11 words) | Piaget introduced cognitive dissonance theory. (5 words) |
| In my essay I will demonstrate how the Government's most recent policy contradicts the findings of major research projects in the area. (22 words) | I will demonstrate how policy contradicts current governemental research. (9 words) |

Another way to help you reduce extraneous words is to edit your paragraphs in a different format. If you lay them out so that they're in a column only about 40 characters wide (you can do this by resetting the margins), you can see the number of lines really clearly. Then, instead of trying to think about cutting out words, aim to reduce the number of lines but keep the meaning. Because of the layout, you see a more dramatic result than when you try to trim words off here and there with the normal layout. If you're a visual learner, this is a satisfying way to edit.

In trying to cut out words, take care not to end up with a stiff, terse essay. It needs to flow and read well, so don't simply chop words out. Read your essay through and check that it sounds reasonable and not robotic.

# Don't not do that . . .

As you write, avoid double negatives because this is an unnecessary complication that confuses your message. See the better alternatives in italics:

✔ The idea is not ineffective. *The idea is effective.*

✔ Research is never a useless activity. *Research is a useful activity.*

✔ Twenty of the children were not absent. *Twenty children were present.*

## *Steering clear of complicated sentences*

Your reader's going to thank you for writing simple, clear, declarative sentences. Simple and clear sentences aren't always very short, but they definitely shouldn't be really long. A sentence of more than 40 words can be difficult for people to understand. You need to be sensible and aim for clarity.

One way to shorten unwieldy sentences is to break them into shorter ones. Look at where you have commas and see whether a full stop and a new sentence are more effective. Don't overload your sentences.

Imagining who you're writing for as you go along can sometimes help. Picture a small group of your fellow students. Are they going to understand what you're saying? Is your work eloquent enough to read out to your tutor?

You should stick to only one main idea in each sentence, and this helps with clarity. Chapter 9 has more info on writing good sentences.

## *Writing statements not questions*

You can easily drift into writing a chain of questions instead of providing statements. This is a particularly dangerous technique if you're writing about something rather controversial, because you lose your grip on the points you're making and leave the reader with a series of queries and nothing firm.

Read this extract from a student's essay. She starts off reasonably and then descends into a list of questions.

> Teachers need to understand enough basic child development to know what behaviours are typical for children in the classroom. Does their training cover the features of learning difficulties? How can they recognise children with problems? If they do not read the texts about behaviour as part of their course, how can they help children? How could they recognise children's problems? How would they know what to do to help? How would they know what was normal?

Now look at this better version:

> Teachers need to understand enough basic child development to know what behaviours are typical for children in the classroom. In order to be able to recognise different and troubling behaviours, teachers need knowledge of what would be considered typical for children at different ages. Through their training, teachers could be helped to learn about the psychology that underpins children's behaviour.

Although the second paragraph lacks quotations and any evidence (it's a first draft), it's a far better attempt than the first one. The first paragraph leaves the reader wondering what point it's making. It's starting to sound like an angry rant and it isn't presenting any solutions to the problem that it's identified.

 Even if you think you've identified some great questions, don't merely list them. If you can't turn them into statements, you either need to increase your research or go back and review what you're trying to say.

# Finding Your Own Voice

When you start writing essays at uni, the academic style can feel awkward and stilted because it's so different from the way you speak. It's different from writing a letter to a friend, for example, because that's chatty and reflects speaking quite closely. You may not have had to write English in this style before coming to university, and you may need a number of attempts before you get into the swing of it. Be patient: by the end of your course, you'll find you've got the hang of this particular way of writing.

## Seeing your writing as part of a process

Don't expect to get writing in an academic style spot on the first time you try. You may do (well done if so), but most students take a while to get into their scholarly stride. Think of each essay as part of your overall degree rather than as a stand-alone piece of work. Essays do stand alone in some senses, but your degree's more about improving and developing than achieving from the first day.

 On many degree courses in the UK, the first year's work is designed as an entry to the subsequent years. Often the marks you get in your first year don't actually count towards the final grade of your degree. Once you're aware of this, you can relax a little and reframe your early essay writing as a formative experience where you can explore a little and try out different ways of working.

 Be really clear about your academic regulations. You need to know whether your marks do count and how many attempts you can have if you don't make the grade first time. You should also find out your tutor's views on late work, extensions and deferrals.

## Working with feedback

In Chapter 17 we take you through dealing with the feedback that your tutor provides on your essay. You need to engage with that feedback, but you can go further.

If your university runs writing courses or seminars, join up and share your writing with others. Alternatively, initiate a more informal writing group among people on your course. Meeting up regularly to review one another's work can be really helpful. If you're working on similar projects, it's useful support, but more relevant here are the emerging differences between your work and that of your fellow students. When establishing your voice and personal style, try to identify what tends to be typical of your writing and approach. See how this varies from what your colleagues say and do in their essays.

 Sharing your work helps you identify your emerging voice and forces you to build on your own strengths as well as face up to areas that you need to improve.

## *Taking it at your own pace*

Developing your academic voice is a complex process. It's about language, of course, but it's also about building your knowledge and familiarity with your discipline. That involves discovering new structures and formats, as well as new ideas and concepts. You're being initiated into a new sphere of understanding, and you need time to get on track.

Follow the advice in this book to ensure that you manage the conventions of your new field, but try not to let the rules suffocate what you want to say. You may be thinking about the ideas in colloquial language, for example. When you write, you need to sharpen up your style but still get across what you want to say.

Give yourself time – good academic writing is often painful to produce because it has to be clear, accurate and thorough.

# Part IV
# Tightening Your Structure and Organisation

'Hullo...Guinness Book of Records?...
I've just written the world's longest essay.'

## *In this part . . .*

In this part, we deal with the nuts and bolts of putting your essay together. We show you how to structure and write each part of your essay: beginning, middle and end. Each part is quite distinctive, and we explain these differences and what you need to do with each to get top marks.

We also guide you through the tricky business of using quotations and compiling comprehensive and accurate bibliographies or reference lists. You've nearly finished!

# Chapter 11

# Preparing the Aperitif:
# The Introduction

## In This Chapter

▶ Finding out what your introduction needs to do
▶ Reviewing alternative approaches to starting your essay
▶ Weeding out common errors

**Y**our introduction is the first part of your conceptual frame-work and helps put your essay into context. You need to make an effort with your introduction because it sets the tone for your essay. You're setting the mood for the person marking your work, and you want him or her to be in a good frame of mind and feel favourable towards you, not immediately put off your work.

In this chapter we talk you through introductions, helping you understand what to cover and how, and what to avoid like the plague.

 You must write the title in full. Not only does it remind the tutor what he or she's marking, but it helps you keep in mind what you should be writing about, ensuring that your work stays relevant.

## Understanding the Aims of Your Introduction

Your introduction's like an opening shot of a film or an overview map at the start of a journey. It provides a sense of what's to come and places your work in a context. It should give the reader a feeling about what's to follow.

In the introduction you need to cover the basic outline of what you're writing about, the rationale for the essay, and some information about the kinds of arguments you want to make.

You should start by clearly addressing the title, question or theme of your essay. Your introductory paragraph needs to establish the main ideas of your essay. If you write it well, the introduction can achieve this interestingly, capturing the reader's attention and making clear why the topic's important.

If you make the opening of your essay clear, direct and succinct, your reader feels that the essay's likely to address relevant issues. This is a good start.

By the end of your introduction, the reader should understand the following:

✔ Your interpretation of the question or title and your understanding of what you have to do

✔ Reasons for bothering to discuss the question, and your explanation of the value of the area under discussion

✔ Any main theories or theorists you may be relying on and a suggestion of the direction you're heading in when answering the question

# Knowing What to Include

Unsure where to start? Don't worry – we've got the lowdown on how to write an interesting, effective intro.

## Covering the conventions of intros

In your introduction you usually need to:

✔ Confirm the topic area or context.

✔ Verify the purpose of your essay.

✔ Identify the main issues or concepts.

✔ State the relevance or importance of the topic.

✔ Give a sense of the structure and/or coverage of your essay.

Here are some pointers for going about these tasks:

✔ Without repeating the question, you can interpret it, showing what it's about. You translate it as you put it into your own words, reinforcing that you know what each part means and what you need to do to provide an answer. You're trying to identify the central assertion or claim in the question.

✔ You can say why the question's important in the field by contextualising it and raising the main issues. You're picking out the key areas for discussion (or 'problematising' the topic) and considering which aspects you can challenge.

✔ You can provide a sense of the viewpoint or perspective you're adopting in your answer by mentioning any specific thinkers or schools of thought to which you refer.

✔ You may summarise how you answer the question, saying what you cover in order to satisfy the criteria.

✔ Depending on the question and your work, you can reveal or hint at the conclusion in your introduction.

Here are some ideas of phrases you can use in your introduction:

✔ **Showing the importance of a topic:**

   • One of the most significant issues in X today is . . .

   • Since the incidence of X has increased, Y has become a vital . . .

   • The key factor in X is the development of Y, which . . .

✔ **Pointing out a concern or problem:**

   • Various theorists have questioned the role of X in Y . . .

   • Unfortunately, despite the developments in the field, X has suffered . . .

   • Despite the success of X, Y has become . . .

   • Findings from X have been contradictory . . .

✔ **Showing your viewpoint:**

   • I will argue that . . .

   • In this essay I will show . . .

   • The aim of this essay is to support the . . .

   • This essay presents a critique of . . .

✔ **Revealing the structure of the essay:**

   • Starting with an overview of X, I go on to . . .

   • Initially I will show X, before explaining . . .

   • The first part of the essay will show how . . .

Sometimes, essay questions give you a certain amount of choice, such as picking either one example or another for the main focus (for example, 'Discuss difficulties in speech and language development in toddlers by using a case study of *either* a child with a hearing impairment *or* a child with a physical difficulty.'). In these cases you should be specific in the introduction about which choice you've made. Similarly, if you have a very wide topic to discuss, you can let the reader know that you're aware of the broad issues but have chosen to focus on one or two areas for reasons that you outline.

You're probably also wondering how long your intro should be. Chapter 3 gives you a basic rule of thumb for chapter introductions: about 10 per cent of the total word count. If you're worried that your introduction's too long, check your essay against this rule. If you're worried that it's too short, stop worrying! Tutors much prefer to read an essay where the student gets stuck into the argument rather than long, rambling, irrelevant waffle.

## Defining keywords and terms

Opening an essay with a list of definitions of key terms and words is very tempting. Doing so seems logical because you're preparing the ground for your discussion and you do have to make things clear for the reader.

However, you need to take care with providing definitions in your introductory section. A list can easily develop where you say:

> 'I am going to discuss the idea of X, which is defined as Y, and then go onto review Q, which means P. I will then show how Z is important, interpreting Z as defined by W.'

Introductions like this are no more than a catalogue of definitions, and they're really dull to read.

Generally, unless the title specifically asks you to provide definitions, you're best to avoid them. What you understand by the question should be clear in your more general writing, and you may cover it through your interpretation of the question.

However, instances do exist where you need to define key terms and words in the intro, such as when you find conflicting ways of describing an important concept for your work. In these cases you briefly state which understanding you're using and its source. For example, if you want to talk about a child who's hearing impaired but who lives and communicates largely with hearing people, you may use *deaf* with a lower-case initial letter. If you're talking about the community of hearing-impaired people, you may use the word with a capital letter: *Deaf.* These different nuances of description are important, and tutors expect you to explain them.

## Answering the question that your tutor's set

The author Carrie recently marked an essay where the student put as the title 'Dealing with underachievement in schools', whereas the title she set asked 'What is the nature of underachievement, and how can teachers support children at risk of failing to achieve?'.

What Carrie asked and what the student answered were two different things. The essay dealt with underachievement in a broad sense but didn't provide a definition of the area and didn't talk about what teachers can do either.

The result? The student failed. What the student wrote was reasonable for the title he adapted, but on this module students were required to use one of the titles Carrie presented. If he'd copied out the title correctly, the student would have realised that he'd completely forgotten to tackle the aspects about the teacher's role.

Here are ways to introduce definitions, if you think you need them:

In this essay, when describing Y, I am using the term X as introduced by W, because this is the version usually understood by nurses in NHS hospitals.

X is a controversial issue that has been described in a variety of ways, and in this essay I will predominantly be using the work of Y and her critics and will therefore use the term W to refer to the discussion of X.

For this paper, I am referring throughout to X, because this is now the accepted term in the field (Theorist, 2000:35).

It is necessary to clarify what is meant by X.

In the field of psycholinguistics, several definitions of X can be found.

Theorist's 2003 definition of X is commonly used (such as by Y, W and Z).

## *Writing a thesis statement*

A thesis statement is less grand than it sounds! It's the sentence (or two) where you state your view on the topic. It's your viewpoint or argument – literally your statement on the *thesis* (that is the argument, hypothesis, notion or idea).

A thesis statement:

- Lets your tutor know your interpretation of the question
- Gives a sense of what you plan to cover
- Shows that you've directly addressed the set question

If you can't summarise your ideas into a couple of sentences for a thesis statement, rethink what you're planning to cover, because it may be too wide.

The nature of your thesis statement depends on the type of essay you're writing:

- **If you're analysing,** you break down ideas and make some of kind of judgement. You back up your thoughts with evidence and illustrations.

- **If you're making an argument for or against something,** you make claims that you substantiate with evidence. You need to try to convince your tutor that your position is logical and that you support it sufficiently.

- **If you're explaining,** that is, writing an expository paper, you demonstrate your thorough understanding with many examples and illustrations.

Deciding what your ideas are is the first stage on the road to writing your thesis statement. Often students claim that they aren't sure what they think about an essay title, but some simple questions help them hone their ideas and isolate their views. They have the ideas all along but aren't sure how to access or express them confidently.

Consider the following if you're a bit stuck on what you think:

- What's the question actually about? Do you really understand it? How can you reword it so that it makes more sense to you?

- Is your best friend, mum or neighbour likely to agree with your view? How can you persuade these people that they're wrong and you're right?

- Do you care about this topic? If so, why is it important? If not, why does the tutor feel that it merits an essay question? The tutor must have chosen to ask this for a reason – what can that be?

✔ Can you convince your tutor that you are able to back up your viewpoint?

✔ What can you read or research to support your case?

✔ Do you have any evidence to back up what you think about the question? Where do your views come from? Can you support them?

## Exploring alternative openings

You may want to introduce your essay in a more original and interesting manner, and this can be a great way to engage your reader from the outset. Here's a selection of possible alternative essay openings. You can start with:

✔ **A concession:** Open by showing the opposite view from the one you plan to argue yourself. You can say: 'Piaget demonstrated that very young children can only view the world from one perspective: their own (1936). In this essay I will show how his critics have proven that his age-related stages are too rigid to usefully describe cognitive development in the under-fives.'

✔ **A paradox or irony:** Show how views have changed over the years. For example: 'Freire was exiled from Brazil in 1964 for his groundbreaking work in educating the poorest classes, only to be brought back as São Paulo's Minister for Education in 1988.'

✔ **A quotation:** You may have the perfect sentence to set the tone for your paper, and this can be a dramatic way to kick off. Be sure to reference clearly (see Chapter 14), or you destroy the effect completely!

✔ **A table or chart:** You may want to make use of the visual impact of a graph or pie chart to show where your essay's located and how it develops. If you're starting with a table or chart, be sure to include at least a sentence explaining what the table's about and a clear heading.

✔ **An example or illustration:** Starting with an example can bring a sense of immediacy to your essay, showing how and why the area's important through focusing on practical applications of ideas.

✔ **Dialogue:** If it links to your topic, some illustrative discussion can be a lively way to begin the essay. Keep the discussion short and relevant, however.

✔ **Some detailed background:** Make links to other essays you've written (without plagiarising yourself), so that you can show how this work builds on your previous essays and on interests you've explored.

✔ **Your rationale:** This is an explanation of your reasons for writing the essay. It must be more than 'I am writing this essay because it is part of my course' and is most appropriate when you have to design your own essay title. In such cases, you may start: 'In this essay I have chosen to focus on the X aspect of Y because it links directly to my work placement/ career plans/reasons for choosing this degree . . .'

Although these are all suitable introductory ideas, not all tutors necessarily welcome them and they certainly don't suit all essay titles. Choose with care and be sure not to use an idea that your tutor may frown on. If in doubt, keep to more conventional ideas.

# Coming Back to the Introduction at the End

If your introduction's the first thing you write, you may find that your writing's really waffly and bland because you aren't sure what you're writing about yet. If that's the case, abandon the introduction for now and get stuck in to the main body of your essay. Rather than sitting with a blank screen and a flashing cursor, get on with organising your notes and writing your argument. You can come back to your intro later on.

In fact, some people deliberately leave writing their introduction until they've completed the rest of the essay. They find ploughing on with the main argument easier.

Whether you've had a go at a first draft of your introduction or not, come back to your introduction once your essay's almost complete. You can review what you wrote and adjust it to reflect your new, improved understanding. You can also change the tone, which is probably more tentative than you now feel, because you have evidence to support your ideas.

Some people think that you shouldn't start writing until you have a really clear idea of what you want to say, while others don't mind starting off a little vaguely. Whichever way you like to work, coming back to the introduction at the end is a good idea.

## What if I don't need an introduction at all?

Some academic staff prefer an essay that launches straight into the argument. That's better than having a poorly written, rambling introduction, of course, but most essays benefit from some scene setting or early explanation to help the reader get his or her bearings.

We always advise checking with the tutor who's likely to mark your work before you decide to be too radical.

# *Avoiding Common Mistakes*

Tutors see the same errors in students' introductions time and time again. One of the most prevalent problems is stuffing intros full of empty nonsense and bland nothings.

Here are some actual student examples of empty essay openings that don't say anything at all. They aren't exactly wrong, just pointless (although some are very poorly expressed):

> The Science Museum is a museum about science that people visit when they want to find out about science and this essay is about the Science Museum.

> In this essay I will show how Piaget thought that children are young and innocent and they should be allowed to think and learn.

> Plato was important as a thinker and his thinking is still thought about now as much as it was when he was alive.

> In this essay I will discuss gifted teenagers based on the fact that there are many very bright teenagers who are clever and intelligent.

 Generating a great deal of empty waffle through saying nothing is easy. If you haven't anything to say that's general and meaningful then don't write anything. You may find that later in the writing process you can clearly see what's missing.

In addition, be careful with the following ways of writing introductions. They're all fairly common in student essays and none is really effective. They betray a lack of direction and show that the students have probably not come back to check their introductions once they've finished their essays.

✔ **Dictionary lists:** Here students provide a series of definitions of each of the keywords in the title. While dictionaries are useful for finding the meanings of words, they're less good at providing nuanced understandings of technical vocabulary. As well as a dry list, you end up with a series of definitions that don't reflect the meanings in your field.

✔ **Rewriting the question and nothing more:** Often the person marking your essay is the very same person who spent ages perfectly crafting the question you're answering. Put yourself at his or her desk for a moment and consider the dullness of rereading 50 versions of the same question slightly rejigged as everyone's opening paragraph. Not great.

✔ **Wikipedia facts and fun:** In these cases, students open with some 'interesting facts' that they've usually gleaned from an Internet site (and they're often not quite accurate; see Chapter 5 for details). The childhood experiences, star sign and home town of your main theorist are rarely relevant to your essay, so don't put them in your introduction.

# Chapter 12

# Serving the Main Course: The Essay's Body

. . . . . . . . . . . . . . . . . . . . . . . . . . . . . . . . . . . . . . . . . .

## In This Chapter

▶ Working out your opinions

▶ Writing descriptively, analytically and reflectively

▶ Developing your argument and keeping it balanced

▶ Including quotations

. . . . . . . . . . . . . . . . . . . . . . . . . . . . . . . . . . . . . . . . . .

*I*n this chapter we get down to the nitty-gritty of the main body of the essay. You need to get to grips with your argument and structure what you're going to say.

You may also find Chapter 3 on essay frameworks and Chapters 8, 9 and 10 on writing style useful as you create your essay.

## Developing a Position

The main body of your essay is all about having an opinion (a position) and arguing your case.

But expressing what you think is difficult if you aren't sure of your opinion in the first place. Take some time to work out your viewpoint, and writing the main body of your essay becomes far easier. You need to take a stand, and in order to do so, you need to question yourself about what you think in relation to the question you're answering or the title you're discussing.

When looking at an essay title, consider the following:

✔ **How much does the area interest you?** Is it an area that you already know about? Does it link in any way to your own life? If you have practical examples that may help later, you should make a note of them now.

✔ **Do you want to look at this topic from a particular perspective?**
Does it make a difference to your view that you're a woman or
a man, a parent, a person of a particular race or from a different culture to the mainstream? Identifying something that you
can bring to the question may help you decide how to progress, so if you are an experienced white-water rafter you may
have a quite specific view on the value of swimming lessons.
This could direct you to a particular angle on the essay..

✔ **How can you be objective?** You don't want to turn your essay
into a rant or personal opinion piece, so you need to step
back from your views after you establish what they are. Think
about the aspects of the topic that really grab you and those
that don't. Can you be completely dispassionate about the
whole area? If you can't, consider how you're going to manage
to be as objective as you need to be for academic work.

You have to gather evidence for your essay (see Chapters 4 and 5
and the later section 'Knowing what counts as evidence'). Let the
evidence influence your views on the topic, and don't necessarily
be hard and fast about what you think at the moment. Prepare for
your opinion to shift as your research deepens.

We encourage you to get in touch with how you feel about the
topic so that you can be sure to make a statement when you're
writing. At no point do we suggest that you can merely present
your opinion, unsupported, and that this is enough for an essay. It
isn't. However, starting with an idea of where you stand is good so
that you can see whether your position changes.

Generally, you can more easily write a strong argument if you take
a position on the topic in question. You should know the key sup-
porters and detractors of the position you adopt. You should also
be aware of the quality of the evidence that they use to support
their contentions.

You may want to present two sides to an argument as evenly as
you can. This is a good, balanced approach to take. (Whatever
your views, you need to present both sides of an argument.) If you
choose to adopt a very even approach, you still need to reach a
conclusion eventually, so bear in mind that you're looking for the
weight of evidence to help you decide one way or another.

Your ideas may change as you go along, but as soon as you've got
enough evidence, you should make up your mind about what you
think and get on with the essay. After all, you can change your
mind again once you've submitted your paper, but you do need to
get a move on now!

# Using Different Types of Writing

University-level essays demand three different styles of writing: descriptive, analytical and reflective. You need to be able to use these styles effectively in the main body of your essay, so in this section we outline how each of them works.

## Descriptive writing

You may use descriptive writing in your essay to tell the reader about the constituent parts of the concern you're discussing and to set the scene and context.

You use descriptive writing for:

✔ Answering the questions 'what?' 'where?' 'when?' and 'who?' (not 'why?' questions, however)

✔ Describing relationships

✔ Identifying factors

✔ Showing the order of something

✔ Stating, telling and explaining

Descriptive writing's useful for necessary context and background, but your tutor's most likely to prefer more analytical work for you to demonstrate your thinking.

Here's an example of descriptive writing. Notice that it's rich in adjectives and there's little evaluation. The words used are quite interesting (more what you'd expect in a novel than an academic text insome ways) words, but quite impartial in general as they describe rather than judge:

> The adult education centre was buzzing when I arrived to sit in on the Spanish class. During the day, the centre is part of the local Community College, but by night and at weekends adults are the focus. People with rolled-up yoga mats milled around the reception area together with others laden with Tupperware pots stuffed with ingredients for their cookery classes. I was trying to get a feel for the range of classes and consider the demographic some of which I did through the glossy brochure before arriving. The range of sessions reflected the local environment; not catering certificates, but Thai dinner party food; not English for Refugees, but Spanish for holidays. The cars in the parking area reflected the lights of the building as well as the affluence of the area; recent, shiny models . . . .

Take care, because in some essays descriptive writing doesn't attract the high grades that analytical writing does (see the following section). Your university provides you with criteria for assessment that highlight this, so do check what's expected of you.

## Analytical writing

Analytical writing is reasoned argument. It requires you to break something down into parts. What you're analysing may be any created work from a text, film or dance performance to a theory, policy or poem.

When writing analytically, you're:

- ✔ Considering the reliability of the source
- ✔ Evaluating the strengths and weaknesses of a position
- ✔ Identifying significant factors
- ✔ Picking out any underlying assumptions
- ✔ Showing the importance of something
- ✔ Weighing up the evidence

Critical argument is, by its nature, rather complex. Your structure must be really clear otherwise your reader can get lost in your work. The rules of thumb are as follows:

- ✔ Make your key point with clarity.
- ✔ Explain what you mean by breaking down some of the terms.
- ✔ Provide exemplars and explain these if required.

You need to build a logical sequence of points that lead to one another, and each point should deepen the argument. You should stick to one point per paragraph (see Chapter 9 for more help with writing paragraphs).

As you weigh up the evidence, consider these points:

- ✔ Think about the focus of the argument. What's your view on this? You should be able to summarise your position in a sentence or so.
- ✔ You need to be convincing, making thorough use of reason and argument.
- ✔ You need to provide evidence and evaluate this evidence in your essay, showing clearly how you're harnessing it to support

your points. This is the part that tutors are most interested to read. They like you to spot anything wrong with the research methods, for example. Perhaps you think that others have wrongly interpreted a theorist, and you have some evidence to back up your claim.

You're engaging in critical analysis and should be actively evaluating what you read. You're deciding how important or useful the research is and how it links to practice (where relevant). Most academic arguments are fairly subtle, and different views may seem close together, so you really need to read and reread to make sense of these ideas.

And don't forget to engage with any disagreements and counterarguments. If you pretend they don't exist, your tutor may point them out to you assuming that you weren't aware of them. You do need to mention them, demonstrating their inherent weaknesses and showing how your ideas and logical argument are considerably stronger.

You can anticipate some of the objections to your own work and ideas, even if you don't come across direct challenges in what you read. The best way to do this is to discuss the issues in class or with other students and your tutor. If you can't get hold of some genuine opposition, you can put yourself in the position of someone with the opposing view and try to pick holes in what you've presented.

If you aren't in the habit of trying out your ideas in a public arena (such as by speaking up in class), you can slip into the assumption that your ideas are so tame and sensible that everyone must definitely agree with you. Really think through potential objections and then boost your argument so that you win in any circumstances.

Here's an example of analytical writing. Compare the style to the descriptive writing a few paragraphs above this one:

Adult Education classes are frequently held in buildings such as schools or other community centres with teaching and sports facilities. It is not cost effective to have centres that are predominantly in use during evenings and weekends only and so it is better to combine functions. By evaluating the nature of classes available it is possible to draw conclusions about the demographic of the area, evaluating the wealth and social standing of the participants.

At Centre A most of the courses were leisure based and focused on hobbies, indicating people who have time available to pursue free-time activities. Centre B, by contrast, runs mainly award-bearing courses such as health and safety certificates, computer training and basic literacy and numeracy support (for the unemployed). The people attending Centre B are making up for gaps in their education rather than pursuing leisure activities.

Here's some of the language you may find useful when analysing:

✔ Why is X considered important?

✔ What does Y actually mean?

✔ How useful is X?

✔ What is the value of Y?

✔ How has X been developed/created?

✔ How does X work in Y context?

✔ Why is Y as it is?

✔ How is X structured?

## Reflective writing

Reflective writing uses a written exploration of personal experiences to inform current ideas and practices and sometimes to make suggestions for improvements for the future. In some practical fields such as child care or health, you may be asked to reflect on your experiences of a placement or work experience or your observations of a professional place or activity.

## Don't be afraid of being critical

Some students struggle with critical analysis because they wrongly define *criticism* in the same way that you may think about being negative, rude or unpleasant. You don't have to be an argumentative sort of person to construct a clear argument. You do need to be reasoned and thoughtful.

In scholarly work, *argument* means looking at pros and cons of an idea and weighing up evidence. What you're trying to do is present a persuasive and strong case that supports a particular viewpoint. You have to support the contentions you make with reasons and evidence, and these need to be valid and appropriate.

In an academic essay, you can write a critical paper that completely agrees with the theories you're discussing – what you're doing is showing how the argument is strong and supported by evidence.

Reflective writing's about:

- ✔ Exploring questions and concerns that you identify through observations and experience in the field

- ✔ Examining your ideas, thoughts, feelings and views following an experience

- ✔ Challenging existing perceptions and understandings

Reflection can be ongoing, where you jot down notes as you're having the experience, or you can do it after the fact. You can combine your notes from different occasions to show how perceptions change over time.

The nature of reflective work can be quite wide-ranging because the spectrum runs from very specific, focused reflection to broader, looser reflection. Its nature depends on the purpose of the work, but usually you need also to include some descriptive work (see the earlier section on this) to explain something of the setting in which the activities took place. You may also need to use analytical writing (see earlier), such as when reflective writing requires you to refer to literature.

If you've never had a piece of reflective writing marked, you should see whether your tutor's willing to meet you or look at a draft to check that you're on the right lines. Give him or her plenty of notice if you want help of this kind.

Sometimes your tutor may require reflective writing in different formats, some of which are more like essays than others:

- ✔ Diary entries

- ✔ Focused discussion of an event

- ✔ Narrative description and reflection

- ✔ Portfolio of experiences

- ✔ Summaries of diary entries

- ✔ Web entries or discussion

You need to think carefully about what to include. This list will help you review what's needed:

- ✔ Identify the issues you are considering

- ✔ Why are the issues significant?

- ✔ How do you feel about these issues?

- ✔ How involved are you in this situation?

✔ How does your involvement affect your responses?

✔ Why do you think you have these feelings?

✔ On balance, are the issues positive or negative?

✔ What further information might you require to improve or develop the situation?

✔ What further issues are raised through this reflection?

You are likely to be writing about something you have done and so a way of structuring this is to have:

✔ A very short description;

✔ Some detailed interpretation of what you have done (here's where you might refer to theory);

✔ A summary of the outcome; some consideration of future developments.

Here's an example of reflective writing:

> We had to design a poster to show some of our research about children playing and we divided the tasks up as equally as possible. We wanted to explore the ideas we read in Bruce (2003) about the importance of outdoor play for pre-school children. One of the team worked in a play centre and arranged to take photographs (with permission from parents). At first I was concerned that they would not really match the theories and I was not sure how valuable that part of the process would be. By the end, however, I realised that the photographs were actually the most important part of the poster as they made it eye-catching and people wanted to read what we had written.

Reflective writing is more informal than other types of academic essays and asks you for your viewpoints in ways that aren't applicable in more usual university essays. Because this type of writing's about personal experience, it requires self-awareness along with analysis and an open mind.

# Keeping a Balanced View

You can keep a balanced view only if you've read enough about the subject and examined relevant information. You need to consider viewpoints other than your own, present them fairly and analyse them critically.

Throughout your writing, you present your own view balanced with those of others. You should use recognised thinkers in the field (they're the ones listed in your course bibliography) – their views form the evidence for your considered evaluative view.

## Knowing what counts as evidence

Different fields use different forms of evidence. Evidence doesn't have to be the results of an experiment or a massive research project with thousands of subjects; more important than this type of evidence is careful and thorough sourcing, and the quality of the source.

Evidence can take various forms:

- Critics' views on artworks or performances
- Data from subjects, even a small number (think of case studies, for example)
- Formal research
- Ideas and arguments of recognised theorists
- Passages of writing in literature

Your golden rules for evidencing are:

- Make sure that the evidence is appropriate to the field.
- Present the full reference – see Chapter 14 for more on this.

## Reading with critical eyes

If you're going to undertake analytical writing, don't forget that you need to read work critically in the first place. For evidence to count for anything, it needs to be scrutinised. Students (and academics too, for that matter) frequently allow well-written argument to seduce them, and fail to engage with the work very critically.

As you're reading, keep asking yourself what point the writer's trying to make and assess whether he or she is achieving that aim. Evaluate the writer's evidence with your critical eye and decide whether the conclusions are based on solid ideas and evidence or whether the writer is making leaps and showing gaps in his or her logic.

The more carefully you assess the work you read, the better you become at detecting bias and pulling out points that don't add up. You find you become more sceptical of the works you review, but this is a positive development because you can be more discerning. You're better off with a few good texts, examined in depth, than a large number of weaker texts that you've only managed to skim.

## Stating your opinion

Ask yourself this: have you explored enough other views to know truly what you think? If the answer isn't a resounding 'yes', go back and do some more research.

When you're clear on your opinion, you're ready to begin writing – but remember that you must back up all your claims with evidence. Your tutor doesn't want to know what you feel about what you've read; he or she wants to know what you can prove about what you've read. If you can show that a study's flawed because the author's making general claims after interviewing only a very few subjects, that's a great point to make. If you want to say that you did or didn't like the paper, that's really of no interest to a tutor.

All your tutor wants to know is that you can present research and weigh it up based on the facts about it and other related evidence and research.

# Incorporating Quotations

Sometimes you have to use the author's words because no others suffice. A considerable number of students, particularly early on in their university careers, tend to quote too often and too lengthily. That's often a sign that you have doubts about your ability to paraphrase and/or summarise (see Chapter 7), or that you're not quite sure what the really important part of a passage is, so you quote the whole thing, hoping that you hit the target somewhere!

Guidelines for using quotations are as follows:

- ✔ Use quotations if you're going to pull apart what the writer's said, not to add padding to your argument.

- ✔ Use quotations in small quantities; they're less effective when their presence dominates your essay.

- ✔ Keep quotations short and cleverly woven into the warp and weft of your sentences; they interfere when overlong and intrusive.

✔ Present quotations correctly: clearly signal them with quotation marks and indent them if they're longer than approximately three lines, otherwise contain them within your paragraph.

✔ Make sure that quotations are absolutely accurate (check this meticulously); you shouldn't change or distort them in any way.

✔ Don't use quotations to make a point on your behalf; you make the point first then use the quotation to back up what you're saying.

Beware of plagiarism (see Chapter 7)! Always include an in-text reference immediately after the quotation, and give full details at the end of your essay in the list of references. (For more on referencing, turn to Chapter 14.)

When calculating the word count, short quotations embedded into your sentences fall into the total number of words. Longer quotations (four lines or more) are indented and you shouldn't include them in the word count. Tutors really don't like long quotations because they often suspect that students are trying to pull the wool over their eyes and fool them into thinking that they've written a lot when in fact a large proportion of the essay's taken up by quoting! By all means use quotes to back up what you're saying, but keep them short and try to embed them into your sentences. That's good style.

# *Using Visuals*

You can use visuals in two main ways: referring to other people's visual information or presenting your own information visually.

---

## Highlighting your argument

Here's how the humble highlighter can help you sort out your material:

✔ Write out your ideas and colour code different bits of your argument. As you build up evidence, colour code that and match it to your main existing sections. This gives you the option of moving things around without arguments getting muddled up; often too much cutting and pasting causes a jumbled structure.

✔ Use highlighters to denote the ideas and evidence that stack up for and against certain ideas. Once you've gathered all your evidence, look at the relative weights and see whether you have enough argument on either side to say that what you've presented is balanced.

## Presenting visual information

Tables, charts, diagrams and graphs can be great ways to present data succinctly and systematically. Graphs show relationships between different components in a compelling manner, and the impact of the visual representation of data can be powerful.

You accompany visuals with two types of text:

✔ **Labels on the diagram:** Including the scales, titles, keys and so on.

✔ **Commentary about the visual:** What it depicts and what that means. You need something like: 'Significant growth in literacy has arisen, as can be seen from the graph (Figure iii).'

You do need to comment on the visual. If you just present the chart, your reader doesn't necessarily understand what you're trying to demonstrate.

Number your graphs and charts in your essay. Use Roman numerals so that neither you nor your reader confuses them with the page numbers.

You must reference the visuals you use as scrupulously as you reference your quotations. Even if you adapt material and make your own chart, you need to acknowledge the source of the information. Label the chart 'adapted from . . .' and include the name, date and page numbers from the original text. See Chapter 14 for more on referencing.

## Interpreting visual information

If you need to interpret tables, charts and graphs, make sure that you take your time and understand the labels and keys. If you're not sure what the titles mean, you can't get much out of the table. Read each heading with care and look at the scales on the axes or column headings.

Take care with photocopies or screen colours. If the key in the original makes subtle use of colour, you need to be sure that you have a copy or version that doesn't distort what you're trying to interpret. Wherever possible, look at the original or a good-quality copy and use this either for your data or to improve your poorer version.

Approach the interpretation of the graph systematically, working your way carefully in a logical manner. Where you can, use your fingers and a slip of paper to block out sections or follow lines to be sure you're getting the elements properly lined up when you're reading.

If the graph doesn't include any totals, make sure that you tally up the scores to help you draw conclusions.

## Summarising information in charts

When you need to create your own table or chart, be sure to use language that's as succinct as you can make it. You can't use bullet points in your essay, but now's your chance to make short phrases work for you.

Think carefully about such features as column headings and labels on axes. Can your reader interpret what you're trying to show? Make sure that your title encapsulates what your table's trying to present.

One of the main points of presenting information in a table is to cut down on words, so ensure that the chart is small and tightly structured.

Flip to Chapter 16 for details on how to present your visuals.

# Chapter 13

# Dishing Up Dessert: The Conclusion

● ● ● ● ● ● ● ● ● ● ● ● ● ● ● ● ● ● ● ● ● ● ● ● ● ● ● ● ● ● ● ● ● ● ● ● ● ● ●

## In This Chapter

▶ Finding out the exact function of the conclusion

▶ Knowing what to put in and what to leave out

▶ Making clear and convincing points to finish off your essay

● ● ● ● ● ● ● ● ● ● ● ● ● ● ● ● ● ● ● ● ● ● ● ● ● ● ● ● ● ● ● ● ● ● ● ● ● ● ●

The end of your essay's in sight! You're at the stage where you need to round off your writing with a strong, clear ending. In this chapter we show you how to craft a conclusion that encapsulates the essence of your essay, frames your ideas and leaves your reader with a sense of fulfilment.

# Knowing How to Conclude

Before you get stuck in to writing your conclusion, familiarise yourself with the conventions for ending a university essay.

## Understanding what a conclusion does

You conclude by explaining what the original question was, how you explored it, and what you discovered. As well as giving a sense of rounding off your essay, conclusions have various functions:

✔ **Summarising your main points:** You need to provide an overview of the ideas in the main body of your essay.

✔ **Reiterating the aims of the essay:** You can reaffirm the rationale for the essay, emphasising its purpose. Your reader can then decide whether you've fulfilled your aims.

✔ **Realising your argument:** Your conclusion should provide the last stage of your argument – the realisation or deduction, where you show that what you're stating is based on the logical development of what you've already written.

✔ **Giving your opinion:** If your essay title asks you to express your views about a topic, you should include these in your conclusion. For example, if it asks you to 'evaluate' or 'assess the worth' of an idea or action, you need to ensure that you present your response in the conclusion.

✔ **Leaving a strong impression on the reader:** You want your reader to have a good sense of your overall argument, and you can reinforce this with a well-crafted conclusion. Think about the lasting impression you want to give.

✔ **Recommending and suggesting further research:** You may have some idea that contributes to a solution for particular problems you've discussed, and you may want to speculate about future directions in the field.

Which of these functions you employ varies depending on the style of your essay and the question you're addressing. No matter what the nature of your essay, however, you must incorporate these two main aims:

✔ Summarising the ideas in the essay

✔ Making an evaluation, judgement or final comment on what you've presented

Some tutors consider that summaries are a waste of words because they're repetitious. Others think that summaries should be used to clarify any evaluations you make. Whatever your tutor's views, your conclusion should always be *more* than a mere summary of the essay. The evaluation or critical comment is always required and the summary is generally part of this process. Whether it's a completely separate section or whether it's more integrated into the conclusion is up to your tutor and your course expectations.

Make sure that you actually do reach some kind of conclusion. If you think that you can't resolve the issues raised, you need to state what your reservations are and show that you need either empirical or conceptual work to complete the task. You should make suggestions to solve the problem, rather than merely stating that you can't reach a conclusion at all.

# Getting the content right

So what do you put in your conclusion and what do you leave out?

## Keeping it relevant

Your conclusion's no different to the rest of your essay in terms of the relevance of the material you should include. A common misconception among students is to think that tutors are impressed to see evidence of all the reading and research they have done around the essay theme. In fact, students presenting work that doesn't link to the question, even when it's obliquely related to the topic, is quite irritating. Ironically, although they may be trying to show off that they've done lots of research, they end up demonstrating a lack of effort in organising ideas and evidence in relation to the title.

Your conclusion should be succinct and directly linked to your essay title. Even when you have to summarise your previous points, these should clearly relate to the title. Always ensure that every point you make has something to contribute to answering the question.

If your title asks for a judgement, here's where you make it. Look at the title; if it asks you 'How effective is . . .?', 'To what extent does . . .?' or 'How useful or relevant is . . .?' you need to make sure that you've answered clearly. Don't evaluate things that aren't part of your essay, however – you have no need to review elements that aren't requested or aren't linked to the topic in hand. They're irrelevant.

## Leaving out new ideas

Never introduce a new idea in your conclusion. You don't have the word space in your conclusion to develop a new idea, and you leave your reader hanging with a tantalising suggestion of something useful that never gets off the ground. If the idea's an interesting and vital aspect of your essay, you should feature it early on and investigate it appropriately.

Sometimes students save up a great idea for the end as a kind of dramatic effect. While we can appreciate the intention, both as tutors and as writers, doing so is not appropriate for an academic essay. You end up appending a great idea as an afterthought, which doesn't have the desired effect of hitting the reader between the eyes with a startling revelation.

The other common reason for introducing something new in the conclusion is to do with poor time management and last-minute desperation. Sometimes students have just about finished their work when they discover that they've left out an important point or they suddenly come across a great idea in their reading. If they can't be bothered to restructure the whole essay (or have run out of time), they introduce this new aspect in the conclusion. This reads as rushed and betrays a lack of forethought and attention to detail.

# Writing the Conclusion

Now that you understand *how* to write your conclusion, the time's come to get down to business, putting pen to paper and bringing a sense of closure to your work.

You need to check your conclusion carefully to ensure that it's well written, accurate, relevant and concise. Chapter 15 helps you edit and proofread your writing.

# Drawing all the threads together

You don't have to leave writing the conclusion until the end of your essay. Some people find that they write the outline of their conclusion alongside working on the introduction, and this makes them feel more comfortable about getting on with the whole essay. Others prefer to let the essay unfold a little as they write.

You can get started on drawing the threads of your argument together as you're going along. Jot down readings or references that have helped you change your view or that have confirmed your original ideas.

When you're redrafting sections of your work, you can sometimes benefit from storing some of the earlier versions in a folder, because they may come in handy for your concluding section.

In thinking about the conclusion to your argument, consider these additional questions:

- What's noteworthy about what you've shown?

- Does ignoring this topic have any negative implications? (Here you can emphasise its importance.)

- What other aspects might you have considered that only came to your attention as you were doing this essay?

# Acting on advice

Universities and courses have varied policies on tutors reading through drafts of students' work. Some have strict guidelines limiting the number of words tutors can read and the number of attempts and redrafts that they can comment on, while others have an ad hoc approach where tutors help if they have time. In other places, a dedicated support tutor is available to comment on structure and writing but not on content.

In the authors' experience, arrangements have altered over the years, but one aspect's remained true: how students respond to support comments is indicative of their eventual grade. If your tutor reads your essay and identifies that you've failed to mention a key point that's vital in addressing the title, you're pretty silly merely to tack a sentence or two onto your conclusion.

Similarly, if the essay's reasonable, but the tutor picks up on a weak conclusion, only making it longer isn't enough: you really need to start all over again. Surprisingly, restarting your conclusion from scratch rather than redrafting and editing a passage that's poorly conceived can actually take less time (and result in better quality work).

Here are some phrases that help you get a sense of how your conclusion should sound:

> In this essay, I have explained how . . .

> The question asked whether X was as important in Y. In this essay, I have shown . . .

> The purpose of this essay was to evaluate X, and through the evidence and argument, it has been shown that . . .

> Through examining the evidence for X, I have demonstrated that . . .

Your conclusion should eventually read something like this:

> In light of the evidence, I conclude that X is vital for Y. I have shown that arguments generally support the view that X. From this basis it can be confirmed that X. The arguments/data presented persuasively show that X, and so finally it can be determined that X. Future research may one day demonstrate the possibility that Y, but, for now, the only logical conclusion is X.

 In order to present a great conclusion, plan an outline of what you need to include. This helps you avoid drifting off the topic, and instead ensures that you provide a pithy, concise finish to the essay.

## *Pointing forward*

Depending on the length of your essay and its layout, you may or may not need to provide some ideas about future areas of study and further research.

If the title doesn't ask you to give ideas, you can merely state the aspects you're interested in pursuing in the future. Another tactic's to highlight the issues that may have a much wider impact and which you're likely to meet again in further studies during your degree.

But you may be expected to do more than this and to identify areas for further research and development. You need to consider this in the light of your evidence and pay attention to different aspects of your work, as follows:

✔ **Noting significance of research:**

- These findings show that X needs to be reconsidered . . .

- My research will be a useful starting point for a future, more detailed study on . . .

✔ **Providing ideas and recommendations for further investigations:**

- Having shown where gaps exist in X, it would be useful to . . .

- In order to establish X more convincingly, work on Y should . . .

✔ **Mentioning implications for practice:**

- It is clear from this research that practical concerns of . . .

- A specific need for X has been demonstrated by Y . . .

Before you get too carried away criticising leaders in the field for not having researched this or that, check that you haven't simply missed a key study on that area!

## *Striking the right tone*

Chapter 10 takes a detailed look at the tone and style you adopt in academic essays. Here, we look at specifically at issues concerning tone in your conclusion.

Your conclusion should have a distinct and clear tone, but it shouldn't be markedly different from the rest of your essay. You need to present an assured, convincing quality of writing that strikes the right balance between too reticent and overconfident.

While you can point out some of the limitations in your essay, don't be apologetic. You need to show that you understand that your essay's making a small contribution to the discussion, but you shouldn't be trying to excuse yourself for aspects that you've legitimately not covered.

Look at these different ways to express the extent of a study, and decide which is most appropriate:

1. I was not able to cover it all in my essay because the word limit was short.
2. The current study has examined only X and Y. Z would be an important aspect were the essay to be extended.
3. Since the sample size discussed here was small, the results should be considered with caution.
4. There is not much value in this work because there are far more texts than have been mentioned.
5. I was unable to examine all the variables such as X and Y, but, based on the existing study, I would suggest that . . .
6. Although the essay does try to answer the question, most of the research highlights a slightly different area, but it is still applicable.

Number 1 makes an excuse. Numbers 2, 3 and 5 are fine. Number 4 undermines the essay that's gone before, and 6 seems like the student's suddenly realised he or she hasn't actually done the right essay, but can't be bothered to put it right.

What you're trying to accomplish is a sense of ending and finality; you don't want to leave the reader feeling up in the air. Return to the question, reinforcing its value. Mention the context of the work and show how your journey through the argument has clarified the discussion, showing where you've contributed your own ideas or examples and how you've refined your existing thoughts. You can show how your understanding of main ideas has shifted or been reinforced.

If you get the tone right, your ideas resonate with your reader after he or she has read your paper. This is what you want, so spend time crafting the final lines to give a sound ending.

## Getting the length right

In Chapter 3 we recommend that, like the introduction, your conclusion forms about 10 per cent of your essay (that is, 300 words
for a 3,000-word paper).

This is just a guide, so don't stick to it rigidly if your essay meets the
requirements better with a slightly longer or shorter conclusion.

If your conclusion's very short, you can't have included all the elements. Use the checklist in the later section 'Checking your work'
to run carefully through your conclusion and identify where you
have gaps. Meeting all the points in the checklist without writing
a few sentences on each one is difficult, so this should solve your
problem. If it doesn't, your essay may be too thin, without sufficient
depth in your argument. This requires a more drastic rethink (see the
later section on how the conclusion can affect your whole essay.)

If your conclusion's too long, you need to cut out anything unnecessary. Before you delete useful paragraphs in error, first check
whether some of the writing's simply in the wrong section. If you
can move some text, you may find that your conclusion's now the
right length after all. If it's still too lengthy, you need to scrutinise
what you've written and delete (ruthlessly) anything extraneous.

Here are some typical extras that students often include
unnecessarily:

- ✔ **Too much repetition:** While you need to refer to the title, you
  needn't write the whole thing out word for word.

- ✔ **References:** You should cover these through your text and
  your bibliography or reference list, not in your conclusion.

- ✔ **Lists that should be in the appendices:** Students sometimes
  mistakenly present bullet points and models that don't quite
  fit into the flow of the essay in the conclusion, instead of in
  the appendices.

- ✔ **Too much personal opinion:** Sometimes students only say what
  they think about a topic in the conclusion, which becomes like
  reading a stream of consciousness with everything they've
  ever thought about a topic presented in a long, unstructured
  paragraph. Keep your opinion succinct and light.

- ✔ **Your feelings about writing the essay:** While you may want to
  mention that the research was interesting, or that doing the
  essay resulted in your changing your viewpoint, you shouldn't

use the conclusion as a confessional. 'I found that this essay helped me grow and I have faced up to some of the problems I had at school with essay writing through the course experience.' This is unsuitable for an academic essay.

## Realising that writing your conclusion can change your essay

When you get to the point of drawing together the threads of your argument to reach your conclusion (see the earlier section 'Drawing all the threads together') you may find that you've shifted your position from when you set out on the journey of your essay. No hard-and-fast rule exists about exactly when you need to be sure of how to end your paper, but you do need to keep a check on how your ideas are developing so that you can make adjustments as you go along.

Most students probably don't encounter a dramatic shift but a clearer idea of what they first meant. You may have found more compelling evidence than you anticipated and need to emphasise slightly different points than you intended. Therefore, you need to go back over your work to check that you've led up to your conclusion appropriately.

Don't let your conclusion contradict all the evidence you've gathered and presented. If your research led you to a different conclusion, you need to rewrite – don't twist the evidence to support something spurious.

If you've completely flipped your ideas or moved away significantly from your original position, you need to rethink your whole argument carefully.

As you're writing, you should think ahead to your conclusions. You're usually better to be a little cautious with your predictions (unless the essay's particularly short).

## Evaluating Your Conclusion

After you've written your conclusion and are feeling quite happy with it, review your words and be sure that you're on the right track.

## Checking your work

Your essay conclusion should be fine if you can honestly say that it meets the requirements on this checklist:

✔ You provide more than only a summary.

✔ Where appropriate, you summarise the answers to the set question.

✔ You mention the title or question and answer it fully.

✔ You show that you've done all you set out to do by relating logically to your introduction.

✔ You include some kind of practical application and a thoughtful response to the essay title.

✔ The conclusion follows on from the essay, matching ideas rather than contradicting them.

✔ You have no new ideas in your conclusion.

✔ You establish a viewpoint that the evidence in your essay supports.

✔ You emphasise the importance of the area the essay's covering.

✔ You reinforce your ideas without using repeated phrases and sentences from the main body of your essay.

✔ You ensure that the style and tone link to the main body of the essay.

✔ You've written no more than 10 per cent of the length of the essay, and the conclusion's more substantial than a brief couple of sentences.

✔ Either in your conclusion or in a dedicated section, you've made suggestions for further related research, directing your reader forward (if your tutor expects this).

✔ You aren't being apologetic, nor are you being arrogant. You're positive and assured.

✔ You cover only the key points and don't mention the less important aspects.

✔ You round off well and don't leave anything hanging unresolved.

Your conclusion's part of the conceptual framework that the reader requires to understand your argument. It must be more than a couple of bland paragraphs at the end of your work.

# Asking yourself 'So what?'

This is the main question us tutors ask when we're marking work. A student makes a statement, and if they present no evidence, we ask 'How do you know that's so?' Then, when we have the evidence, we ask 'So what?'

If you've really researched the topic and have a view on why it matters, you can pre-empt this question by saying *why* the area's important. You want to demonstrate that the issue matters to people and has value.

Try to avoid raising rhetorical questions in your conclusion, because they weaken your essay and make you sound vague. You need to get off the fence!

# Making the final check

You need a kind of Gestalt attitude to the conclusion, in which the whole is more than the sum of the parts. What we mean by this is that you need to ensure that all the elements of your conclusion are there – it needs to meet the requirements of a conclusion – and then you need to reread it and decide whether it's an apt conclusion to your essay. In doing this final check, you're looking for tone, style and general feel, not just all the elements; thus a Gestalt approach.

# Chapter 14

# Acknowledging Sources of Information

- - - - - - - - - - - - - - - - - - - - - - - - - - - - - - - - - - - - - - - -

### In This Chapter

▶ Knowing why correct referencing is paramount

▶ Quoting indirectly and directly

▶ Look at different bibliographic methods

- - - - - - - - - - - - - - - - - - - - - - - - - - - - - - - - - - - - - - - -

**A**nyone reading your essay should be able to follow up references in your work by using the bibliographic data you present. Your data must be accurate enough to allow readers to go and find the exact source you've used. For this reason, academic writing uses agreed conventions to which you need to conform within your own essays. This chapter shows you how to master the mechanics of referencing and clears up some misconceptions and confusions.

'Who cares whether my references are perfect?' you may be thinking. 'It's the writing within the essay itself that counts.' Stop right there. Proper referencing's essential and valuable, and in this chapter we show you why.

## Understanding the Importance of Referencing

Reflect on the reasons for careful referencing to be sure that you know why you're taking the time to meet the requirements. Here's why we make such a fuss about acknowledging sources of information:

✔ If readers need to check the reliability of a source, they're able to do so with ease.

✔ Where you're presenting someone else's views and thoughts, you're courteously acknowledging where they come from.

✔ You're being honest about where the ideas originated and not pretending that you thought them up for yourself when in fact you read them in someone else's work.

✔ If you need further information from the same source, you have all the required details to find the original work.

✔ If you carefully present your sources, readers have more faith in the quality of your claims.

✔ By being able to reference effectively, you demonstrate attention to detail and an understanding of how your discipline presents knowledge. This is one of your ways into your particular professional field. Being able to adhere to the conventions of your discipline is part of becoming a professional and so it will help you in your developing career (whether you choose further study or not).

# Bearing in Mind Some Basics

Later sections get stuck into the fine details of referencing. But before we delve too deep, here are a few important points to keep in mind. When referencing you need to:

✔ Acknowledge your sources, both as you use them and also at the end of your work. As you go along, you need only minor details, but, at the end, you provide a full and comprehensive list.

✔ Acknowledge all sources, not only books. That means that you must provide the full details for all websites, television programmes, journals, newspaper articles and so on that you use for your essay.

✔ Follow guidelines with extreme care. Organising references and bibliographies always takes longer than you anticipate, so allow double your first estimate.

You're responsible for filling in all the gaps in your referencing, even if you have to head back to the library just to find the date of publication of something. Here are some ideas to help you track sources as you go:

✔ Each time you find a source, put the reference in a special file.

✔ Use bibliographic software (such as Endnote, Biblioscape, Library Master or Citation), which saves all your sources for you and then produces your list of references at the end. Your university is likely to have access to such software and also to run training courses. Visit www.endnote.com for more information.

Collating sources while you research for your essay saves you hours at the end when you're really pushed for time.

Failing to acknowledge the opinions and ideas from another writer's work is like stealing that person's thoughts and is termed plagiarism (flip to Chapter 7 for more on this). You're responsible for citing the source, even when you've paraphrased rather than directly quoted. Where a genuine gap exists due to missing information, you need to note that data was unavailable.

# Getting to Grips with the Jargon

Referencing comes with its own terminology. Make sure that you know what the different terms mean:

- ✔ **Appendices:** These pages come at the end of your work and contain additional information that's necessary for your argument but interrupts the flow of your writing if you place it within the text. Appendices are most useful for tables, models, examples and diagrams that are valuable but not required.

- ✔ **Bibliography:** This is a list of everything you've read or researched for your essay or dissertation, placed at the end of your work. Depending on your tutor's requirements, the bibliography can include all the reading you've done – whether or not you discuss this directly in your writing – or be a list of only what you've mentioned in your essay. You present the list in alphabetical order, by author, and include all types of sources in one list (so you mix web addresses or newspapers with books and journals in alphabetical order by author). You usually have either a bibliography or a reference list, but not both. You need to list full details of the source.

- ✔ **Citations:** When you cite someone, you're acknowledging a source. 'Citation' is a general word, but can specifically describe instances when you need to refer to a secondary source – when you need to note the original source even if you found the information from a different book or journal. The aim is to show exactly where the idea was presented. Citations are most common in undergraduate essays when students want to say that they've used one writer's interpretation of someone else's thoughts or theories.

- ✔ **Direct quotation:** Here you're using someone else's exact words. You should enclose these in quotation marks. You must state the source, date and page number.

- ✔ **Footnotes and endnotes:** You must check your course policy on footnotes and endnotes because these may be disallowed or required. They're additional comments, notes or references at the bottom of the page or at the end of your essay. If they're allowed, you can use them to elaborate on the main ideas without digressing from the main themes and arguments.

✔ **Further reading:** Sometimes you're asked to provide a reference list that includes only what you've referred to directly and then augment this with a list of further reading to show your additional research.

✔ **Indirect quotation:** Here you paraphrase or summarise (see the later section 'Quoting indirectly'). You adapt the original text or refer to it using your own words, and so you have no need for quotation marks. You need to cite the source (author and date) and in some cases – usually when you're raising a very specific point – you should put the page number(s) as well.

✔ **List of Works Cited:** This is what it says! You provide a list of every work that you have cited in your essay. It's the same as a reference list.

✔ **Reference list:** This catalogues all the sources to which you refer in your essay. The reference list and in-text citations should match exactly in terms of author and date, so if you mention a source in the main body of the essay, you must include this in the reference list entry. Similarly, no source should be in the reference list that doesn't feature in the main text. The list should be at the end of your document and ordered alphabetically by author, and you need to list full details of sources. You usually have either a bibliography or a reference list, but not both.

✔ **References in the body of the text:** Here you're referring to the sources that come up as you go along; they're the mentions within sentences of people in your text, or quotations that you use to illustrate ideas. You usually include only the author and date (and page number if you use a direct quotation). You include in-text references as you write as well as in either your bibliography or reference list.

Use the terms that your tutor recommends – if these disagree with the terms we use in this book, stick to your university's definition. Here we present the common definitions, but understandings and conventions may vary.

# Pinning Down Your Referencing Style

All references include the following:

- ✔ Author(s) and/or editor(s)
- ✔ Date of publication
- ✔ Title of chapter, paper or resource
- ✔ Title of book, journal or collective programme
- ✔ Publisher
- ✔ Place of publication or URL
- ✔ Date you accessed the work (if Internet source)

Where references differ is in their presentation. Many different systems for referencing exist. Here we look at two of the more common styles for referencing, but you should rely on your university and course guidelines for full details of what your tutors expect. Even academic fields differ in their approaches. For example, the British Education Research Association, has webpages with guidelines (they use a style called APA):

> www.bera.ac.uk/data-collection-reviewing-research-literature/referencing-and-citation/

The British Psychological Society have a style guide of their own:

> www.bps.org.uk/downloadfile.cfm?file_uuid=1B29ADB1-7E96-C67F-D51D3ADFC581A906&ext=pdf

... and the British Medical Association's version is different again,

> www.bma.org.uk/library_medline/electronic_resources/factsheets/LIBReferenceStyles.jsp

Be clear which style you have to use. Consult your course booklets for details about this and attend study skills sessions wherever possible so that you're certain that what you do meets the regulations on your university course.

# Using Harvard (a.k.a. author/date)

This book can't show you all the different methods in operation, so we've stuck to the most common method generally found in science, humanities and the social sciences. This system's known as 'author/date' because that's how it works: you put the name of the author and then the date of the publication. More than one 'author/date' system exists, but the Harvard system's the one you encounter most widely.

With the Harvard system, you present full source details in the reference list or bibliography at the end of the essay. You include minimal information in the essay text. To see Harvard in action, skip to the section 'Quoting Within Your Essay'.

# Working with footnotes

Most undergraduate courses don't encourage the use of footnotes. For example, in English literature, footnotes are often used, whereas in education studies they're generally discouraged. If you are allowed to use footnotes, you're given clear guidelines about whether the footnotes are for references or for additional material.

Footnotes are additions to the main text and are usually found at the bottom of the corresponding page. If they're at the end of the essay, they're called endnotes. They're used to elaborate on the main ideas in the essay without interrupting the flow of information in the main text.

If you're explaining a key idea and you have an obliquely related concept that you want to acknowledge, the footnote or endnote's the place to present your ideas. If you have an illustration or example, however, you usually put this in the main text so that it doesn't distract from the flow of your discussion.

You number footnotes and endnotes (whether for references or not), and you can do this either in parentheses or by using a superscript.

> According to Bowles [3], the interpretation of melody by some singers . . .
>
> Bowles[3] observes that such singing is tantamount to being out of tune . . .

The following sections in this chapter help you reference using the Harvard style. If your university wants you to use footnotes for references, then you're using a different system to Harvard (such as a numeric system). So ensure that you're clear what you have to do.

# Quoting within Your Essay

Any university-level essay includes within the body of the text quotations from sources and references to sources. In this section, we dissect how to weave references into your essay.

## Citing the author in the text

When you refer to a writer's ideas in your text, you need to provide the name, date and page reference. The reference should look something like this:

> Following initial discussions held at the National Portrait Gallery (Wright, 2004:5-11), it could be concluded that . . .

When you're citing the author in the text as you're going along, use the name if it occurs naturally within the flow of the text:

> Kempston (2006) reports that even careful use of quality veneer is inferior to using solid wood (p.2).

Or:

> Kempston (2006:2) reports that even careful use of quality veneer is inferior to using solid wood.

## The golden rules for quotations

While quotations can have an impact and can make an essay richer and more exciting to read, you need to be circumspect. Don't scatter them liberally around your paper without good reason. Here are some key guidelines on using quotations:

✔ Use quotations only to emphasise or support an idea or argument.

✔ Quote people who are recognised as relevant to your field.

✔ Keep quotations succinct and precise.

✔ Make sure that you fully understand what the quotation's saying.

✔ Keep the quotations in context – don't cut out key words or shorten quotations so that they're unrecognisable.

✔ Make sure that your quotations actually link coherently to your own writing.

✔ Never use a quotation without embedding it in your text. You need to introduce and analyse it, linking it convincingly to the points you're making.

Sometimes the name doesn't fit into your sentence structure. In such cases, put the name in brackets at the end of the sentence:

> . . . solid wood will always give a better finish due to the grain (Kempston, 2006:2).

You usually don't need to mention the author's first name. If you are asked to include first names, do this only once, the first time you introduce the author, and then revert to the convention of using surnames.

If the work's by two people, name them both:

> Brookman and Mair (1988:26) have shown that light opera is a valuable format for students wanting to develop . . .

With instances of multiple authors (three or more), you can use the shorthand of *et al.* which means 'and others' (you provide the full list of authors in the bibliography):

> Andrews et al. (2007) list the main effects of the first months of the presidency . . .

When you're referring to an organisation, this is often in place of a specific author. Unless the organisation specifies the author, it generally retains the rights to the work and so it *is* the author for the purposes of your referencing. Avoid abbreviating an organisation's name the first time you mention it, otherwise your reader may not know what you're referring to.

> The simpler version has been created for teachers (Department for Children, Schools and Families, 2003). It is designed to help them adapt the theory to the classroom. In a further model, this is highlighted (DSCF, 2004:14).

You need to express secondary sources very clearly, so that your reader can see how they match with your bibliography.

> Violet (1999) suggests that watching the news can disturb younger children who do not understand the context of the stories (cited in Sobrina, 2000:10).

When you can't find an author for a particular source, list it as *Anon;* when a source has no clear date, recognise this by stating *no date*.

For page references, consult your course guide to see whether it gives a preference. Here are some common conventions:

(2004:4-11)

(2004, p.4-11)

(2004, p4-11)

(2004, pp4-11)

On websites, you may have trouble locating page numbers. Instead, you can indicate the line number if that's easy to find, or use the screen number if appropriate. This is only possible when you have a site with several screens on the same topic and they are numbered. It's usually the case if someone has adapted a PowerPoint presentation onto a website, which happens with conference proceedings and keynote addresses, which are often useful to reference. Sometimes stating 'near the end of the document' or similar is sufficient.

## *Quoting directly*

*Direct quotations* are the use of an author's words directly copied from the original text and incorporated in your essay. You must match the original word for word, and you have to be painstaking about getting the source details accurate.

Use direct quotations sparingly and with the utmost care. They need to be directly focused on the point you're making. They should add to your essay rather than detract from your ideas. An essay with too many direct quotations ends up as little more than a stitched-together version of other people's ideas.

Avoid using bland quotations that really add nothing to your work. If the book you're reading on psychology includes a statement about psychology being important, this is hardly surprising, nor is it a viewpoint unique to that book. Quoting it is pointless, so don't.

Used carefully, direct quotations are a great way to emphasise a point you're making. You can also use quotations as exemplars of your main points.

When you're introducing a direct quotation, certain phrases can help you link things together:

✔ The following quotation from X demonstrates that Y is '. . .'.

✔ X states that '. . .'.

  ✔ As X verifies, '. . .'.

  ✔ According to X, '. . .'.

  ✔ In 1851, X argued that '. . .'.

## Quoting indirectly

When you use indirect quotations, you're not using someone's exact words but paraphrasing or summarising what they've said or written:

  ✔ *Paraphrasing* is when you put a passage of writing or speech into your own words, generally trying to condense the original. You must cite the original source with clarity or else you're not paraphrasing but plagiarising (stealing others' words and ideas and passing them off as your own).

  ✔ *Summarising* is cutting out any exemplars or illustrations and providing a much reduced version with only the main points highlighted. A summary's sometimes known as a précis. Again, you must provide full reference details including page numbers. If you've used several pages or a whole chapter, you can cite the entire chapter or area of the source you used.

Chapter 7 provides more detail on paraphrasing.

Being able to integrate indirect quotations smoothly into your writing shows that you've understood what you've read, but if you fail to reference effectively, you appear to have lifted other people's ideas. If you don't understand a point, leave it out rather than risk a misinterpretation.

## Slotting a short quotation into your sentence

If your quotation contains fewer than around 20 words, you can incorporate it into your sentence by enclosing it in quotation marks. You don't need to start a new line or indent the text. Take care that your sentence reads smoothly and works as a whole.

> This point is supported by Lowe who contends that one should maintain fitness through 'practising the headstand for ten minutes per day' (1978:65).

You may need to adapt the quotation slightly to make sense in your context. You use square brackets for this and for when you need to clarify a point. Here, you don't know who's being discussed without the clarification in the square brackets:

'She [Ella] was the most inspiring person we had known.'

You may also need to add a word so that the quotation reads more smoothly:

'We noted the teacher's exhortation to "pick up [their] paint-brushes at once" . . .'

Be scrupulous: copy the punctuation of the quotation as well as the words.

## Dealing with longer quotations

If your quotation's more than around 20 words, you should intro-duce it with a colon and indent it in place of using quotation marks. It looks like this in the text:

In 1961, when they arrived, it was the most severe winter for some time, and there were regular thick fogs that made travel difficult:

You'd have ice inside the window every morning and you couldn't see your hand in front of your face for the fog. We kept the baby warm by insulating her with newspaper and putting her in the cot fully dressed with a hat! (Hazelwell, 2000:34)

When a quotation's longer than a few lines, you need to think fas-tidiously about whether you really need it at all. If you do need to use the quotation, you have two choices:

✔ **Using the quotation in full:** If shortening the quotation changes its meaning or reduces its impact, you should go ahead and use the full version, but remember that you then have fewer of your own words available to get your ideas across.

✔ **Shortening the quotation:** You can leave out some unnecessary words if you wish, but not in a way that changes the meaning. If you do need to leave out a few words, replace them with a row of three dots (known as an ellipsis). This shows where you have deleted some text. Doing so is acceptable only when it doesn't alter the meaning.

## Simplifying with Latin shorthand

Here are some handy shortcuts that can save you time in your essay writing. Rather than copying the full in-text reference again and again, these two little words are shorthand for saying 'Here's one I mentioned earlier':

✔ **Ibid.** means 'from the same source' and refers to a source that you've only just used. It's useful if you want to use different pages from the same document. After the first mention you put, for example, (Cusack, 1984:34) and then when you want to use the same text, in the next line or so, you merely put (ibid.:94).

✔ **Op. cit.** means 'already cited' and refers to the most recently cited work by that particular author. So if you've written about one source in an early paragraph and then wish to refer to the same source at a later stage, you can simply mention the author in the paragraph and then write (op. cit.) in place of referencing it all again.

# Listing References at the End of Your Work

At the end of your essay, you need to present all your sources in your reference list or bibliography (the earlier section 'Getting to Grips with the Jargon' explains these). This is an essential component of the essay, validating what you claim in the body of the text. You must follow the accepted conventions to ensure that the reader can find the original sources to assess them personally and decide whether they agree with your interpretations.

As ever, you need to check your course regulations with care, but generally speaking you must:

✔ Place your bibliography at the end of your essay.

✔ Put everything in alphabetical order (by author).

✔ Avoid separating books, articles and websites, or other sources, unless specifically requested to do so.

✔ Ensure that you format the bibliography to allow easy reading and to meet requirements.

✔ Use appropriate spacing and leave a line between each entry.

Read on to find some standard rules from the Harvard system for referencing books, journals, government reports and electronic sources.

Universities have their own preferences for referencing. Check your course materials to see whether your tutor or your field employs any variations.

## For books

You lay out references for books as follows:

> Author or editor's surname, initials (Year of publication) *Title of Book: Including Subtitle,* Edition, if it's not the first edition, Place of publication: Name of publisher.

Edited book:

> Smith, C.M.M. (ed.) (2006) *Including the Gifted and Talented: Making Inclusion Work for More Gifted and Able Learners,* London: Taylor & Francis.

Book with two editors:

> Hand, M. and Winstanley, C. (eds) (2007) *Philosophy in Schools,* London: Continuum.

Edited book with multiple named authors:

> Wallace, B., Fitton, S., Leyden, S., Montgomery, D., Pomerantz, M. and Winstanley, C. (eds) (2007) *Raising the Achievement of Able, Gifted and Talented Pupils Within an Inclusive School Framework,* London: NACE and LG&T.

Single-author book:

> Montgomery, D. (2006) *Spelling, Handwriting and Dyslexia,* London: Routledge.

Book by two authors:

> Brighouse, T. and Woods, D. (2006) *Inspirations: A Collection of Commentaries and Quotations to Promote School Improvement,* London: Network Continuum Education.

Book with multiple authors:

> Cohen, L., Manion, L. and Morrison, K. (2007) *Research Methods in Education,* 6th edn, London: Routledge.

Book not yet published:

> Winstanley, C. (forthcoming) *The Ingredients of Challenge,* Staffs: Trentham Books.

Chapter in book:

> Winstanley, C. (2006) 'Inequity in equity: Tackling the excellence-equality conundrum' in Smith, C.M.M. (ed.) *Including the Gifted and Talented: Making Inclusion Work for More Gifted and Able Learners*, London: Taylor & Francis, pp. 22-40.

### For journals

Journal references look like this:

> Author's surname, initials. (Year of publication) 'Title of article', *Name of Journal*, Volume number(part number): Page numbers.

For example:

> Freeman, J. (1997) 'The emotional development of the highly able', *European Journal of Psychology in Education*, 12: 479-493.

You reference newspaper articles in the same way as journals. If the article doesn't have a named author, list the entry by the name of the paper (drop 'the' from the name) and note 'no author listed'.

### For government reports

Here's how to reference a report:

> Organisation (date) *Title* (reference number or code), Place of publication: Publisher.

Here's one we made earlier:

> DCSF (2008) *2020 Children and Young People's Workforce Strategy: Evidence and Knowledge Management* (PDFDCSF-01055-2008), London: HMSO.

### For electronic sources

You're likely to use the Internet for your research, and you need to be clear about how to reference web pages. Sites can change and become outdated, so you must note when you accessed the website. Generally, reliable sites have good archives where you can check these details, so be accurate.

Some Internet sources can be very poor quality. Make sure that you can verify the information you're using. Use Chapter 5 as your guide.

For articles that you've found on websites, include:

> Author or editor's surname, initials (or, if no author, name of organisation) (Year of publication) *Title*, URL, Rest of date if applicable. Date accessed.

For example:

> Love, E. (2009) *Suzi Winstanley: An Artist with Roar Talent* www.independent.co.uk/arts-entertainment/ art/features/suzi-winstanley-an-artist-with- roar-talent-1231761.html, 8 January. Accessed 10 February 2009.

Some tutors prefer you to be more concise, as follows:

> Love, E. (2009) *Suzi Winstanley: An Artist with Roar Talent* www. independent.co.uk/arts, 8 January. Accessed 10 February 2009.

If your web addresses run to several lines each, putting a shortened version's better. What you need to check is that someone's able to find the page you're referring to.

For a website from which you took general information, you should put the URL as well as some sort of title for the organisation or individual:

> Challoner, J., www.explaining-science.co.uk. Accessed 10 February 2009.

> Science Museum, www.sciencemuseum.org.uk. Accessed 10 February 2009.

Downloaded pdf files constitute electronic sources, so put the web addresses for these as well.

## For digital media

You also need to reference recordings, films and CD-ROMs with clarity:

> *Title* (Year of distribution) Director [Format (DVD or video cassette etc.)], Place of distribution: Distribution company.

Here's your example:

> *Etre et Avoir* (2002), Directed by Philibert, N. [DVD], Paris: Canal Plus.

### For visual materials

You may need to reference a table, chart, model or illustration in your work. You should reference this with the same level of detail as a quotation, if it hails from a published work of any description. If you have more than one diagram, you need to label them all with figure numbers.

For example:

'Types of Sprinkler', page 469, in Brickell, C. (ed.) (1992) *Encyclopedia of Gardening*, London: Dorling Kindersley.

# Part V
# Finishing with a Flourish: The Final Touches

'He's just dividing his essay into manageable chunks.'

## *In this part . . .*

*N*ever spoil the ship for a ha'penny worth of tar: The last stage of the writing process – editing and proofreading – can make the difference between a good essay and a great one. Here we show you how to grab those extra marks by sheer attention to detail.

We then look at the aftermath of the essay, showing you how to use feedback to your advantage. By understanding how you might have done things better, you'll improve as a writer. We show you how.

# Chapter 15

# Editing and Proofreading: It's All in the Detail

## In This Chapter

▶ Understanding how to edit your text for content, structure and style

▶ Fixing an essay that's too short or too long

▶ Knowing how to proofread

**T**his chapter focuses on fine-tuning the content of your essay. It's about putting the finishing touches to what you're saying and how you're saying it.

Have you ever read a news report about the howlers people commit in their CVs? Or the comments that recruitment officers make along the lines of 'people today can't spell' or 'nobody knows their grammar any longer'? In the real world of work, first impressions count and a CV showing that you pay no attention to detail and take no pride in your work can cost you a job interview. Handing in your essay is similar. A well-organised, tidy piece of work already puts your tutor in a positive frame of mind, while a sloppy effort has the reverse effect.

This chapter introduces you to editing and proofreading techniques that help you review the content of your essay so that you present your ideas logically and in good English.

# Knowing the Difference between Editing and Proofreading

Where does editing end and proofreading begin? What do these terms really mean, and which order do you do them in? Confused? We have the answers . . .

   ✔ **Editing:** This is the first part of the polishing process. You look at content, structure and style – checking that you have a logical flow of ideas that make sense and ensuring that you've answered the question. You may also have to edit your essay to ensure that it's the right length. You need a clear head.

✔ **Proofreading:** This is your final job. You look at spelling, punctuation and grammar, and check language for problems like inconsistency and repetition. You need a dictionary, a grammar reference book, maybe a thesaurus, and a sharp pair of eyes.

Both processes are essential if you want to present a tidy and professional piece of work to your tutor. However, you're best to keep the editing and proofreading processes separate because they require different skills. Besides, unless you're good at multitasking, focusing on several things simultaneously is hard, and you're going to be more accurate if you do one at a time.

Editing for content and flow should be done on one day or in one writing session. Perhaps leave the essay overnight or at least until after your coffee break and then do another sweep where you may look at punctuation, and yet another read-through for spelling errors, and so on. The more you can separate and stagger these sweeps, the more effective they should be.

# Editing: Casting a Critical Eye over What You're Saying

When you edit your text you focus on four areas: content, structure, style and length.

## Considering content

Your aim when editing is to revise the content of your writing so that the argument comes across as well developed. You check that:

✔ You give a balanced, objective response to the question.

✔ No patches of writing go off at a tangent, add nothing to the argument or detract from the flow of ideas.

✔ Your facts are accurate.

✔ Your meaning's clear.

✔ Your points are fully developed and don't need expanding.

✔ You back up your points with examples.

✔ Your examples are relevant.

Look back at the precise wording of the essay title and pick it apart one more time to ensure that you've interpreted it accurately. Then go through your work paragraph by paragraph, ruthlessly questioning whether what you're saying is directly relevant to the essay title.

You may be upset if you get your essay back and see paragraphs struck through with the word 'irrelevant' scribbled in the margin. Apart from the fact that your feelings may be hurt, irrelevant passages can affect the word count and lose you marks if you're way over the word limit. Or they take up valuable space that you should be devoting to considering other aspects of the argument. In either case you lose out.

Turn to Chapters 11, 12 and 13 for more on your essay's content.

Checking the content also includes being absolutely certain that you've acknowledged every source you've used correctly and fully, both in the text and in your list of references. Meticulous and rigorous attention to these details is called for at this stage. Look at Chapter 14 if you need to refresh your memory about referencing, and Chapter 7 if you need to improve your summarising or paraphrasing skills.

## *Examining structure*

When you edit, you look at the structure of your essay as a whole and ask yourself whether it's logical and well organised.

You need to think about your reader and put your ideas in an order that's helpful. If your ideas jump around, your reader finds them difficult to follow. You should endeavour to make things as easy as possible for your tutor. After all, he or she may be facing a mountain of essays to mark, and patience does wear thin!

Chapters 9, 11, 12 and 13 help you with structuring. Here are some of the main things to look for as you edit. Over time you find that you commit the items on this list to memory, so that checking for them becomes automatic.

- ✔ In the light of the question, are the sections are in the right order? Can you reorder parts of the essay to achieve a better effect? Do they build up to a logical conclusion, or should you rework the order to achieve the conclusion more smoothly?

- ✔ Do you have a beginning, middle and end? Each essay should have these, each section of an essay should too, and on a smaller scale each paragraph as well.

- Look at the introduction and the conclusion. Do they balance? Does the conclusion answer the question(s) that the introduction raises?

- Have you used one main idea per paragraph?

- Does each paragraph follow on logically from the one before?

- Does each sentence follow on logically from the one before?

- Do you use appropriate linking words between paragraphs and sentences? Are any of your linking devices superfluous?

Be particularly careful if you want to move chunks of text around when editing your essay. You can easily get lost doing this, and you need to guard against bits of text disappearing all together!

If you're using Word, turn on the **Track Changes** function and use the different colours that identify deletions and additions. They do help. You can then see what you've deleted or moved and go back to the previous version if need be.

Save your versions as you go along and number them Essay v1, Essay v2, and so on. If you do lose some text or are unhappy with your changes and want to revert to an earlier version, you can do so. Playing around with a piece of text in a copy rather than the one and only version of your essay is a sensible strategy!

## Addressing style

Another aspect of editing is to do with the actual language you use and being critical about the words and style on the page in front of you. Does the essay come across as academic? Or is it no different in style and feel from a letter to a friend?

'Control' sums up what we mean here. When you write you're continually making choices. Good style implies having an awareness of the different choices then making your selection in the full knowledge of the effect that decision has. For instance, you choose one word over another with a similar meaning because it suits the context better. You decide whether to write a long, complicated sentence or a shorter one, again aware of the situation and the way the different sentences sound. Whichever situation you find yourself writing in, you have to conform to the rules and make choices that are appropriate.

In Chapter 10 we show you how to write in the academic style. Here are some key things to look out for as you edit:

- **Bias:** Check that your argument is balanced and your terminology's politically correct.

✔ **Jargon:** Do you use specialist terms correctly? Do you define any ambiguous terms? Don't assume that the reader knows what you mean.

✔ **Language:** Is your writing formal and in keeping with the academic style?

✔ **Padding:** Be ruthless and cut out words that are superfluous and that you can eliminate without changing the meaning.

✔ **Slang:** Make sure that informal, slang words haven't slipped into your essay.

✔ **Tone:** Do you strike the right tone or do you come across as overconfident?

## Ensuring that your essay's the correct length

Don't forget the word count! With the Word Count feature in your Tools menu, this is easy to calculate.

Tally the number of words in the body of the essay only and don't include the words in any appendices. Strictly speaking, you don't count any long quotations in the body of the essay, or any footnotes. But remember to check your course guide for the requirements at your university.

So how many words have you written? Is this more or less than required? Many tutors tolerate 10 per cent over or under, but anything beyond in all probability incurs a penalty of some kind (again, check your course guide). This means that if your lecturer asked for 2,000 words, anything between 1,800 and 2,200 is acceptable. Go above or below these limits and you're in the danger zone.

Email your tutor if you are in the danger zone and see what his or her reaction is. In some cases it doesn't matter too much, but in others it does. The acceptable number of words depends on your tutor and the nature of the work you're submitting.

Here's how you can edit your work if you've fallen short of or overshot the target.

### 'Losing' words

So how can you go about getting rid of some of your text so that the essay falls within acceptable word count limits? Try these steps – start at the first one and work your way through until you hit your target word count.

1. **Look for chunks of text that are unnecessary.**

   Go back to the essay title and your plan. Make sure that every section of your essay adheres to that plan and that you're answering the question in a direct and logical fashion without going off at a tangent. You have to be rigorous here. Sometimes you can be quite pleased with a paragraph you've written, but if it isn't strictly necessary and you can take it out without affecting your line of reasoning, this is one to eliminate when the word count's too high.

2. **Look for a section or part of one that you can hive off into an appendix.**

   Remember, the words in an appendix aren't part of your word count. Lengthy additional information that isn't absolutely necessary to the flow of your argument, such as a page of biographical details, comes into this category.

3. **Analyse each paragraph and see whether you've unnecessarily repeated any ideas.**

   Sometimes you want to say things twice in order to emphasise your point, but this is a feature of speaking, and you don't have to do it in formal writing. Look to see whether you can turn around any sentences and express the ideas in fewer words without compromising meaning or grammar.

4. **Eliminate words at sentence level.**

   Do this without, of course, changing the meaning or disturbing the grammar of the sentence. As a very rough rule of thumb, if you've been asked to write a 2,000-word essay and have 2,300, eliminating one word per sentence should bring you down to 2,200, which should be acceptable. Look for words that repeat without adding any new information. Especially look for adjectives and adverbs, which in many cases you can pare away – you may even improve your style in the process.

Students often find the fourth step the hardest. Here's an example of it in action. Look at this sentence:

> Writing 'in real life' often imposes limits on the number of words you can use and so it's really a very useful skill to have so that you can condense what you want to say into a much smaller number of words. (42 words)

With a little thought and playing around with the sentence structure, you can write instead:

> 'Real-life' writing often imposes word limits. Thus condensing a message into fewer words is a useful skill.

This contains 17 words. Notice that you can use 'real life' adjectivally and place it in front of the noun 'writing'. You can turn around 'the number of words you can use' into 'word limits'. Similarly, 'what you want to say' becomes 'a message' and 'a much smaller number of words' becomes 'fewer words'. The adverbs 'really' and 'very' have disappeared.

In addition to eliminating words, you're also improving the tone of your writing. Academic style is formal and impersonal. Unlike *For Dummies* books, it avoids addressing the reader as 'you' and using the word 'your'. Similarly, academic style avoids joining two sentences together with the words 'and so', which can sound too colloquial. Notice that our rewrite uses two separate sentences instead of the original one and begins the second with 'thus', a more formal variation on 'so'.

Having too many words may be a signal that your style's a little informal and therefore more wordy. By trying to write in an academic tone, you may well be able to eliminate a considerable number of words and meet your word count. Chapter 10 helps you get to grips with the academic writing style.

### Adding in words

If your word count's too low, you need to try to pad out your sentences. But that doesn't mean adding in the words we help you to remove in the previous section!

Lengthening your essay isn't about adding waffle and superfluous language. If you've fallen short of your target word count, this means that you're not developing your points fully enough.

Here's what to do:

1. **Go back to the question.**

   Break it down and make sure that you're accounting for every single idea that it contains. You may have missed something.

2. **Look to see that you've developed and explored every point fully.**

   You may benefit from looking back to what we say about writing a paragraph (Chapter 9). Do you discuss every point in all its aspects, and have you given examples to illustrate what you want to say?

If you've considered all of this and find that your word count's still way off the required number of words for this assignment, you must talk to someone – either a classmate or your tutor. Clearly you've missed something, and you need to find out what that is.

Tutors have a pretty clear idea of what's possible, and if they stipulate a certain number of words for an essay, they know that's a reasonable request. After all, they've probably set the same question in previous years and know from past experience that a first-year student can write 2,000 words on X. Therefore, if you're struggling to find something to say, you must have missed something, and you need to talk to a fellow student or, better still, your tutor.

# Proofreading: Dotting the Is and crossing the Ts

Proofreading means paying close attention to the actual words you're using, their spelling and so on. You need to proofread because you become blind to your own errors when you write. When you reread your work you often don't see the missing word, the spelling mistake or the repetition, because you're too familiar with the content. You somehow see what *should* be on the page, not what *is* there, or if you do see what's there, it doesn't necessarily fully register with you. Therefore, having a list of things to check for and some suggestions on how to proofread effectively is a good idea.

Never ignore that nagging voice inside you telling you to check your work over one more time. Somewhere deep down you know that you can make an improvement. And putting in the effort's worthwhile. One more mark may make the difference between a 2:1 and a 2:2.

## Knowing what to look for

Even the most proficient users of English can get things wrong and, let's face it, English isn't the easiest language for spelling and words that sound similar. English being what it is, including here every single slip you may make or trap you may fall into is impossible, but we can certainly mention some of the most common. And we try not to be too technical when talking about language.

In no particular order, these are some areas of confusion that seem to crop up time and time again in student essays. Not all may apply to you, so if you can say, hand on heart, 'I never mess *that* up', give yourself a pat on the back! But you've probably got your own little blind spots, so watch out for the things you continually get confused over and add them to your list of things to check when you're proofreading.

These are just a few of the areas where you can check for errors. Don't forget to look at the grammar we outline in Chapter 8 as well.

### *Making sure that every sentence is complete*

In contexts other than academic writing, you can write much more freely and play around with the language. Not so in your essay. 'Not so in your essay' is an utterance and works here because I'm writing in a very similar way to speaking, but such sentences are not normally acceptable in an academic essay.

Every sentence should have a main clause. If it doesn't, we call it a sentence fragment. These are typical of writers whose first language isn't English, but even native speakers use sentence fragments when they forget that they're writing in an academic style.

Sentences to check in particular are ones beginning 'because', 'which', 'when' and 'if'. These often introduce incomplete sentences. Here's an example with 'because' so that you can see what we mean.

> Because English is often the first foreign language taught in many countries in the world.

The student has written this intending it to be a complete sentence, but unfortunately it isn't. It isn't a main clause because it has 'because' at the beginning, which the grammarians among you know to be a word that introduces a subordinate clause, not a main one. The solution is either to eliminate 'because' completely or to add a main clause so that the clause is anchored to something:

> Because English is often the first foreign language taught in many countries in the world, British people tend not to be very motivated to speak foreign languages.

Now the sentence is complete and correctly structured. It also has the advantage of being longer and sounding fully developed.

Watch out for sentences like these as you're proofreading. Ask yourself whether the sentence you're reading is complete.

### *Checking your spelling*

No doubt you have a set of words that give you grief. Make your own checklist of things that you confuse or get wrong, and try to commit the correct versions to memory. 'Separate' and 'desperate' are on author Mary's list, together with 'medicine' and 'skilful'. Add to your personal list as you get feedback on your essays through the year, and keep the list handy for the proofreading phase.

# Spellchecker: Friend or foe?

One of the first things that springs to mind when you think about proofreading is using your computer's spellchecker. Why not get your PC to do the hard work for you? Here's why you can't rely on that tool alone:

✔ It doesn't recognise every word in the language, and it can mislead you into changing something that's correct but the spellchecker doesn't realise is correct.

✔ It can't distinguish between words like, among others: 'from' and 'form'; 'there', 'their' and 'they're'; and 'weather' and 'whether'. Therefore, it can tell you whether a word's correctly spelt, but not whether it's correctly used. For example, your spellchecker won't flag up a sentence like this one: The bra was nosy and full of smock. (The bar was noisy and full of smoke.)

By all means use your spellchecker, but do so discerningly and then print off your essay and proofread it.

Find out what your tutor's pet hates are language-wise. Does he or she despair of people who confuse 'lose' and 'loose'? Or 'quite' and 'quiet'? Or 'accept' and 'except'? Well then, you know especially what to check for. Here are some handy phrases to remind you of which word means what:

✔ You may lose your trousers if they're too loose.

✔ You need to be quite quiet when you're proofreading.

✔ We all accept your criticism, except for Kevin.

Ensure that your spelling's consistent throughout your essay. So if you spell 'proof-reading' with a hyphen on page 1, don't spell it 'proofreading' without the hyphen on page 2. And if you use realise, realising and realisation in your essay, don't also include realize, realizing and realization (with a 'z' rather than an 's').

## Weeding out abbreviations

In academic writing, avoid abbreviations such as 'etc.', 'e.g.' and 'i.e.', even though they're frequently used in other circumstances. They're not formal enough for this situation. Alternatives are 'and so on', 'for example' and 'that is', although the structure of each individual sentence affects your choice to a large extent.

A word of advice about 'etc.' is that even the more formal 'and so on' may not be acceptable. Take a look at this example:

D.H. Lawrence wrote short stories etc.

You may change this to:

D.H. Lawrence wrote short stories and so on.

That's still vague, isn't it? What exactly does 'and so on' mean? Academic writing requires you to be precise, so in a sentence such as this, you should try to find a general word or expression that you can use to complete the sentence:

D.H. Lawrence wrote short stories and other types of literature.

'Other types of literature' suggests the novels, poems and letters that he wrote during his career.

You may want to use the abbreviation for the name of a society or organisation, especially if it's too long to write out in full every time. The procedure to follow is that the first time you refer to the organisation or whatever it is, you write the name in full with the abbreviation in brackets. After that you can use the abbreviated form throughout. Like this:

These statistics have been taken from the World Health Organization (WHO) website. The WHO conducted this survey in 2007.

### Looking at numbers

Numbers come up everywhere: even if your course is literature, you include dates in your writing. Double-check all numbers and figures, be they dates, percentages or statistics, and written in numerical form or in words. Slipping up is so easy.

And check that the numbers are consistent throughout the text. Look at the way you write the numbers. Words or numerals? Fifteen or 15? Five thousand or 5,000? Hard-and-fast rules are tricky to suggest, but we can give some general pointers.

Write the following in words:

✔ A number that begins a sentence:

- Eight people were injured in the fire.
- Two thousand people were left homeless after the floods.

> ✔ A number made up of one or two words:
>> • The fire claimed the lives of eight people.
>>
>> • The floods left two thousand people homeless.

Put the following into numerals:

> ✔ A number made up of more than two words:
>> • The plane crash claimed the lives of 124 passengers.
>>
>> • The earthquake killed 350,000 people.
>
> ✔ Currency, time or dates: £64,000; 8.45 a.m.; January 10.

 The best advice is to look at books and journal articles from your subject and imitate the way they deal with numerical information. And, above all, be consistent!

## Using different proofreading techniques

Proofreading isn't a question of simply reading through your work a second time, but rather it's about actively using different techniques to see where you may have slipped up. The secret to effective proofreading is to change your behaviour and interact with your essay in a way that may seem counter-intuitive – something that you don't normally do.

First, print off your essay. Don't proofread your work from the computer screen. On the screen it looks different, you read differently, and the number of words your eyes take in can be different. So you pick up on different aspects of your writing when you have the hard (paper) copy in your hands.

Now, set the scene. Proofreading can be really intensive and you need to be able to concentrate well. The coffee bar isn't necessarily a good place. You need to:

> ✔ Find a quiet corner so that you can concentrate and don't get disturbed.
>
> ✔ Take your time.
>
> ✔ Take a break if your concentration slips.

So, with printout in hand, seated in a quiet, comfy spot and with your mobile switched off, what techniques can you try?

### Reading slowly

You train yourself to read as quickly as possible in order to get through the mountains of books on your reading list. But proofreading's the one activity when trying a different technique's advisable. Instead of taking in several words in a single fixation (flip back to Chapter 4 for more on reading), focus on one word at a time. Go slowly. Carefully. Really think about what you're saying.

Use a ruler as a guide to make sure that you read every line and prevent your eyes from racing ahead.

### Reading aloud

By reading aloud what you've written, you have to go at the speed of your speech as opposed to the much faster speed at which you read silently. This helps you pick up on the little things your eyes may otherwise slide over too quickly.

Even better, ask someone else to read your essay aloud to you. That really does make you pay attention to what you've written (and maybe squirm with embarrassment, too!). Failing that, read your essay aloud into a voice recorder and play it back to yourself.

### Reading backwards

This must seem a strange thing to suggest! People are trained to read from left to right, and the idea of reading a script that goes from right to left as in some languages seems unnatural. For the very reason that it's unnatural, it's sometimes used as a technique in proofreading. Your eyes going in the wrong direction across the line feels strange, but they can sometimes pick out the little things that they skip over too quickly when you're reading in the normal direction. This technique seems to work for some people better than others, so give it a go!

At word level, reading backwards is particularly effective when you're checking for spelling mistakes. Some people claim that reading along the line backwards also helps them to identify a repeated or omitted word, or even a grammatical error. And at sentence level, reading sentence by sentence backwards, so starting with the last sentence, may highlight gaps in your continuity of thought.

When you do this you're trying to cheat your eyes and force your brain to process what it sees differently from when you're actually composing the text. In this way, slips and imperfections may stand out.

### Changing the look of what you're reading

Like reading backwards (see the previous section), this is a way of tricking your eyes into seeing differently. If you alter the font type, font size or text colour, you can make your brain think that it's processing a new text. The feeling of familiarity disappears when something seems fresh, and the little slips may jump out at you. So make a few changes to the look of your essay and see what they reveal.

Don't forget to change your work back to the standard typeface and font size before you hand it in!

### Reading with a friend

One of the best ways to ensure that your work passes scrutiny is to get someone else to look over it. Having a fellow student or other friend cast a second pair of eyes over your work may help to flag up improvements in three main areas:

- ✔ **Content:** First of all, try a classmate who's able to pick up on inconsistencies in content because they've taken the same course as you. Tit for tat: you can do the same for your friend.

- ✔ **Quality of thought:** Next, find someone who hasn't done the same course and may even be studying a subject from an entirely different discipline. This person has no prior knowledge or expectations. If they can follow what you're saying the first time they read your essay and it makes some kind of sense to them, you must be explaining yourself reasonably well.

- ✔ **Language:** Recruit someone who's good at picking up slips of spelling, grammar and the like to help you. This can be a parent, friend, partner or anyone who's hot on language.

### Reading the next day

Lots of people edit at night and proofread the following morning, and this generally works. What you can see with fresh eyes after a good night's sleep is amazing. What seemed sound the evening before can appear flawed in the morning. And normally, you can be more critical of what you produce and should be more alert to its faults and failings.

# Chapter 16

# Perfecting Your Presentation

● ● ● ● ● ● ● ● ● ● ● ● ● ● ● ● ● ● ● ● ● ● ● ● ● ● ● ● ● ● ● ● ● ● ● ● ●

*In This Chapter*

▶ Getting the look and feel right

▶ Communicating visually

▶ Checking and double-checking before handing in

● ● ● ● ● ● ● ● ● ● ● ● ● ● ● ● ● ● ● ● ● ● ● ● ● ● ● ● ● ● ● ● ● ● ● ● ●

his chapter's all about making a good impression. It focuses on the polish and shine that you give to your essay to make it look good and stand out from the rest. Yes, your essay has to look the part.

Don't get us wrong: you can't hide substandard content but you can make your essay look as if you care and you take your studies seriously. The few extra marks you may receive for a professional presentation may take you from one band into the one above when your tutor's grading your work, so that little extra effort may well be worthwhile! Handing in a piece of work is a pleasure when you're proud of it. Don't let yourself down by spoiling the effect with sloppy presentation. If you've done the very best you can in terms of content, make sure that you reflect this in the look and feel of your essay.

Also, remember that your tutor may have 50 or so essays to mark, possibly late in the evening, and you want the first impression to be a good one. So if yours is the 49th essay, you want your tutor to pick it up, smile and think 'This looks good!' – not groan 'Oh no, not more of the same old *!?*/!'.

This chapter concentrates on surface appearance. However good your work looks, though, you can't fool your tutor if the content isn't up to scratch, so we do recommend that you go back to Chapter 15 to look at techniques for editing and proofreading the content. And if you're pushed for time and have to make a choice between editing the content and polishing the look, go for the content because that's what counts in the end. If your work shows care in its presentation, that's a bonus.

# Looking Good: First Impressions

You often make snap judgements about another person in the first few seconds, taking in clothes, build, facial expression and more in a single glance before the person's said a word. Sometimes your first impression turns out to be inaccurate, and more often than not it's incomplete. But that initial impression does count, and the same with your essays. In just a couple of seconds, the person who is marking glances over the work, already forming an impression of the content from the way it looks. In one sweep, the eyes take in typeface, format, neatness and so on, and the assessment begins before the person reads a word. So make sure that your essay's a winner from the start.

Think of your essay as a product. How does it look? Is the packaging attractive? Does it make people want to buy it? Does it say high quality or bargain basement?

## Picking paper

You're likely to print out on whatever paper's going, which in all probability is 80 grams per square metre (gsm). But if you can get hold of 90 gsm or even 100 gsm, this kind of paper is that bit more solid and professional looking.

Don't use coloured paper: white's the order of the day for your essay. The only exception to this is a situation in which, say, you used different types of questionnaires to gather data, and different colours allow you to distinguish easily between them. You need to attach examples of these questionnaires to your work, but in any case they form part of the appendix and don't appear in the body of the essay, which is uniformly white.

Bear in mind that university essays are usually printed on only one side of the paper, but times change and you (or your tutor) may feel strongly that you want to use both sides of the sheet in order to save paper.

You may be fortunate enough to have your own printer. If so, make sure that you have enough paper and ink or toner! And if you have to use the university's facilities for printing out, don't leave it to the last minute. Hand-in days are rarely sprinkled evenly through the term but instead tend to cluster on certain key dates. You can be sure that lots of students are handing in on the same day as you. So what happens? Right first time: the printers break down under the pressure. The problem may be the volume of sheets to print out, the nervous fingers that transmit stress to the machines, or the printers themselves having their revenge, but so often students hand in essays late 'because none of the printers was working'. Save yourself from haring around campus looking for one that works by printing your essay the day before and not at the last minute.

## Perfecting pages

You should number all pages and position the numbers in the same place on each page.

In a smaller font and in the footer to the essay, include your name and/or your student number, just in case the pages get separated. Tutors do drop piles of essays on the floor! In case of any muddle, make sure that each page of your work is identifiable as yours should they somehow come adrift.

Check that the pages are:

- ✔ All there
- ✔ In the right order
- ✔ The right way up

You may laugh, but in the rush to hand in, these little things get overlooked. You can exasperate your tutor if you don't present your pages in an orderly fashion, and you don't want the assessment to get off on the wrong foot.

Number any appendices, starting at Appendix 1, then Appendix 2 and so on, but ensure that the page numbering continues uninterrupted throughout the essay. Each appendix begins on a new page.

## Binding

Staple or paper clip your pages together and, if your assignment's a lengthy one, you may want to invest in a plastic cover of one sort or another. This really depends on how much the essay's worth in the context of your final grade for this unit and this year. If it counts for a lot, treat the work with the care and respect it deserves by protecting it in a plastic covering.

Whatever you do, make sure that reading the content of your essay is easy – that you haven't punched holes through important figures, for instance, or otherwise made your work difficult for your tutor to read. Leave a left-hand margin of around 3.5 cm or more so that words on the extreme left don't disappear in the binding or in punched holes. This level of attention to detail is necessary. You don't want anything to put your lecturer in a bad mood!

## Creating a cover sheet

Your university may provide you with a pro-forma cover sheet, but if not make sure that you include the following information:

- ✔ Your name and/or student number (depending on whether marking's anonymous)
- ✔ Name and reference number of your course/module
- ✔ Number of the assignment (if you have several to do on the course)
- ✔ Title of your essay
- ✔ Name of your tutor
- ✔ Word count (see Chapter 15)
- ✔ Date of submission

Don't include graphics on the cover sheet unless you have a very good reason to do so. Pretty pictures or designs don't get you extra marks.

# Looking Good: On Closer Inspection

When your tutor looks more closely at the way you present your work, your attention to detail can reinforce the impression of someone who's taken time and made an effort with the essay. If you're a bit slapdash about how you present your work, you may put the marker in a less than positive frame of mind.

Discover how to use the View facility in your word-processing software. You may like to compose in Normal or Reading Layout, but Print Layout is closest to how it looks on paper. Check the appearance of your essay first in this view before you print it out. You don't want to waste paper. Ask yourself whether your work looks good before you hit the print button.

## Choosing the right font and font size

Your department is likely to recommend that you use any of the commonly available typefaces such as Arial or Times New Roman. Each font has a look and feel that sends out a particular message, and you want this message to be appropriate. We recommend that you avoid typefaces that:

- ✔ May be difficult to read
- ✔ *Mimic handwriting*
- ✔ Don't feel very academic

Find out what your tutor likes, because he or she is the one reading your work. Tutors may have definite preferences; for example, some people find reading a long piece of text easier if it's in a serif font (like Times New Roman) while others prefer a sans-serif typeface (like Arial). Both of these fonts are popular choices.

As for the font size, 11 or 12 point is fine for the body of the text, with headings in 14 point:

> This is 11-point Arial.
>
> This is 12-point Arial.
>
> This is 11-point Times New Roman.
>
> This is 12-point Times New Roman.

## Styling headings and subheadings

Use the same font and font size throughout your essay, except when you come to headings and subheadings, which you can style differently. But make sure that you're consistent if you do this. A typical choice is Times New Roman (serif) for the body and Arial (sans serif) for the headings. But if you're not an expert in contrasting fonts, simply use a single one throughout and don't take any risks.

Titles, headings and subheadings (if your essay has these) are usually in **bold**. If you want you can also make them slightly larger than the rest of the text so that they stand out and guide the reader through. You may want to take your inspiration from this and other *For Dummies* books, which are rigorous in their consistent use of emboldened headings and font sizes.

## Using italics

Italics can be very useful in headings, but in the body of the essay you usually reserve them for words in a foreign language and for the titles of works. For example, your sentence may read '*The Great Gatsby,* by F. Scott Fitzgerald, was written in 1925 and is thought by many to be the best representation of the *Zeitgeist* of the 1920s.'

In *Writing Essays For Dummies,* the odd word is in italics for emphasis because the style of this book is chatty and we use italics to replicate the intonation of the voice. We want you to feel like we're talking to you. The style of an academic essay is formal and not at all chatty, so don't use italics in this way in your essay.

## Spacing adequately

Allow your tutor plenty of space for written feedback. Tutors get annoyed if they have no room to write on a student's essay. You then don't get the valuable feedback that you can benefit from, and your tutor may be cross. Not a good way to go.

Leave margins on both the left- and right-hand sides, and double space your essay to leave room to write between the lines. Together these provide the marker with ample opportunity to comment on your work.

Consider how you present your paragraphs. The physical gap between paragraphs on the page or screen should be clear and unequivocal. Two main methods exist: leaving a whole line gap and indenting. Figure 16-1 illustrates how these alternatives look on the page.

---

**Whole line gap**

Iropetio prouieout ioreuiuiou ioiou ioretoieu roteui orteiueior tueioe rotuer utieeot ueoru oierutoierut ieruoitueroutoier utioerutoi ruoitu eroit uerotu oerut oierut ioeru toier uti ouer.

Iropetio prouieout ioreuiuiou ioiou ioretoieu roteui orteiueior tueioe rotuer utieeot ueoru oierutoierut ieruoitueroutoier utioerutoi ruoitu eroit uerotu oerut oierut ioeru toier uti ouer.

**Indenting**

    Iropetio prouieout ioreuiuiou ioiou ioretoieu roteui orteiueior tueioe rotuer utieeot ueoru oierutoierut ieruoitueroutoier utioerutoi ruoitu eroit uerotu oerut oierut ioeru toier uti ouer. Iropetio prouieout ioreuiuiou ioiou ioretoieu.

    Roteui orteiueior tueioe toruer utieeot ueoru oierutoierut ieruoitueroutoier utioerutoi ruoitu eroit uerotu oerut oierut ioeru toier uti ouer.

---

**Figure 16-1:** Laying out paragraphs.

Use whichever methods your tutor recommends (and your course details should tell you), but if no one method is specified, choose your favourite and stick to it throughout the essay. Consistency's very important in this area.

Having got the layout right, make sure that the spacing's uniform and neat. Check for extra spaces that your finger might have accidentally put in between words, because these spoil the overall effect. Similarly, look between paragraphs. One line (an extra hit on the Enter key) is enough.

Check, too, that the spacing and indentation are standardised if you use bullet points. In an academic essay, you don't often need bullet points, but you may include the odd list. Make sure that you use the same style of bullet point throughout. Avoid fancy ones; the plain and simple round ones are best.

Long quotations should be single spaced and indented. See Chapter 12 for full information on dealing with quotations.

For readable text, align the left-hand side and have a ragged right-hand edge (as in this book) rather than justifying it (which stretches the lines so that the right-hand edge is straight, like the left-hand one). Justified text, which many books and newspapers use, can create 'rivers' of white space that detract from the readability of the text and are unattractive.

## Incorporating data into your essay

Long lists of figures or other data can disrupt the flow of your argument, so in many cases you should put them into an appendix at the end of your essay. Or you may be able to convert the data into a visual. Technology makes visuals relatively easy to create, and you may well have expertise in this area. If you do, use it!

### Using visuals

Visuals can be bar charts, pie charts, graphs, tables or pictures, and you should use them to condense data that's otherwise too lengthy to write out in full, for example the results of questionnaires and surveys. In an academic essay, you shouldn't include visuals to prettify, but to convey information. By converting the data into a visual, you clarify patterns and trends that are lost in a glut of words. Use visuals to make your meaning clearer and to help your reader follow your argument.

However, bear in mind that overusing visuals detracts from your main argument. The layout should be clear and simple with no clutter. Ask yourself whether any visual, table or diagram belongs in the body of your essay or in one of the appendices at the end of your work. This is your decision, depending on the importance of the data the visual contains and how frequently you need to refer to it at this point in your essay. If you're talking about the information a great deal, the visual should probably be in the body of the essay so that the reader doesn't have to keep thumbing through the pages to the end.

### Displaying visuals

A common error that students make is to create charts in colour on the screen, forgetting that when they print these out in black and white the effect may not be the same and the colours may end up as indistinguishable shades of grey. If you can't print out in colour, use stripes, dots or hashed areas that are distinguishable in black and white.

Insert the visuals into the text in the order in which you refer to them in the essay, and number them in that order. Try to insert the visual as close as possible to where it first occurs or where you discuss it at length. Check that when you refer to the visual in the text, the numbering's correct. Ensure that the visuals and their numbers are in the right order (have you by any chance switched them around in editing and forgotten to change the numbers?).

Normally, underneath each visual you write a caption and a title, such as *Figure 1 The average price of a loaf of bread in the UK between 1950 and 2000*. A good idea is to make this slightly different visually from the rest of the essay, for example *in a smaller point size of same font and italicised*. Again, check that all the captions are uniform throughout the essay.

Double check! A frequent oversight is in the labelling of items in a chart, for example ages in a bar chart. The temptation is to label columns '20 to 30', '30 to 40', '40 to 50' and so on. If you think about it, if you want to consult the chart in order to find information about, say, 30 year-olds, which column do you look in? You should be writing '20 to 29', '30 to 39', '40 to 49' and so on. Be careful, then, that you don't include any overlap and that you label categories carefully in order to avoid confusion or misinterpretation.

Consider how visuals fit on the page:

✔ Never split a table or chart over more than one page. If you can't get it on one page, you probably have enough data for two charts. If it's overlapping only a tiny amount, you may be able to incorporate a fold-out A3 page, but check whether your tutor's prepared to accept this for marking.

✔ Make sure that you include white space around each visual so that it stands out and doesn't look cramped. But not too much space! Take your cue from books and the amount of space the professionals use.

# Finishing Off

You're on the home straight now – just a little more effort before you're ticking that essay off your to-do list and trotting off for a well-earned drink in the students' union.

## Running through your checklist

You think you've done everything and you're ready to hand in, but before you rush to your department, stop for a moment and double-check your work using the handy checklist we provide in Table 16-1. Don't lose marks needlessly! Take time to check your presentation.

| Table 16-1 | Look and Feel Checklist |
| --- | --- |
| **Action** | **Tick** |
| Cover sheet: have you included all the necessary information your department requires? | |
| Have you included the title? | |
| Are all the pages numbered and in order? | |
| Appendices included? | |
| Have you left enough white space for your tutor to write comments? | |
| Are the layout and spacing consistent and logical? | |
| Are all typefaces and font sizes consistent and appropriate? | |
| Are any visuals correctly placed, sized, readable (especially if in black and white), with accurate captions and numbers? | |
| Have you checked the word count? | |

*(continued)*

### Table 16-1 *(continued)*

| Action | Tick |
|---|---|
| Have you stapled or clipped the pages together? | |
| What message does your work convey from its appearance? | |
| (for you to add) | |
| (for you to add) | |
| (for you to add) | |
| (for you to add) | |

Polish your work to the best of your ability and then sleep on it (not literally with your essay under your pillow!) – go through it again with a clear head and a fresh pair of eyes the following morning before you give it in.

## Kissing the essay goodbye

In the run-up to your essay deadline, check where and when you have to submit it. You may think that the deadline's 4 p.m., but it may be midday, and you don't want to incur a late submission deduction for a simple mistake.

When you do get to the day of submission, say goodbye to your essay – for the time being. Make sure that you put it in the right place for your tutor to collect, and if you're submitting two essays on the same day, make sure that you hand in the right one to the right office. ('I'd never do a silly thing like hand in the wrong essay,' I hear you say. Wanna bet?)

You experience that wonderful glow and feeling of relief when the essay's finally handed in. Enjoy the moment. Plan a treat to congratulate yourself on your achievement, and realise that you're one step nearer to getting your degree. Then, when you're ready, look at Chapter 17, which helps you through getting back your marked essay.

# Chapter 17

# Moving On: Results and Feedback

● ● ● ● ● ● ● ● ● ● ● ● ● ● ● ● ● ● ● ● ● ● ● ● ● ● ● ● ● ● ● ● ●

### In This Chapter

▶ Adopting a positive approach to feedback

▶ Getting to grips with firsts, seconds and thirds

▶ Improving on a disappointing mark

▶ Taking stock and moving on

● ● ● ● ● ● ● ● ● ● ● ● ● ● ● ● ● ● ● ● ● ● ● ● ● ● ● ● ● ● ● ● ●

So you've handed your essay in – is that it? Sorry, no! As this chapter shows, it's just one step along the road to your degree, but one that you should reflect on and gain from. You can easily think that when you've submitted your essay the process is over – and in many respects it is. It isn't truly over, though, until you get the feedback and this brings about a change inside you, which may be to do with content (what more you need to know) or technique (your skills as an essay writer).

The ultimate objective is for you to gain knowledge and expertise in your chosen field, so each essay is a step towards your goal. In this chapter we explain that when you reflect on the process as a whole, from the time you're given the essay title to the moment you find out what grade you got for it, you focus on the things that have gone well for you and the areas where you've succeeded. You may even have enjoyed some of it!

To finish off this particular step, ask yourself a variety of questions. What difficulties have you come up against? What can you do differently next time? What can you gain from this experience? And – most importantly and assuming that you're like most of us and not a genius like Albert Einstein – when you get your marks back from your tutor, what can you do to improve on them? Signing off a given essay can only really happen when you've consciously made a note, mental or otherwise, of what the essay-writing experience has taught you. You're then ready to move on.

# Congratulating Yourself on What You Achieve

Don't be down on yourself and think what you would have done, could have done, if you'd had more time, if you'd managed to get hold of that elusive book, if you'd paid more attention in that lecture.

Try to think glass half full, rather than glass half empty. If this is your first essay at university, then you've come a tremendously long way and you've discovered so much in a short time. You can't expect to get essay writing absolutely perfect first time, and you can't expect it to be easy. If it were easy, loads of people would be sailing through with firsts! So you need a positive mindset, and you should try to have a healthy perspective on the whole reason for being at uni. You're there to get to know more, after all – not just about your subject but about playing the university game, which is what writing essays is all about.

## Noting what you've done well

Soon after you've handed your essay in, find some moments to reflect on the whole process of writing it and be objective about the bits you think went well and the areas you can aim to improve on. Make yourself a list that may include questions such as:

✔ Planning:

- How did I use my time?
- How realistic was my plan? Did I plan for downtime, interruptions, 'life', relaxation?
- How can I manage my time better in future?
- Did I work in the best environment for studying?
- How can I help myself to concentrate better?

✔ Writing the essay itself:

- Did I unpick the title and work out what it was asking of me?
- Did I have enough background information and read around the subject sufficiently?
- Which part of the writing process was easiest? Most difficult?
- Have I got to grips with the referencing system?
- How easy was it to use my sources, summarise and quote, without plagiarising?

✔ Then, in preparation for next time, make a note of things you need to put in place, for instance:

- Get hold of a good thesaurus.
- Learn how to do in-text quotation better.
- Discuss the essay with your classmates early on in the process.
- Allow more time for getting hold of books from the library.
- Remember not to leave printing until the last minute.

Acknowledging what you *did* do well is very important, rather than feeling bad about your weak areas. A lot of us find criticism easier than praising ourselves, making negative comments rather than positive ones. So have this as your golden rule when you evaluate your essay writing: for every negative comment you make about your work and your abilities, you must find a positive one to balance that out. For instance:

✔ I had difficulty structuring my argument . . . but my work had a good introduction and conclusion.

✔ Some of my in-text referencing wasn't perfect . . . but I didn't plagiarise and I did try to acknowledge my sources.

✔ I messed up at the beginning, not understanding what I was supposed to be doing . . . but I retrieved the situation because I planned in enough time to research and write the essay.

A list of negative comments and thoughts only brings you down and makes you feel miserable about taking on the next assignment. A realistic appraisal of how you did, however, with a positive, up-beat and encouraging message, can help set you up to do even better with the next essay.

To help yourself find the good in what you've done, imagine that you're speaking to yourself as your friend does. Is your friend going to say to you, 'You made a real mess of that essay. What you wrote was rubbish. I don't know what you're doing at university.'? Of course not! What he or she may say is something along the lines of, 'Well, maybe you had a bit of difficulty with the essay, but writing the first one's always hard. You did finish it and hand it in on time.' Don't be so hard on yourself!

Remember to be a good friend to yourself and your classmates too. If they're feeling down because they didn't do as well as they expected, you can boost each other's morale by adopting a balanced attitude and finding the positives to weigh against the negatives.

## Focusing on positive feedback

Tutors – bless them! – have a habit of dwelling on the negatives and saying what you didn't get right. This is normal, this is what they do, and you can expect them to comment on the weaker side of your performance. They want you to learn, to do as well as you can, to push you further.

Unfortunately, in the pressure to get all the scripts marked, tutors sometimes forget to mention the good things that you've done, so you have to do that for yourself. In an ideal world, every tutor takes care to praise as well as criticise, but the reality is that feedback of the negative kind tends to be verbalised and the positive tends to be taken for granted and left unsaid.

However, you *will* receive praise; when you do, hang on to it and give yourself a pat on the back. Praise comes in different forms, which may be actual comments or ticks in the margins of your essay or in a grid if your department has a tick-box feedback sheet. If your tutor's written or ticked 'good' then that's what your work is. You obviously like being told that your work's 'brilliant' or 'excellent', but you have to realise that at university 'good' is a very acceptable word indeed and you should be happy about it. Smile! Take time to enjoy the moment, relax and glow. Remember it, and then knuckle down to the next assignment when you're going to do even better.

# Understanding What the Marks Mean

This is particularly important if you're coming to the UK from a different country where the system of grading's quite different. What do tutors mean by the marks they give?

Generally speaking – and you should check your university's grading system to be absolutely sure what applies to you – tutors don't tend to give what appear to be high marks. The marks may seem low, but you have to understand the system and interpret your mark in context.

Here's how it works:

✔ **70 per cent or over:** A first-class grade – a mark over 70 per cent – means that you've produced work of an exceptionally high standard, and if you do this consistently you should get a first when you graduate. Tutors don't mark with numbers in the 80s or 90s very often and reserve these for (a very few) outstanding scholars.

- **60–69 per cent:** Given that only a small number of students gain a first, the vast majority are happy to receive a mark in the 60s, which means graduating with an upper second (or 2:1) and you've done really well. This is an excellent result, and you should be happy with it. Solid marks clustering in the 60s should get you that 2:1, of which you should be immensely proud. But a first's within striking distance if you just push yourself a little bit harder . . .

- **50–59 per cent:** A lower second (or a 'Desmond': 2:2, Tutu – get it?); this means 'good, but could have done better'. If you get something in the 50s for your essay, you really must aim to hit the 60 mark next time. You've done okay, but you can clearly improve on some areas.

- **40–49 per cent:** Any mark between 40 and 49 is disappointing, but you've done the minimum to pass and scraped through with a third. A degree's a degree, when all's said and done, and many employers don't want to know the class of a degree, only that you have one, so in the long run graduating is what counts. Getting a third does matter, though, if you have thoughts of going on to do a master's or further education of some sort.

- **Below 40 per cent:** Anything under 40's a fail. We don't go there, because it isn't going to happen to you!

# Coping with Getting a Lower Mark than You Hoped For

Strangely enough, most of the time you have a fair idea of the kind of mark to expect for an essay. You know deep inside how much work you put in, how well you got on top of the subject, and how skilfully you put everything together. You know when you skimped on the background reading, or didn't probe fully enough into an issue or threw your work together. And you know that your tutor knows! So you can make a rough stab at predicting the range of marks your work may fall into.

If you've done a decent job, you can't help but have expectations of the mark you're going to attain for a piece of work, and sometimes you get a pleasant surprise because you receive a mark higher than you expected. Be especially pleased when this happens! This truly is a cause for celebration, and you should mark the occasion with an extra pint, bar of chocolate or longer lie-in. Give yourself a reward for doing so well.

But the reverse scenario can and does happen – you tried hard with an essay, but when you get the marks back they're lower than you expected. You missed something or didn't quite get your head around the topic. Maybe the issue was more complex than you realised, and what you wrote didn't do it justice. Or you didn't pay enough attention to all the different aspects and techniques that make up essay writing and that we show you in this book. So many things that can go wrong, so many balls to juggle with and perhaps drop. You're only human if you let a few fall from time to time. But when you tried hard and the mark you achieve isn't as high as you want, you may be really disheartened.

Apart from drowning your sorrows in the bar – which is understandable, but you may regret it the morning after – what other practical things can you do to improve your mark next time?

## Dealing with disappointment

After the initial disappointment, you have to pick yourself up and get back to business. Though you may not feel like it, get out the essay and look carefully at the comments your tutor made. Where have you gone wrong?

Some things are easier to put right than others. For example, if you lost marks through careless referencing, this is relatively simple to rectify. Look at Chapter 14 for our advice.

Spelling, punctuation and poor expression are other examples of things that you can improve on with a little help and thought. You may be angry with yourself rather than disappointed for losing marks over these. Dictionaries, grammar books like *English Grammar For Dummies* (Wiley) can help. Friends can read through your work for you and pick up on the passages where you express yourself poorly. So, yes – a low mark for your language is disappointing, but it's not the end of the world, and you can put a lot right relatively painlessly.

If, on the other hand, you lost marks because you didn't understand something to do with the content of your course, this can be disheartening and discouraging. Don't beat yourself up. We all make mistakes and have to forgive ourselves as our friends forgive us. We're often much harder on ourselves than a friend may be. If the feedback and mark for your essay show that you haven't addressed the topic in a satisfactory way, don't take it too much to heart. It doesn't mean that you're the worst student ever, nor that you're going to fail your degree. You've simply experienced a blip in your progress and need some sound advice to set you back on the right road again. The following section can help.

## Talking to your tutor

The comments written on your essay may not be enough for you to understand where you've gone wrong and what you should do next time. As we've said before, your tutor may have a whole pile of essays to mark, and giving specific feedback on every single one is hard. What he or she means may not always be clear, especially if your essay's adorned with vague underlinings, squiggles and question marks, with no actual wording to explain their significance.

You may be able to catch a tutor at the end of a lesson, but often a crowd of students are jostling for attention, or one or other of you has another class to go to so you simply don't have enough time. A better solution is to drop in if the tutor has designated office hours for this purpose, or send an email to make an appointment, explaining that you need help to see where you've gone wrong with your essay.

 Make sure that you come away from this one-to-one meeting with a clear idea of where you lost marks, why, and how you can do better in your next essay.

If you had difficulty understanding the course content, your tutor can tell you which chapters of which books to reread, or which handouts to go through again. If he or she's unhappy with the way you answered the question, you need to know where you should have expanded or developed your argument differently. Your tutor can show you where your ideas are a bit thin, or if you're repeating yourself unnecessarily. Or perhaps you didn't use the best sources, and you need to know what these are. Wherever the weakness in your essay lies, you should come away with practical strategies so that you're less likely to make similar mistakes again.

## Taking action to improve

One thing you can ask your tutor for is an essay written by another student that's a good model for you to study – probably from a previous year, because using one of your classmates' essays as a benchmark may be awkward. Tutors often hesitate to let other students see these, because you can easily misinterpret a 'model' as the only way to answer a question, and imitate it too closely. This can prevent you from writing an essay from your individual viewpoint and can hinder original thought and personal development. At university level, 'cloned' answers are generally not welcome.

If someone in your class has done well in the essay, and you both feel comfortable with the situation, nothing stops you asking to look at your friend's essay so that you can begin to see where you may have gone astray. One way or another, reading an answer that was more successful than yours can help you to see what you should be aiming for.

In an ideal world you find time to write your essay again, but now with improvements. Though you may not be able to do this, what you may find time to do is to go back to your saved file (and I hope you have saved it!) and annotate the original with brief comments (using different colours so that they stand out). In the light of your tutor's comments, what you may have gleaned from reading other essays, and what you now realise to be your weaknesses, go back through the assignment and make it better.

Going through the process of actually changing your essay helps your brain to remember the changes and makes it more likely that you get things right next time. Until now, the 'right' version has come from your tutor's mouth or been in someone else's words. You need to make the changes yourself, and doing it on paper helps each change come about in your head, which is where it really counts.

# *Taking advantage of other support*

What do you do if you have really serious difficulties with your work, ones that are more than your tutor can realistically help you to overcome? You may have a form of dyslexia or serious difficulty concentrating, or you may not be functioning well for some other reason. You probably have a lot going on in your life, after all.

Your university has a host of support services if you need them. Ask in your students' union, look in your student handbook or browse your uni's website. For example:

- ✓ Counselling services exist if you have problems preventing you from studying.

- ✓ Mentoring services can help you with your work in aspects such as time management and getting yourself organised.

- ✓ Medical or well-being services on campus can test you to see whether you perhaps have a mild form of dyslexia or some other medical condition that may be having an effect on your work. Don't forget to have your eyes tested, because headaches may not result from the burden of constant reading but from the fact that you need glasses!

In other words, don't be afraid to use the services your university offers you. They're free, and if you think that someone can help you, you're silly not to take advantage. The services are offered discreetly and confidentially, so no one else needs to know that you're seeking support if you don't want them to.

When the reason for a disappointing performance is nothing to do with your studies but something going on in your private life that's upsetting or distracting you, telling someone – either the lecturer whose essay you've done poorly or your personal tutor if your university allocates you one – really is in your own interests. Universities are full of kind and understanding individuals who want you to succeed. They can take your personal circumstances into consideration in order to help you get through your course, but this can happen only if you let people know in the first place.

To put in a better performance next time around, you may need to call on a number of people to help you – your tutor as well as some sort of adviser, for example – and let others know if you're in any kind of difficulty.

# *Moving On to the Next Essay*

This first experience of writing an essay at university level should reveal to you a considerable number of factors about your abilities and indicate areas to work on. You should by now have a clear picture of what you've already achieved and what remains for you to improve on next time.

You should set yourself a goal of achieving a slightly better mark next time. If you got 57 per cent for this essay then your goal is to hit 60 per cent and get into the band above. If you got a mark in the lower 60s – say 63 per cent – then you should aim for one in the higher 60s, say 68 per cent. Don't be unrealistic: you're unlikely to soar up 20 marks from one essay to the next other than in exceptional circumstances!

In writing essay number 2, you do everything you did well in number 1, but even better. Where you had little wobbles, you work on these to put them right. You can do a lot for yourself (especially with the help of this book), but don't hesitate to bring in the expertise of other people in order to achieve your aims. If you had difficulty interpreting the essay title, get a group of fellow students together to work out what your tutor expects in the next essay. If you had difficulty with the content, check with your tutor that you're reading and focusing on the right things. Many tutors are happy to cast a quick eye over your essay plan if you email it to them. They clearly can't read an entire essay before you submit it, but a plan shows them how you're interpreting the question and organising your answer.

Above all, gain from the comments your tutor makes and try to put his or her advice into practice. That's easier said than done, but as long as you make an attempt and your tutor sees that you're taking suggestions on board then you're doing what university requires and expects of you. You may not get everything right second time around either, but as long as you're making progress then that's what's important. Onwards and upwards!

# Part VI
# The Part of Tens

'What do you mean, you've <u>no</u> confidence in me as a tutor!?!'

## In this part . . .

All *For Dummies* books have a Part of Tens, and this is no exception. Here you can find top tips in handy, bite-sized form, on both troubleshooting your essay crises and writing excellent exam essays.

# Chapter 18

# Ten Troubleshooting Tips

● ● ● ● ● ● ● ● ● ● ● ● ● ● ● ● ● ● ● ● ● ● ● ● ● ● ● ● ● ● ● ● ● ● ● ● ● ● ● ● ● ● ● ● ● ● ● ●

## In This Chapter
▶ Knowing what to do if disaster strikes
▶ Acquiring strategies for putting things right

● ● ● ● ● ● ● ● ● ● ● ● ● ● ● ● ● ● ● ● ● ● ● ● ● ● ● ● ● ● ● ● ● ● ● ● ● ● ● ● ● ● ● ● ● ● ● ●

*W*riting a great essay is no doddle: We'd hardly have written this book if it were. From time to time you'll come across problems, and when you do, this chapter is here for you. Here we highlight ten common crises that striker essay writers and – more importantly – we tell you what to do about them.

## Oops! I've Written Too Many Words

If you're way over your word limit the first course of action is just to be honest with yourself. If you've tried to cram in everything you've ever read or thought, your essay will be wordy and irrelevant in places. You can reduce your wordage in various ways:

- ✔ Check whether your bibliography and references are included in the word count

- ✔ Put descriptions and comparisons into a succinct table (you can use note form in tables)

- ✔ Put models or exemplar into appendices (stick to the limit prescribed, however)

- ✔ Cut out spurious headings and sub-headings

- ✔ Cut out any waffle or padding – try and remove 20 per cent of your whole essay by cutting out words in each paragraph. If that doesn't work, you'll need to reduce words from every sentence.

- ✔ Eliminate any repetition

The key is not to be precious. Your carefully crafted phrases will just irritate your tutor if you're way over the word limit. Chapters 15 and 10 can help you further in reducing your word count.

# Uh-oh . . . My Essay Is Too Short

Essay titles are designed to be answerable within the word limit set. This also means your tutor feels that if you are way under the set target then you can't have done the subject justice.

Go through your essay and make up a sub-heading for each paragraph. First, you're checking for logic and coherence. Your work should flow and make sense. See whether you've missed out or glossed over any steps in the argument. Perhaps you've made the odd leap in logic that you need to fill out more clearly.

Next, go back to your research. You should have a good sprinkling of relevant illustrative and supportive quotations. These may be too short. Can you expand them by including a little more from the original? It's also possible that you've failed to link the quotations into your essay and you can improve on this.

We also advise you to get your list of subheadings for each paragraph and your rough bibliography and either meet your tutor, some fellow students or a support staff member. Go through your overall plan and outline and discuss the references. It's likely that you've omitted a key reference or concept. If you've included them all, you must have glossed over an aspect that requires more attention.

If none of these techniques work, you need to go back to the title. You've probably missed something out or misunderstood the emphasis on one aspect of the requirements.

Flick to Chapter 15 for more pointers on beefing up your essay.

# Eeek! I'll Never Finish On Time!

Of course you know you need to start your essay early. Every student knows they should, but for reasons of life and laziness they don't always start promptly.

If you know you're going to struggle to make the deadline for personal reasons, tell someone. If you have complex personal circumstances, you should see the support staff or teaching staff and explain what's going on in your life and how it may affect your work. People are far more likely to be sympathetic when they're given some notice. If you let them know you have a difficult circumstance, it'll come across as less of a suspicious last-minute excuse than leaving your confessions until hand-in day.

What happens if you feel the tutor hasn't given you enough time in the first place? Your tutor should provide your essay requirements with enough time for you to get to work on it in good time. If the whole class is feeling aggrieved due to a sloppy attitude from a staff member, then take this up with your course leader. However, always speak to your tutor first because he or she may have withheld setting the essay earlier for a good reason. For example, the tutor may want students to have a broad knowledge before settling on a topic, or may want to time the essay so that it coincides with available resources such as a visit to a museum's temporary display.

If the reality is that you have simply started too late, we really recommend that you see your tutor and discuss your options. If it's the first time this has happened and you have an excellent, unblemished record, you may find you get a sympathetic hearing and can negotiate some extra time. Conversely, if you habitually miss deadlines, you have an issue that needs to be sorted out Even so, your tutor will be at least relieved that you have recognised you need some help. There's always a way to sort out these problems and being able to face up to your poor time management is a prerequisite to actually tackling the concern. Take a look at Chapter 2 for some tips on organising your time effectively.

# I'm Having Technological Torments

If you have a technical problem with your computer, printer or memory stick, you're better off if you have a printed out draft version of your work that you can show to your tutor as proof that you've been working on your essay. The authors have accepted draft essays in the past and this has stopped students being penalised for late work. You have to remember that tutors can get pretty cynical over the years. We've heard a range of imaginative and pathetic excuses for failing to submit and technology is a popular choice among the students looking for a handy get-out or making a desperate attempt to win more time.

We know that many people have honest IT emergencies (we're not immune ourselves). If you are a genuine case, you should be able to show evidence of the difficulty. If you experience a problem in your computer lab, be sure to note the exact time and date:

you need this as proof of problems. Many IT staff are brilliant at retrieving documents from failed hardware, so don't throw away your memory stick in disgust just yet. If you're at home, get some technical support in as soon as you can and get evidence that they've been and there's a genuine problem.

To miminise problems, do the following:

- ✔ Save your documents regularly as you're working.
- ✔ Print out versions of your work as you go (you can do this on scrap paper, using a draft setting to save ink).
- ✔ Back up your work on different memory sticks.
- ✔ Save to the university hard drive whenever possible.
- ✔ Keep one of your memory sticks at a friend's home in case you lose yours.
- ✔ Arrange with a couple of friends to regularly email copies of your work to one another. Each set up a folder and store one another's drafts, just in case.

# My Writing Is Just Appalling

How do you know? Before you start to panic you need to discover the extent of your problem. In our experience with students, those who worry the most are often perfectly capable and turn out some great work. It's often the case that there's been a long gap between their last school or college essay and their first university essay and their concerns are unfounded.

However, lack of confidence isn't always the problem so it's important to establish what the situation is. Although some tutors are unable (or unwilling) to read full drafts, most courses provide an opportunity for students to submit at least a short sample of writing for feedback. Take advantage of the help that's available and gain a realistic impression of your strengths and weaknesses.

If you know you have a serious difficulty then avail yourself of the services the university provides and contact your local authority or funding body for help with additional services. You may be entitled to extra time to complete your work, or additional one-to-one proof-reading or essay-writing help. It's up to you to ensure you use these services.

And be sure to read Chapters 8 and 15 which help you develop your writing, editing and proofreading skills.

# I'm Not Sure I've Answered the Question

In Chapter 3 we explain how to answer the essay question. But you may get to the end of a writing frenzy and suddenly realise that you've veered wildly off the point. Try to avoid this by keeping your essay title pinned or stuck where you can see it while you're working. Write the title out in full in your notebook and have it at the start of your draft work so you can keep referring to it as you go along.

If you didn't keep the title in mind and you're off-topic, first you need to establish what questions you've actually answered (if any). It's likely you had a choice of titles and it's possible that you can switch title and have fewer changes to make to your essay as a result. This is an easy option and allows you to get things done quickly. Check with your tutor if necessary.

If you can't hop to another title, you'll need to see what went wrong. Break down the title and see whether you just left out a small section or only swerved off course in one part. Put right as required.

If that's no good, create a subheading for each paragraph and ruthlessly discard those that are irrelevant. You can save what's relevant and fill in the gaps.

# I Think My References Are All Wrong

Referencing is indeed a laborious process, but errors in referencing are liable to irritate your tutor as well as lose you marks. If you think you've got it all wrong, that's a positive step, in that you can have a go at correcting your mistakes.

Take a look at Chapter 14, which runs through the basics of referencing.

Follow the guidance from your university (preferably your course) really carefully. You may think them pedantic, but rules exist about how to use commas, italics and colons in references, and your university expects you to learn the rules and apply them to your work.

If you know you've made a mistake but you aren't sure how to correct it, a good tactic is to try to make an appointment with your tutor or, better still, support staff and go through where you think you've gone wrong. Staff won't take kindly to you turning up and asking them to sort out your references for you, but will be far more helpful if you've identified your problems and want some directed help.

# I Don't Really Understand the Reading

Some students fill their essays with quotations that they've simply failed to understand, and the tutor can spot such students a mile off because they use quotations wrongly. If there's a word you aren't quite sure of, but you have the general sense of the quotation, get to work with your dictionary and make sure the quotation fits in well in your essay.

If the entire sentence is crammed with words that you can't define, don't use the quotation at all. What's the point if you aren't sure what it means? The obvious course of action is to read something different on the same topic because that may have clearer or more appropriate text for you.

If you can't find clarification in other material, speak to your fellow students or your tutor. Most tutors are happy to help someone who has a specific question. Don't say 'I don't understand the reading' – that's just too vague and there's no way of helping. Instead, ask something specific, like 'I was looking at Chapter 2 as you suggested and I just can't see how I can link Durkheim's ideas to this concept as you mentioned. Please can you just point me in the right direction to follow this up?'

# I Hate My Course and Can't Be Bothered

If you're so de-motivated that you aren't bothering at all and are just turning in weak work that you know will scrape a pass, you need to rethink your university studies completely. As tutors, students often ask us for advice on what modules they should choose or what books to prioritise in an additional reading list (with everything else being equal – no essential texts). Our advice is generally to stick to what piques your interest.

If you're really keen on learning about something you're more likely to put in the effort and time required to ensure or encourage success. Unless you have courses that you must cover for the sake of a professional qualification, you're often freer to change your situation than you may first think. (By the way, if you're stuck with professional modules yet you're struggling to be motivated at university, have you really made the right career choice?)

Most successful people have a wonky trajectory to where they've arrived. For example, the author Carrie's background is in education and no one's really asked her why she chose ethnomusicology as a module on her MA in philosophy and history of education – she just fancied doing it and it was terrific fun. She'd rather explain that at an interview then try and make excuses for poor grades arising from poor motivation in general (and resulting poor grades).

Students often tell us they're a few marks off a good grade. It may be true, but it makes for a boring, defensive story to keep repeating what you almost achieved. In the end you didn't achieve it and that's that. What would you rather: take some time out, find the right path and succeed; or stay where you are, do badly or far less well than you could, and then spend the rest of your life telling people what you *could* have done rather than what you actually did?

# *I Can't Find Any Mistakes – Is That Really Okay?*

This is really an issue of effective proofreading. It can be impossible to pick up errors in your own work but others' mistakes stick out like flashing neon signs.

Try all the techniques in Chapter 15 and check you've really answered the question directly. Most of students can keep improving up to the deadline, tweaking here and there, but you need to know when to stop. If you're honestly satisfied you've done all you can, then you're done.

# Chapter 19

# Ten Tips for Writing Essays in Exams

## In This Chapter

▶ Using your time effectively before and during the exam

▶ Finding the best revision strategies

▶ Planning, writing and polishing your essay

*H*ave you ever revised for an exam but not come away with the result you hoped for? Have you struggled to gather your thoughts together and produce an essay under exam conditions: on an uncomfortable seat in a large lecture theatre? Have you considered that the techniques that served you well at school – such as cramming at the last minute and parroting prepared answers – may not be the right ones to use now that you're at uni?

In this chapter we help you bring about the changes you may have to make in order to produce well-written essays under exam conditions. We also give you our top ten pieces of advice to ensure that you're in fine fettle for the big day.

## Planning for Exams from the Start

You know from the beginning of the course whether you have to sit an exam at the end or whether assessment's based on course-work alone. Your exam isn't going to be a surprise, so plan for it from the very beginning. Above all, don't leave revision until the last minute.

In Chapter 6 we encourage you to be systematic in your note taking and this is where that pays off. Good storage and retrieval of notes from the start of term, with separate files for the notes for each unit and dividers to separate the sections, all make revision easier. When your material's organised and already presented in chunks, you have a head start in the revision process.

Reading and rereading your notes on a regular basis throughout the term or semester is an excellent idea, rather than leaving everything to the end. When you come to the end of a section or part of the course, you retain more of the content if you read through notes and handouts and ensure that all the documents are in an order that makes sense to you.

At the beginning of your course you probably receive a handbook or an online document giving you all the information about the unit, including things called 'learning outcomes'. These indicate what you should know and be able to do when you've finished the course. Referring back to this document at odd moments as the weeks go by and reminding yourself of the stated learning outcomes is useful. Often you can get so tied up in the minutiae of your subject that you miss the big picture. The general over-arching statements of what the unit's fundamentally about can help you see how the pieces fit together and get a perspective on everything.

The unit handbook also contains criteria for assessment that can remind you what your teachers are looking for. Bear these in mind as you're thinking about the exams to come.

# Managing Your Time

You often need two types of planning documents:

- **Overview:** Thinking of all the exams you have to prepare for, you need to apportion certain times or days to revision for each. As soon as you get your exam timetable and find out which one's first, plan backwards, allowing enough time to revise for each exam.

 Be sensible and plan time off for relaxation. Nobody can revise solidly without a break.

- **Detailed plan:** Thinking of one particular exam, make a list of what you have to revise (the 'chunks' we refer to the previous section) and the times you've set aside for these in your overview. Divide the time by the number of chunks to give you an idea of how many hours you can devote to each chunk in order to get through all the revision. We don't need to say that you shouldn't spend too long revising one aspect of your unit to the detriment of the others. All areas require roughly equal time if you're to present yourself in the exam with a fully rounded knowledge of all aspects of your subject. If you plan your revision in this way, you can avoid starting one thing then jumping around to reread something else, which isn't the most efficient way of managing your time.

Once you've got your overview and the more detailed plan of what you intend to do, plan where exactly you're going to do the revision. Look back to Chapter 2 for detailed advice on getting the location right and helping yourself to concentrate. Above all, deal with possible distractions so that you can get the most out of your revision time and not be interrupted or disturbed.

Don't plan to find out new information right up to the last minute. The night before the exam you can refresh by looking through your exam revision notes, but you can't internalise new information at this late stage. Go to bed early instead!

# Trying Different Revision Techniques

After you form a plan (see the previous section) you know *what* you're going to revise and *when*. You now need to think about *how*. This can help to avoid the frustration that students can feel if they don't think carefully about how they're going to revise.

Revision isn't simply rereading course material, but engaging with it actively, looking for patterns and connections. So revision for the exam essay requires you to make notes, but these are different types of notes from the ones we look at in Chapter 6: notes you make on your reading and while planning an essay.

Your revision notes are based on your lecture notes and reading notes, but in rereading all of these you boil them down and condense them into about a page (maximum two pages) of keywords and ideas. Use different colours (see Chapter 6) to highlight different types of information. Then place this summary at the front of the appropriate section in your file.

Following the timetable you've drawn up, you should plan during any revision session to reread your 'chunk', reflect on it and produce your revision notes on that chunk straightaway during the session, while it's fresh in your mind. This is a unit of revision, with a beginning, middle and end. It has a given, short amount of time that you need to manage, and an objective (your revision notes) that's the physical product of the activity. This technique helps you to feel in control of the process and you have something to show for the couple of hours you've spent during the session.

To fine-tune the strategy, you can perhaps use a different-coloured paper for your revision notes so that you can immediately recognise them. Yellow paper's easy to come by and can be pleasant for the eye to work on.

When you start your following revision session, the first thing to do is read through the revision notes from the previous session, refreshing your memory and reminding yourself of the good work you did last time in reviewing your work and consolidating your knowledge. In succeeding revision sessions you can glance through revision notes to get yourself in the mood. Every time you look at them you give your brain the chance to consolidate knowledge and be supported in the process of memorisation, and most importantly you allow it to perceive links and patterns at a deeper level.

Finally, in the build-up to the exam, pull out all the revision notes and, with as clear a mind as you can possibly summon up, go through them calmly.

An alternative format to A4 pages for your revision notes is to use index cards. These have the advantage of being more portable – you can pull them out of your bag more easily on the bus journey to uni, say, and make good use of the time you spend travelling. Some students find them very user-friendly, especially as part of their revision. Other alternatives are wall charts or spidergrams of key ideas. Write or draw keywords and concepts on large pieces of paper. Cluster your thoughts together, draw circles round your thoughts and then lines to link the circles. Stick your diagrams on your wall and look at them frequently. Let your mind make the connections and take you to a different level of comprehension.

If you respond aurally more readily than visually, try recording on a digital voice recorder your thoughts or key facts and keep playing them to yourself. You may feel silly the first time you start 'talking your course', but nobody else has to hear and if the technique works for you and helps you marshal your ideas, it's one to adopt.

Do whatever helps you to revise. Don't feel embarrassed. If you remember best by standing on your head with a carrot in each ear, then go for it!

# Using What's Gone Before

In your revision, use what you've already written on the subject and past papers, an invaluable source in preparing for writing exam essays. Both are tremendously useful, but you need to use them with caution.

With essays you've already written, gain from your mistakes and omissions. Consider the feedback you received from your tutor, whether regarding content or structure, and reflect on how you can write the essay better.

Don't memorise your essay. You're not going to have the same question on your exam paper. Always remember that at university you're not being tested on your ability to know by heart, but on your depth of understanding. Memorising essays or course content can get in the way of showing your ability to demonstrate the application of your knowledge. If you regurgitate a memorised answer in your exam, hoping that by chance you hit on some of the required points, your tutor spots it immediately and getting much of a mark for the answer becomes difficult. Memorise facts, dates, names and the odd quotation by all means, but not entire essays.

The same thing goes for past papers, which are available in your university library and/or online. These are a valuable insight into the different types of questions that have been asked. Look for patterns and for what keeps coming around again and again. Check with your tutor that the forthcoming exam's on similar lines, but expect that in composing the exam paper your tutor puts a spin on something that you may not predict, or approaches an issue from a slightly different angle. That's why you can never fully prepare an answer to an exam essay question in advance.

Some tutors are willing to go through a past question in class to highlight the kinds of things they're looking for in exam essays. If you're unsure of yourself you can write up an answer, hand it in to your tutor and ask for feedback.

Another practical thing to do is get together with classmates and make an exam revision group. As well as being a pleasant social occasion, you can discuss past questions over a coffee (nothing stronger – exams are serious business) and compare ideas. You gain from one another and the whole process of revision, which can seem stressful and solitary, becomes more enjoyable.

When you come back home after a meeting of the exam group, a good tip's to sit down and write up the essay you've been discussing. Do this in real time, because 'real-time' practice for exam essays is extremely helpful. Simulating the exact feelings and conditions of the examination room (the butterflies in your stomach and the hard seats) is hard, but at least once before the big day try to write an exam essay in the required time with no notes and no breaks. This helps you to gear up for the occasion and feel in control. If you've run out of time and your plans have gone haywire, then write an outline of the essay, bullet-point style, even if you don't flesh it out.

# Being Good to Yourself

Throughout the revision process, try a little TLC and don't be too hard on yourself if things don't go according to plan. Especially in the days leading up to your exam, you need to:

- ✔ Make sure that you have all the sleep you need

- ✔ Plan for relaxation and exercise so that you feel good about yourself mentally and physically

- ✔ Try to eat well and avoid alcohol (well, definitely none on the eve of the exam)

- ✔ Keep your body hydrated – your brain needs water to function well

Above all, keep your attitude buoyant and your spirits up. This is especially important if you've had bad exam experiences in the past and the memories come back to haunt you. History doesn't have to repeat itself, and besides, you have all of the support this chapter has to offer you! If you tell yourself you're going to do badly, then you do. Instead, try to make your internal voice speak confidently and positively about the upcoming exam. Focus on the good work you've done in your revision, and tell yourself that you're ready for the exam.

A good attitude is key, but don't set yourself unrealistic expectations. If the subject's new to you and you have, admittedly, struggled a little along the way, then you're silly to expect a brilliant mark. What you can expect is a creditable performance, confident that you've done your best and made significant and valuable steps forward along the path towards your degree.

# Gearing Up

Several days before the exam, make sure that no last-minute changes have taken place. Check and double-check the day, time and place of the exam. It may be in a building you're unfamiliar with, so you need to find it a couple of days before. Don't waste time and energy on the day of the exam running around trying to find a room that you've never been to before. You may also have to think through how you're going to get there. Check your bus times and mentally go through your journey. Allow yourself plenty of time to get there so that you're not in a fluster.

The day before the exam, make a list of everything you need to take with you and prepare your bag with the necessary equipment. This includes items such as:

- ✔ A bottle of water

- ✔ Food (especially an energy bar to snack on and keep you going)

- ✔ The pens and pencils you want to use during the exam (this can be really important to some students)

- ✔ Your lucky fluffy toy

- ✔ Your ID – essential when you take the exam (imagine having to run home to find it?)

- ✔ Your watch – you should be able to see the clock in the examination hall, but glancing at the watch on your wrist is easier (synchronise it with the clock in the exam room when you enter)

Then go to bed at a reasonable hour and get a good night's sleep. Don't forget to set your alarm clock if you need to get up earlier than usual, and adopt a 'belt and braces' approach. In other words, have a second alarm clock or arrange with a classmate to phone each other to make sure that you're both up and about and raring to go!

# Writing by Hand

In the examination proper, a problem that a number of students experience when writing their essays is that they have to write by hand. Nowadays, much of your writing is actually typing, on the PC or in the form of text messages. You may make notes for essays or in lectures by hand, but how often do you write for a couple of hours solidly? How often do you write a ten-page letter to a friend by hand, for instance? People are getting out of practice in writing at length and at speed with pen in hand.

Before computers were commonplace, students submitted even quite long essays by hand and only typed up an important piece such as a dissertation. They were therefore in the habit of writing at length and their hands were used to it. Today's students often complain about not being able to write quickly enough in the exam. Tutors similarly complain about the ensuing legibility! No doubt a time will come when students do exams on a computer, but at the moment universities are in a transition phase between the technology of the hand and that of the PC. And so difficulties exist.

So what can you do? Practise writing by hand for long periods. You need to exercise the muscles in your hand just like any other muscles in the body. Your fingers, hands and arms may ache after an exam. If you have another exam the following day they may stiffen up, making writing slower or more painful. The solution's to flex the muscles and keep them supple. Treat them like any other aching limb after a serious workout. Muscle-relaxant oils, warm water and above all massage can really do the trick. Get someone to massage your lower arms for you. This can really hurt, but the pain may be worthwhile if you have to scribble like fury the next day.

# Dealing with Exam Nerves

Sometimes nerves are worse before the event – when you sit down and the exam begins, you're so busy concentrating on the questions that you don't have time to be scared. But many people have butterflies around exams.

Things to tell yourself before the exam are that to get to uni you've done exams successfully, so no reason you can't do well now you're there. You may have had the odd bad experience, but if you've got this far then poor exam performance can't be a permanent feature of your make-up. Don't dwell on memories of a previous bad experience in an exam. Things don't have to be the same again and on other occasions you did do well, so think about those. Concentrate on the successes that have brought you to university, not on the odd blip along the way. And in any case, everyone has to experience problems from time to time or you don't truly appreciate your successes.

You aren't alone. Just remind yourself that most students feel a bit nervous even though their exterior may not reveal the queasiness within. And a student who's genuinely not nervous isn't sufficiently focused on the task. Nerves are normal and even useful – you do need a little adrenaline to get and keep you going. Too much isn't helpful, but none at all isn't a good sign!

When the exam's under way your nerves should settle down, but they can bubble up again. Looking at other people scribbling away when you (naturally) pause for a second or two when writing isn't a good idea. You begin to ask yourself what they're writing about and your thoughts stray from what you should be writing yourself. You start to imagine that what they're writing in their essays is better than what you're putting down on paper. Don't go there!

Don't compare yourself or ask yourself what they're writing about. For all you know they're writing rubbish. Take a deep breath, look back at the title of the essay you're doing and refocus. Look at the time on your watch, not the clock in the examination hall (which means looking at other students as they work while you locate the clock). Breathe deeply again, pull your wandering mind back in and give yourself over entirely to the question in front of you.

The other classic panic scenario in the exam is blanking out. You've nothing in your head and the question in front of you seems entirely unrelated to what you've studied. The first, very practical thing to do is to check that you've been given the correct exam paper. Seriously! Students from several different disciplines can be taking exams together in the same large examination room (for reasons of numbers and logistics). Are you in the correct seat according to the seating plan? Look at the course code and name on the front cover of your paper. Is it in fact the paper you should be sitting? Mistakes such as this do happen. Invigilators can, and do, occasionally slip up when distributing papers.

Having checked that you have the right paper, look at the questions again. Mentally run through the sections and main themes of your course, trying to see how the questions are related. Write down these main themes if you need to. Visualise your revision notes, the spider diagrams on your wall, or hear again in your head the notes you recorded for yourself. The course content and the questions in front of you have to marry up. Breathe deeply and calmly, scribble any thoughts down that come into your head (you can cross these through later), but write something so that you've started. With a few moments of calm and controlled breathing, you should begin to see the links and the ideas begin to flow.

Your tutor isn't a monster who wants to see you floundering. No tutor feels satisfaction when students can't do their best in an exam. Each question asks you to reflect on some aspects of what you've been studying, and with a cool, clear head you can summon up a response. You've done the reading, the studying, the reflection and the revision. The question isn't a trick but a vehicle for you to demonstrate the best of yourself.

# Answering the Question

If you follow our advice in the earlier section 'Using What's Gone Before', you've looked at previous exam papers and know how many questions to expect. However, read the instructions carefully. If the paper says 'answer every question', then do so. If it says 'choose two of the five essay topics', do that. Don't answer all five. And so on. Double-check that you understand which and how many questions you have to answer.

Then look carefully at the number of marks allocated for each answer. This indicates the relative weighting and consequently the amount of time that you should allocate to each question. Make a plan and apportion your time accordingly. For instance, if you have to write one long essay (50% of the marks) and two shorter ones (25% each), then spend roughly half your time on the first one and a quarter each on the other two.

If you have an hour in which to write an essay, allow 10 minutes for planning, 40 for writing and the remaining 10 for checking and polishing. Scale up or down accordingly, for example 5, 20, 5 if you only have half an hour.

Read all the questions, and then read them all again. If you have a choice, think deeply and choose wisely, obviously going for the areas you feel strongest in. If you're having difficulty choosing, underline the keywords and ask yourself how you feel about having to write about them. This may help you decide.

Keywords and function words are what you should focus on (Chapter 3 gives you the lowdown on these). You may be tempted, given the pressure of the clock, to read too quickly, let your eyes alight on a single word and start putting pen to paper straightaway. This is often too hasty. Try not to do this, but instead circle all the keywords in the question (you may see several) and underline all the function words. The function words tell you what kind of essay you're expected to write. Is the question asking you to discuss a topic, or compare and contrast? Does it require you to evaluate something? (And if it says 'illustrate', don't draw a picture!)

You can answer the questions in any order you like, but you probably feel best if you start by doing the one you're most confident about. Get that out of the way and leave till last the one that seems the trickiest.

The way to answer the question once you've chosen it, circled the keywords and underlined the function words is to brainstorm every idea that tumbles out of your mind and dump it onto the page. Scribble and abbreviate. The notes are for no one but you. As long as you can understand your shorthand and code, that's all that matters. The function words indicate the shape of your essay (see Chapter 3 for more on this) and from this you can develop your plan, clustering together your ideas for the various sections. Subdivide ideas into groups and these form the basis for your paragraphs. Look back at the brainstorming and see what examples you can use. Think of a few more examples if you can.

When you've completed your plan, compare it with the question. Does your plan account for every keyword and function word in the question? If it doesn't, amend the plan. Do it now, before you start writing. When it does account for keywords and function words, note how many words you're supposed to write, then begin your answer.

The process of writing an exam essay is exactly the same as when you write one for an assignment as part of your coursework. As you write, remember the following key points:

- ✔ You're not writing 'all I know about X' but instead putting forward a coherent and logical argument in response to a question. Keep reminding yourself of that argument as you write. Refer to Chapter 12 for more on forming and conveying your argument.

- ✔ Chapter 9 shows you how to write paragraphs. Don't forget to focus on one main idea per paragraph and to ensure that your paragraphs flow logically from one to the next.

- ✔ Always write an introduction, a body and a conclusion (see Chapters 11, 12 and 13). Common weaknesses of essays written under exam conditions are missing or inadequate introductions and conclusions: the student either plunges straight in to the question or comes to an abrupt halt without rounding off.

Missing conclusions, in particular, usually indicate that the student's run out of time and stopped when told to do so. An essay that sounds finished comes across as controlled, and conveys a very positive impression to the examiner. The writer has been in control and has managed time well. Throughout the exam you should be keeping an eye on the clock and making sure that you stick to your timings. Don't be tempted to spend too long on one essay and leave yourself short on another. Stick to your timings and all will be well!

However, what if the worst happens and you do run out of time? Two minutes to go and no way you can finish. Then – and only in an emergency – outline what you wanted to say in the form of bullet points. Your examiner doesn't like this and you don't get full marks. But if you show that the content is there, you just didn't have time to write it up in complete sentences, then you may get a few extra marks. That's better than nothing.

# Presenting the Examiner with a Polished Product

The advice we provide in Chapter 15 on how to tidy your essay up by proofreading and editing applies similarly to essays you write in exams.

Remember that the person who marks your paper has a pile of similar scripts to mark. How many students are taking the same paper as you? Does a single person have to mark all of them? Your tutor may be marking late at night and be really tired, so take pity on him or her and do everything you can to make the task easier. Make your essays stand out from the rest by taking the time to check for simple mistakes and problems.

In the previous section we recommend that you plan to have 5 or 10 minutes to check through your essay at the end. Do check your spelling, particularly terms key to your topic and names of people and places. Shakespeare may have spelt his name 15 different ways in his lifetime, but only one version's generally accepted now!

Similarly, check your punctuation. Watch out for commas, or the lack of them, and make sure a full stop's at the end of every sentence. Don't go for complicated punctuation, just try to get the basics right.

Check that your writing flows. This may mean adding a linking word or expression to make your train of thought absolutely clear. In your haste to write you can easily miss out words, so do look out for omissions as you're reading through.

The final thing to attend to is the crossings out. Cross through the notes you made at the beginning of the essay so no possible confusion exists between these and your answer proper. Then check that you've clearly crossed out alterations to individual words and sentences and written corrections clearly and neatly. Do try to avoid asterisks and arrows going all over the page. If you've planned efficiently as we suggest in the previous section this shouldn't happen, but if it does, make sure that the signs are crystal clear and that the tired examiner doesn't get lost.

'Stop writing now and put down your pens.' You can comply with a smile on your face, knowing that you've done your best and deserve a little celebration!

# Index

# FOR DUMMIES

*Making Everything Easier!™*

## UK editions

## BUSINESS

978-0-470-51806-9

978-0-470-77930-9

978-0-470-71382-2

## FINANCE

978-0-470-99280-7

978-0-470-74324-9

978-0-470-69515-9

## HOBBIES

978-0-470-69960-7

978-0-470-77085-6

978-0-470-75857-1

Body Language For Dummies
978-0-470-51291-3

British Sign Language
For Dummies
978-0-470-69477-0

Business NLP For Dummies
978-0-470-69757-3

Cricket For Dummies
978-0-470-03454-5

Digital Marketing For Dummies
978-0-470-05793-3

Divorce For Dummies, 2nd Edition
978-0-470-74128-3

eBay.co.uk Business All-in-One
For Dummies
978-0-470-72125-4

English Grammar For Dummies
978-0-470-05752-0

Fertility & Infertility For Dummies
978-0-470-05750-6

Flirting For Dummies
978-0-470-74259-4

Golf For Dummies
978-0-470-01811-8

Green Living For Dummies
978-0-470-06038-4

Hypnotherapy For Dummies
978-0-470-01930-6

Inventing For Dummies
978-0-470-51996-7

Lean Six Sigma For Dummies
978-0-470-75626-3

# FOR DUMMIES

## A world of resources to help you grow

## UK editions

### SELF-HELP

Cognitive Behavioural Therapy
978-0-470-01838-5

Neuro-linguistic Programming
978-0-7645-7028-5

Emotional Freedom Technique
978-0-470-75876-2

### HEALTH

Overcoming Depression
978-0-470-69430-5

IBS
978-0-470-51737-6

Low-Cholesterol Cookbook
978-0-470-71401-0

### HISTORY

British History
978-0-470-99468-9

Twentieth Century History
978-0-470-51015-5

The Ancient Greeks
978-0-470-98787-2

Motivation For Dummies
978-0-470-76035-2

Personal Development All-In-One For Dummies
978-0-470-51501-3

PRINCE2 For Dummies
978-0-470-51919-6

Psychometric Tests For Dummies
978-0-470-75366-8

Raising Happy Children For Dummies
978-0-470-05978-4

Reading the Financial Pages For Dummies
978-0-470-71432-4

Sage 50 Accounts For Dummies
978-0-470-71558-1

Study Skills For Dummies
978-0-470-74047-7

Succeeding at Assessment Centre For Dummies
978-0-470-72101-8

Sudoku For Dummies
978-0-470-01892-7

Teaching Skills For Dummies
978-0-470-74084-2

Time Management For Dummies
978-0-470-77765-7

Understanding and Paying Less Property Tax For Dummies
978-0-470-75872-4

Work-Life Balance For Dummies
978-0-470-71380-8

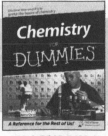